Learning Resources Center
Collin County Community College District
Spring Creek Campus
Plano, Texas 75074

WITHDRAWN

GE   Nadeau, Robert,
170   1944-
N335
2006   The environmental
              endgame.

$24.95

THE
ENVIRONMENTAL
ENDGAME

THE
ENVIRONMENTAL
ENDGAME

Mainstream Economics,
Ecological Disaster,
and Human Survival

ROBERT L. NADEAU

Rutgers University Press
New Brunswick, New Jersey, and London

Library of Congress Cataloging-in-Publication Data

Nadeau, Robert, 1944–

The environmental endgame : mainstream economics, ecological disaster, and human survival / Robert L. Nadeau.

p. cm.

Includes bihlingraphical references and index.

1. Environmanetal policy–International cooperation.   2. Environmental responsibility.   I. Title

GE170.N335   2006

304.2′8–dc22   2005020078

A British Cataloging-in-Publication record for this book is available from the British Library.

Copyright © 2006 by Robert L. Nadeau

All rights reserved

No part of this book may be reproduced or utilized in any form or by any means, electronic or mechanical, or by any information storage and retrieval system, without written permission from the publisher. Please contact Rutgers University Press, 100 Joyce Kilmer Avenue, Piscataway, NJ 08854 – 8099. The only exception to this prohibition is "fair use" as defined by U.S. copyright law.

Manufactured in the United States of America

This book is dedicated to the memory of Professor Garrett Hardin.

CONTENTS

INTRODUCTION

This book convincingly demonstrates that the crisis in the global environment is rapidly becoming a zero-sum endgame in which the winners or losers could be all of the humanity, but it also promises to reveal how this game can be won. Obviously, this discussion is not the final word on what will be required to resolve this crisis, and any author who claims to have answers to all of the complex issues involved is either hopelessly naïve or terribly misinformed. The intent here is not to provide those answers. It is to open a conversation predicated on two assumptions that must be foundational to any successful attempt to prevent an ecological disaster that, if not prevented, will make the terms of human survival very harsh indeed: (1) the international community must begin very soon to develop and implement institutional frameworks and processes capable of coordinating large-scale human activities in environmentally responsible ways on a global scale; and (2) this effort must be predicated on our best scientific understanding of how this can be accomplished in the most prudent and responsible manner in the least amount of time.

During the course of this discussion, it should become quite clear that the crisis in the global environment is menacingly real and must be resolved with all deliberate speed. And it will also become very obvious that the success of this formidable enterprise will be entirely dependent on our willingness to hear what science has to say about the causes of this crisis and the manner in which it can be resolved. The first step in this direction, as Edward O. Wilson puts it, is to stop referring to our best scientific understanding of the complex interactions between human systems and environmental systems as the "environmentalist view" and to start calling it the "real-world view."[1] Scientists have attempted to make this view real by disclosing the dynamics involved in the interactions between humans and the environment, interactions based on the best scientific theory and evidence. However, this real-world view is rarely communicated in ways that can be readily understood by those outside the scientific community, and another of the large ambitions here is to translate this view into a form that readers without any background or training in the sciences can readily understand and appreciate.

In *The Dream of the Earth*, Thomas Berry made the following comment about the crisis in the global environment: "It's all a question of story. We are in trouble now because we do not have a good story. We are in between stories. The old story, the account of how the world came to be and how we fit into it, is no longer effective."[2] In this discussion, the frame tale for the new story that can serve as the basis for resolving the environmental crisis is science. On the most obvious level, scientific knowledge has gifted us with the means and methods of positing and implementing viable solutions to this crisis. What is not so obvious is that this knowledge has also revealed that we have entered a new phase of human history in which the old stories about the sources of human identity and the relationships between groups in both political and economic terms are badly in need of revision.

The new story as it will be told here incorporates relevant material from a broad range of fields in the sciences and social sciences. The first two chapters of this story explain why there is no basis in the present system of international government and in the economic theory that now serves as the basis for coordinating virtually all large-scale economic activities, neoclassical economics, for resolving the environmental crisis. The third chapter describes the dynamics involved in the interactions between human systems and environmental systems as they are now understood in the scientific community.

Chapter 4 enlarges the framework of older narratives about human history to include what science has to say about this history, with particular emphasis on three recently discovered scientific truths. The first truth is that all of the 6.4 billion people on this planet are the direct descendants of about two thousand individuals who were part of the small lineage of hominids that evolved the ability to acquire and use fully complex language systems about sixty-five thousand years ago. The second, related truth is that all the descendants of this first group of fully modern humans are profoundly the same in genetic, cognitive, and behavioral terms. And the third truth is that the collective activities of our species have always been embedded in and interactive with the global environment. In this more realistic account of human history, it is also quite obvious that interactions, or "feedbacks," between biological and cultural processes have massively conditioned historical developments and that fully modern humans have been in the process of massively transforming the entire ecosystem since the emergence of the first complex human societies about 10,000 years ago.

The chapters that deal with the origins and history of neoclassical economic theory will demonstrate that there is no basis in this theory for positing viable economic solutions to environmental problems. Chapter 5 demonstrates that assumptions about the lawful or lawlike dynamics of free-market systems in the mathematical theories used by neoclassical economists were originally articulated by three eighteenth century moral philosophers—Adam Smith, Thomas Malthus, and David Ricardo. These philosophers posited the existence of natural laws that allegedly govern the movement and interaction of economic actors in free-market systems in much the same way that Newton's laws of gravity govern the movement and interaction of masses of material bodies. The creators of classical economic theory were Deists who firmly believed that the natural laws of economics originated in the perfect mind of the Creator of a mechanistic universe. There are two scientific truths that readers will be obliged to confront in this portion of the new story. The first is that the classical economists predicated their belief in the actual existence of the natural laws of economics on metaphysical assumptions, and the second is that Smith's metaphor for the collective actions of such laws, the "invisible hand," is a metaphysically based construct.

Chapter 6 demonstrates that the creators of neoclassical economics (Stanley Jevons, Leon Walras, Maria Edgeworth, and Vilfredo Pareto) developed their theories by substituting economic variables derived from classical economics for physical variables in the equations of a mid-nineteenth-century physical theory. A number of mathematicians and physicists told the economists, all of whom were trained as engineers, that the economic variables are utterly different from the physical variables and there is no way in which one can assume that they are in any sense comparable. However, the economists apparently failed to realize how devastating these arguments were and proceeded to claim that they had transformed the study of economics into a rigorously scientific mathematical discipline like physics. Strangely enough, the fact that the creators of neoclassical economics borrowed their mathematical formalism from the equations of a soon-to-be-outmoded mid-nineteenth-century physical theory was completely forgotten; the totally specious claim that neoclassical economics is scientific was almost universally accepted; and subsequent generations of mainstream economists proceeded to bury metaphysically based assumptions about the natural laws of economics under an increasingly more complex maze of mathematical formalism.

Chapter 7 deals with an attempt to graft a green thumb onto the invisible hand in a subfield of mainstream economics called environmental economics, which is taught in universities and practiced in government agencies and development banks. When mainstream economists are asked whether there is any basis in their mathematical theories for resolving environmental problems, they typically argue that the practitioners of environmental economics deal with these problems very effectively. This chapter conclusively demonstrates that this argument is bogus. The primary reason why this is the case is that the mathematical theories used by the environmental economists are fundamentally the same as those used by other mainstream economists. Consequently, the economic solutions proposed by the environmental economists invariably promote the growth and expansion of market systems at the great expense of the global environment, and there is no basis in these theories for reducing the overall destructive environmental impacts of economic activities. This discussion also demonstrates why it is not possible to extend the framework of neoclassical economic theory to include the environmental costs of economic activities, by examining some failed attempts to do so by a diverse group of interdisciplinary scholars known as ecological economists.

Chapter 8 describes the manner in which belief in the actual existence of the nonexistent natural laws of economics became foundational over the last two decades to the Washington or market consensus. It is well known that this alleged consensus has served to legitimate a program for economic globalization that can fairly be described as a recipe for ecological disaster. But virtually nothing has been said about the fact that the Washington or market consensus is premised on metaphysical assumptions and functions as a quasi-religious belief system. The primary article of faith in this belief system is that the natural laws of economics will necessarily result in a new global order in which all national economies will be free-market systems and all governments will operate in accordance with the principles of democratic capitalism. This chapter examines the origins of this teleological view of the human future in mainstream economic theory and the large role played by this quasi-religious belief system in the political process in Great Britain and the United States over the last four decades.

The primary objective in chapter 9 is to explain why the resolution of the crisis in the global environment may well be dependent on two extraordinary developments—the fairly rapid displacement of the present system of international government with a supranational federal system, and the simultaneous development and implementation of an environmentally responsible economic theory. In the beginning of this chapter, the case will be made that we are witnessing something like a phase change in geopolitical climate that may greatly enhance the prospects that these developments will occur. The primary reason why this may be the case is that the numbers of studies in environmental science that clearly indicate that abrupt, large-scale changes in the global climate system could easily threaten the lives of billions of people are increasing exponentially. In this situation, it is reasonable to assume that a new geopolitical climate can rapidly emerge in which concerns about the crisis in the global environment will rise to the top of the political agenda in virtually all countries. This chapter also describes in some detail how a fully functional system of international government can emerge in a timely fashion and what will be required to simultaneously develop and implement an environmentally responsible economic theory.

The scientific truth that is most pervasive in this discussion is that the crisis in the global environment exists because fully modern humans evolved the capacity to acquire and use fully complex language systems and to organize their experience in a language-based symbolic universe. In this universe, the prospects of survival were greatly enhanced by the ability to externalize ideas as artifacts and to invent new narratives that coordinated collective human activities in increasingly larger and more complex social systems. For reasons that will be examined in some detail later, this not only explains why our numbers increased much beyond the roughly 5 million individuals that would have been possible during the normal course of evolution. It also explains why recent generations of fully modern humans could use their collective knowledge and expertise to create global systems of production and exchange that are rapidly undermining the capacity of the system of life to sustain our existence.

When the environmental crisis is viewed in these terms, it becomes quite clear that the origins of this crisis and the manner in which it can be resolved are the same. This crisis exists because fully modern humans had the ability to coordinate collective activities in increasingly larger and more complex social systems and to externalize ideas as artifacts. And the crisis can be resolved by using this extraordinary and utterly unique ability to accomplish three formidable objectives. The first is to develop and implement, in both economic and political reality, institutional frameworks and processes capable of coordinating large-scale human activities in a sustainable global environment. The second, related objective is to displace environmentally destructive technologies with technologies that have relatively benign environmental impacts. And the third is to enlarge the bases for mutual recognition and cooperation between peoples and governments in ways that will allow for the totally unprecedented levels of cooperation in the international community required to accomplish the first two objectives.

This book is intensely interdisciplinary, and the discussion of material from any of the academic fields will probably not be detailed or nuanced enough to satisfy all the scholars in these fields. In my view, however, any effort to make sense out of what is required to resolve the crisis in the global environment must be intensely interdisciplinary and should appeal to as broad an audience as possible. If this is the case, the relevant question for these scholars is whether the discussion of material in their fields is substantially correct and not whether it could be published in a scholarly journal designed to be read by experts in these fields. If scholars are willing to read the book in this way, they should be satisfied that this requirement has been met.

In an effort to ensure that this would be the case, I asked scholars in the hard sciences, the social sciences, and the humanities to carefully read this book in manuscript form, to make suggestions for revisions, and to provide whatever advice and counsel they felt was needed. Some of the names of these individuals, particularly those of Garrett Hardin and Herman Daly, should be familiar to anyone who has been actively concerned about environmental issues. Hardin, best known for a 1968 article on the "tragedy of the commons," established a new field of study known as human ecology and was instrumental in creating a new discipline in economics called ecological economics.

During the entire course of his adult life, Hardin worked unstintingly to raise awareness about the environmental crisis, and he did so with a blend of intellect, eloquence, and passion that was utterly unique. This seminally important figure in the environmental movement died recently, and he will be greatly missed by those of us who have long relied on his wisdom and foresight. In humble recognition of his enormous accomplishments, this book is dedicated to Garrett Hardin. Herman Daly, widely known for his seminal work in ecological economics, was among the first economists to systematically demonstrate that there is no basis in mainstream economics, or in neoclassical economic theory, for realistically accounting for the environmental costs of economic activities. I am extremely grateful for his invaluable assistance in writing the chapters of this book that attempt to disclose why there is no basis in the economic theory that we now use to coordinate global economic activities for positing viable economic solutions to the environmental crisis.

The contributions of Kirk Jensen, a sciences editor who provided invaluable assistance in preparing two of my previous books for publication, are apparent on virtually every page of this one, and there were several occasions when I could easily have abandoned this project without his encouragement. I am also grateful to Karim Ahmed, a physicist who has been a major force in the environmental movement throughout his career, and to Patricia Warner, a population biologist who has directed a number of environmental programs at the National Science Foundation, for their invaluable assistance in writing the material that deals with environmental science.

Brack Brown, a scholar in public policy and international relations, provided many useful suggestions about how to deal with the material in these fields, and Jack Censor, a world-class historian, was kind enough to comment on the material that deals with historical developments. I also wish to thank my coauthor of three previously published books, the astrophysicist and cosmologist Menas Kafatos, for carefully reviewing and commenting on the material that deals with modern physical theory. Last but certainly not least, allow me to express my heartfelt gratitude to my wife, Kathy Wax, for putting up with me while I was writing this book and never complaining, even when I insisted on working on it over the weekend and into the early hours of the morning.

THE
ENVIRONMENTAL
ENDGAME

1

THE MAKING OF THE GODGAME
Winners Take All

There was things he stretched, but mainly he told the truth. That is nothing. I never seen anybody but lied, one time or another.

— MARK TWAIN, *ADVENTURES OF HUCKLEBERRY FINN*

The "Godgame," the in-group term for an online computer game that over one hundred software engineers are developing at Electronic Arts, the industry leader in the computer game business, is not designed for use by testosterone-driven males under the age of twenty-five. The designated players are social scientists, and their interactive playing field is a virtual planet Earth generated by sophisticated imaging software from photographic data gathered by satellites and high-altitude reconnaissance aircraft. The players will be able to look down on this revolving planet and observe the environmental impacts of large-scale human activities by zooming in and out on any region from the tropics to the poles.

The goal in this high-stakes competition is to coordinate large-scale human activities in ways that will lead to the emergence of a sustainable global environment by articulating coherent and workable proposals for changing the institutional structures and processes that coordinate these activities. Equally remarkable, the social scientist players will be constantly reminded that this must be accomplished prior to the point at which large-scale changes in the ecosystem are projected to occur. Another anxiety-producing aspect of this game is that the amount of time that remains before these changes are likely to occur will not be arbitrary. This projection will be made by a large group of internationally known environmental scientists based on simulations of the global environment generated by state-of-the-art climate modeling software running on a network of supercomputers.

When players of the Godgame click on any location of the virtual planet, they will be able to access a nested series of images, diagrams, graphics, and charts that describe the complex web of interactions between large-scale human activities and the environmental impacts of those activities. For example, integrated computer models on population density, socioeconomic behavior, and the dynamics of the ecosystem serve as the basis for describing the impacts of the growth of cities on water use, nutrient distribution, and biodiversity. Other, equally sophisticated computer models will be used to depict the impacts of economic activities on wetlands that filter contaminants, the hydrologic cycle that maintains supplies of freshwater, and the climate system that regulates and sustains temperature, precipitation, sea level, estuaries, and fisheries.

Players can learn more about an environmental issue or problem by clicking on particular regions of the virtual planet or accessing menus at the top of the screen. If a player clicks on rain forests, the present condition of these forests will be described in multimedia format, and the impacts of human activities on these ecosystems will be simulated at various scales and times. Simulations of these impacts on a global scale will include graphical illustrations of feedbacks between changing conditions in this ecological system and those in other major ecological systems. When a player clicks on a particular rain forest, the complex interactions between the interrelated aspects of this ecosystem will be described and imaged, and descriptions of particular aspects will be synthesized from the best available data from diverse research fields. For example, the material on biodiversity is based on data on all known species in a particular rain forest, including their genetic diversity, and the functional interdependence of these species, including microorganisms. Simulations of the complex web of interactions associated with human impacts on this rain forest, or other complex ecosystems, are synthesized from an analysis of data in the following fields: ecology, geology, molecular biology, genomics, soil sciences, conservation biology, hydrology, environmental engineering, and geographic information systems.

The players will be able to ask environmental scientists specific questions and engage other players in dialogue by e-mail, instant messaging, and Web-based videoconferencing. These interactions will be facilitated by electronic Delphi tools for collective discussion and decision making, shared notebooks and databases, and interactive maps and graphs. When a player or group of players feel that they have sufficient background knowledge to articulate changes in institutional structures or processes that can coordinate large-scale human activities in ways that will reduce destructive environmental feedbacks, the next step is to develop a detailed proposal. But before a move can be made, or before the proposed changes can be entered into the integrated system, two important requirements must be met.

First, a select group of other players in the relevant disciplines must agree that the changes are feasible or workable within the context of the geopolitical realities, social norms, and economic conditions in the countries or regions where they would occur. And second, a panel of scientific experts must rule that the proposed changes are specific or concrete enough to serve as the basis for making quantifiable projections of their impacts on the ecosystem at local, regional, and global levels. The obvious intent of the first rule is to enhance the prospect that the changes can be implemented in the real world, and the rationale for the second is that it will allow changes that meet the first criterion to be translated into numerical data that can be factored into computer-generated simulations of future states of the global environment.

After a proposed change passes these tests and the projected environmental impacts are incorporated into the simulations, an integrated system of modeling software calculates the cumulative effects of this change (and all previous changes) on baseline measures for sustainability in the entire ecosystem. The baseline measures are derived from sophisticated computer simulations of conditions in major subsystems of the global environment that could allow the entire system to sustain itself in relative equilibrium. Based on these simulations, scientists will make reasonable projections of amounts of arable land, potable water, groundwater, levels and mixtures of atmospheric gases, maximal extinction rates, degree of species diversity, and so on, that would allow for the emergence of a sustainable global environment. The challenge to the players is to coordinate large-scale human activities in ways that enhance the prospect that conditions for sustainability can be restored.

In a small rectangular graphic display at the bottom of the players' screens, the collective environmental impacts of human activities on measures of sustainability in the global environment will be represented by a black line, and the baseline measures that would allow for the emergence of a sustainable global environment will be represented by a green line. Because these impacts are now rapidly moving the ecosystem away from sustainability and undermining its capacity to support human life, the black line when the game begins will be much longer than the green. The challenge for the players will be to reduce the length of the black line and increase that of the green until the first is equal to or less than the second. They can do this by making changes in the institutional structures and processes that coordinate large-scale human activities. If these changes are implemented and improvements in the baseline measures of sustainability indicate that they have been effective in producing the desired results, the black line will become marginally shorter and the green line marginally longer.

Two digital clocks located in the right-hand corner of the display will constantly remind the players that sustainable conditions must be in place prior to the point at which large-scale changes in the global environment become irreversible. The red clock will display the number of years in whole numbers and fractions before these environmental changes are projected to occur in the real world, outside the virtual reality of the game. On this most recent version of a doomsday clock, the amount of time that remains before an ecological Armageddon is projected to occur will be periodically adjusted as more accurate predictions become available and environmental conditions change. A blue clock positioned next to the red clock will represent the time that the environmental changes will occur if the proposed changes in human institutional structures and processes that have been implemented in the virtual reality of the game actually occur in the real world and produce the desired results.

If computer simulations indicate that real-world reductions in the destructive environmental impacts of large-scale human activities have enhanced the prospects of achieving a sustainable global environment before major environmental disruptions are projected to occur in the real world, the amount of time on the red clock will increase. But if the changes in the institutional structures and processes that coordinate large-scale human activities are not implemented in the real world and the scope and scale of these human activities continues to expand at the current rate, the time remaining on the red clock will continue to decrease. If the game began today, this clock would be initially set at 18.9 years, an alarmingly short period in which to put our global household in order.

While it is impossible to imagine how the Godgame will actually be played, it is possible to illustrate how it might be played. Imagine that a player or group of players is attempting to fashion a set of proposals that will facilitate the rapid development and dissemination of alternative energy resources by making changes in markets, legal structures, regulatory agreements, and international conventions. Now suppose that some of these players are working on proposals that could result in a rapid transition from a global transportation system based on fossil-fueled vehicles to a system based on fuel cell vehicles.

The advantages of this new transportation system are easy to appreciate—fuel cells utilize the chemical energy of hydrogen to produce electricity, and the only emission is water vapor. The players know, however, that the full implementation of this technology will require additional breakthroughs and that the most optimistic estimate of the time frame in which these breakthroughs could occur is ten years. Given that the computer simulations of the environmental impacts of the present global transportation clearly indicate that something must be done immediately, some players develop proposals that will promote the more widespread production and use of hybrid vehicles. Meanwhile, the group of social scientists working on the transition to a global transportation system based on hydrogen decides that the first phase of this transition will feature a technology that is not as environmentally friendly as fuel cells—hydrogen combustion engines.

In these engines, hydrogen is combusted in the same manner as gasoline, and there is no emission of carbon dioxide. The combustion process produces significant amounts of nitrous oxides, a greenhouse gas produced by reaction with nitrogen. But this technology is proven, and there are no technological barriers to its widespread use. BMW is already selling hydrogen-powered cars with conventional engines, Mazda has converted its rotary engine to run on hydrogen, and Daimler-Chrysler, Ford, Honda, and General Motors are in the process of developing hydrogen-fuel-cell cars. And it is also conceivable that ample supplies of hydrogen can be extracted from water with the use of renewable energy resources such as solar, wind, and biomass.

The prospect that a technological solution to this transportation problem exists seems comforting until one considers what would be required to implement this solution in a timely fashion on a global scale. First, a global transportation system based on hydrogen combustion engines would require enormous financial investments in a massive new infrastructure that has four major components: (1) a hydrogen production system based on thermal, electrolytic, and photolytic processes; (2) a hydrogen distribution system consisting of a network of pipelines, trucks, barges, and fueling stations; (3) a storage system of tanks that can contain the hydrogen at high pressures and ambient temperatures; and (4) the widespread availability of vehicles powered by hydrogen combustion engines.

The most obvious problem that the players will face in planning for the rapid development of this infrastructure is the enormous capital costs.

President Bush pledged in his 2005 State of the Union speech to make the transition to a hydrogen-based transportation system a national goal and committed $1.7 billion over the next five years for research and development. However, this represents a small fraction of the costs of this transition. For example, Shell announced in March of 2003 that it would retrofit one gasoline pump in the Washington, D.C., area to supply six experimental General Motors vehicles. The cost of outfitting this one station with two nozzles, several compressors, and an underground storage system that can store hydrogen at 425 degrees Fahrenheit below zero is $2 million. If all oil companies retrofitted their stations for the sale of this fuel, the cost per station would drop considerably. But there are about 180,000 service stations in the United States alone, and the current estimate for retrofitting all of them is about $100 billion.[1] The costs of developing and implementing the production and distribution systems that would provide these stations with hydrogen fuel are not known, but there is no doubt that they would be many orders of magnitude higher.

As the players of the Godgame contemplate changes in institutional structures and processes that might allow this infrastructure to emerge, they must also take into account the vested interests that would be threatened by these changes, such as oil companies, automobile, truck, and heavy equipment manufacturers, governments in which oil revenues are a large portion of GNP, and investors with large interests in oil-based or oil-related businesses. The players must also contend with the fact that the global economic system is now utterly dependent on the widespread availability of cheap oil, that much of the capital in this system comes from oil revenues, and that the production of a large number of goods and commodities, including plastics and chemical herbicides and pesticides, could be disrupted by major changes in the production and supply of oil. In this analysis, the players would also be obliged to contend with the realization that the transition to a global system based on hydrogen combustion engines could be massively frustrated by those who believe that any attempts by government to regulate, control, or otherwise interfere with the dynamics of market systems will imperil the global economy.

In their efforts to conceive of viable pathways through this maze of socially constructed systems and processes, individual players will rely on their own discipline-based knowledge. Those with a background in mainstream economics might favor schemes involving public-private partnerships with heavy reliance on government subsidies and tax incentives. Players in public policy might favor schemes in which governments impose new taxes on fossil fuels and tighter emissions standards on greenhouse gases and other pollutants. Experts on international law and inter-governmental agreements and protocols might champion proposals that would promote the growth and expansion of the alternate transportation system with the use of these instruments. Similarly, players with expert-ise in social, political, and economic conditions in second- and third-world countries might articulate proposals that could promote the emergence of the new system in these countries with capital investment and low-cost technology transfers from first-world countries. Those with a background in social or industrial psychology might conceive of public relations cam-paigns that would advertise the benefits of a hydrogen-based transporta-tion system, assuage concerns about safety issues, and convince those who are enamored of the conventional automobile that this love affair must come to a timely end.

The designers of the Godgame are aware that large numbers of social scientists are already attempting to posit solutions to environmental prob-lems and that a small percentage of these scholars are involved in group research projects than span a wide range of disciplines and include ex-perts on environmental science. But they also know that virtually all so-cial scientists, including those engaged in the group research projects, do not have any advanced training in the hard sciences and have great diffi-culty understanding scientific descriptions of the environmental impacts of human activities. Hence one rationale for creating the Godgame is to provide a learning environment in which social scientists with little or no expertise in the hard sciences can quickly acquire a fairly robust under-standing of the complex web of interactive relationships between human systems and environmental systems.

The designers of this game have also attempted to check the tendency of academics to posit theoretical solutions with no real-world conse-quences by requiring the social scientists to formulate proposals that stand a reasonable chance of being implemented and that are specific enough to be translated into quantifiable environmental impacts. But what may prove to be the most singularly important aspect of the God-game is that it obliges social scientists with expertise in diverse fields to work closely together to fashion coherent and workable proposals in which differences between discipline-based assumptions and biases are reconciled and minimized.

All the scholars who have been invited to participate in this unprece-dented research project have an international reputation in their field, and most are associated with universities, research institutes, and non-governmental organizations outside the United States. These scholars should feel honored to be included in this elite group, but it is very doubtful that the experience of playing the Godgame will have much entertainment value. The relative lengths of the black and green lines displayed at the bottom of their screens and the numbers on the blue and red digital clocks displayed in the top right-hand corner will serve as constant reminders that the stakes are enormous. In one scenario, the descendants of the world's current 6.4 billion people will live on a planet that is capable of sustaining human life in hospitable natural environments for a very long time. In the other, the survival of billions of people will be imperiled by our refusal to coordinate collective human activities in ways that are commensurate with the terms of human survival.

A BIG SCIENCE PROJECT FOR THE HUMAN FUTURE

The software program that the hundred or so software engineers at Electronic Arts insist on calling the Godgame is obviously not capable of supporting the sophisticated functions and interactive capabilities described here. Far from being a stand-alone package, it is designed to interface with a vastly more complex system that does have such capabilities. This system has been under development for some time and is known as the Global Ecosystem Modeler, or GEM. Conceived in January of 1992 and developed at a cost of $620 million, GEM has functioned thus far as an elaborate computer-based research tool that facilitates the efforts of physical scientists to understand the complex nonlinear system of the global environment. The project now has 449 full-time employees on its technical staff with an additional 113 full-time employees in support roles, and about 3,000 research scientists worldwide are active participants.

The proposal to create the GEM system began as an impromptu conversation during the first session of a conference for high-level physicists on some of the more arcane aspects of dynamical systems theory at the Los Alamos Laboratory in New Mexico in January of 1992. Samuel Kaufman, a physicist at Columbia University, interrupted the proceedings and asked to read portions of a recently released document with the ominous title "World Scientists' Warning to Humanity." After the other conferees assented to his request, Kaufman noted that this was the first time that a representative group of senior world-class scientists, sixteen hundred from seventy-one countries, had issued a warning to all of humanity. They did so, he said, in response to the failure of the largest gathering of heads of state in history—at the Earth Summit in Rio in December of 1991— to fully recognize, much less adequately deal with, the crisis in the global environment. Kaufman then proceeded to read the following passage from this document: "Human beings and the natural world are on a collision course. Human activities inflict harsh and often irreversible damage on the environment and on critical resources. If not checked, many of our current practices put at serious risk the future that we wish for human society and the plant and animal kingdoms, and may so alter the living world that it will be unable to sustain life in the manner that we know. Fundamental changes are urgent if we are to avoid the collision our present course will bring about."

After briefly summarizing the major crises in the global environment detailed in this document, Kaufman read the passage in which the senior scientists issued their warning to humanity: "No more than one or a few decades remain before the chance to avert the threats we now confront will be lost and prospects for humanity immeasurably diminished. We the undersigned, senior members of the world's scientific community, hereby warn all humanity of what lies ahead. A great change in the stewardship of the Earth and life on it is required, if vast human misery is to be avoided and our global home on this planet is not to be irretrievably mutilated."[2]

Because the twenty-three physicists at the Los Alamos conference had devoted a considerable amount of time to the study of the environmental crisis, Kaufman's intent was not to raise their awareness of the magnitude of this crisis. It was to create a context for asking the following question. "Why is it," he asked, "that the vast majority of educated people, including global economic planners and representatives of national governments, are so unwilling or unable to deal with the prospect that we could well be only a few decades away from a situation in which large-scale irreversible changes in the global environment will occasion human loss and suffering on a scale that is difficult to imagine?" As a case in point, Kaufman commented on the responses in both print and electronic media to the release of the "World Scientists' Warning to Humanity" document. He said that only a few European newspapers, and only in their back pages, announced the release of the document; that all major newspapers in the United States, including the *New York Times* and the *Washington Post*, deemed the event "not newsworthy"; and that only a handful of radio and television stations worldwide made passing mention of the warning's contents.

Kaufman's question sparked a heated debate that continued virtually nonstop until well past midnight on the first day of the conference. Some participants in this debate attributed the lack of concern about the crisis in the global environment to the abysmal failure of even developed countries to provide their citizens with a basic scientific education. This ecological illiteracy, said Stewart Kahn, a physicist from the University of Chicago, is everywhere present in decisions made by politicians, policy makers, and economic and social planners. At this point Richard Ogleby, a physicist on the faculty at the Los Alamos Laboratory, made the case that the sources of resistance to resolving the environmental crisis are much deeper and far more intractable. He argued that the vast majority of people, including those in highly industrialized countries, attribute the natural order to the benevolent agency of supernatural forces and are unable in both intellectual and emotional terms to entertain the prospect that life on the entire planet can be disrupted by human agency.

Sensing that this philosophical debate was going nowhere, Kaufman decided to refocus the discussion. He said that the business of physical scientists is not to engage in endless speculation about all the reasons why the crisis in the global environment is not fully understood or appreciated. It is to provide a scientifically valid description of the conditions required to achieve a sustainable global environment and an empirically sound basis for coordinating human activities in ways that would allow those conditions to emerge. "The role of the scientist," Kaufman concluded, "is to use the best available theory and evidence to describe the terms and conditions for human survival in a sustainable environment and not to dictate how this can be accomplished."

Two of the younger scientists, physicists Fred Johnson and Tim Rose from the University of Massachusetts at Amherst, took issue with this traditional view of the role of the scientist. They argued that given the magnitude of the crisis in the global environment, perhaps the scientific community should abandon its usual resistance to political activism and become more engaged in the messy business of raising public awareness and promoting meaningful change in the political process. But the consensus view was that if the scientific community was perceived as advocating any political agenda, this would completely undermine its ability to meaningfully contribute to a timely resolution of the environmental crisis. And this quickly led to the conclusion that the only way in which physical scientists could hope to make this contribution was to continue to function as dispassionate and objective purveyors of scientific truths in accordance with the rules and procedures of science.

On the second day of the conference, the physicists concluded that they could best serve these truths by drawing on their collective expertise in dynamical systems theory. Over the next three days, the group decided that they would attempt to create a virtual university in cyberspace in which scientists with a broad range of expertise would collectively develop computer-based models of the present and future state of the nonlinear system of the global environment. The primary goal in this incredibly ambitious project would be to create models that could simulate the complex interactions between classes of human activities most responsible for the disruption of major systems in the global environment and the impacts of those activities on the environment.

The assumption was that if this could be done with a reasonable degree of accuracy or, as the physicists put it, within an acceptable range of statistical probabilities, it would no longer be possible for government leaders and global economic planners to act as if the crisis in the global environment does not exist. The scientists were convinced that an enhanced scientific understanding of the actual relationships between large-scale human activities and the large-scale changes in the global environment occasioned by those activities would not only constitute a clarion call for collective global concern and action. It would also provide an empirical basis for articulating international initiatives and programs that could coordinate these activities in environmentally responsible ways and for developing and implementing technologies that could dramatically reduce the environmental impacts of these activities. The unstated belief behind this optimism was that the truths of science have more authority than any other truths and, therefore, that scientific truths about the impacts of human activities on the global environment would necessarily result in a massive restructuring of these activities.

The planning committee that was created at the end of this conference decided to use the resources of the Los Alamos Laboratory and some limited but readily available funds from environmental groups to sponsor a series of four week-long conferences in 1992. These meetings attracted a large number of scientific researchers on environmental issues from major universities and government research centers worldwide. After six hundred of these scientists indicated that they wished to participate in the last session, the planners were obliged to move the meeting from Los Alamos to a large convention hotel in San Francisco. At the end of a three-week planning session in June of 1992, the development program for the GEM system had been articulated.

The first of the ambitious goals of this program was to create multi-layered dynamic models of the nonlinear system of the global environment using sophisticated software that would run on supercomputers in Europe and Japan. The second was to establish a high-speed telecommunications network that would allow developers and researchers to access and manipulate the models and that would link the supercomputers to a wealth of data from an array of earth-observing satellites and ground-based observation systems. Thanks to some sizable grants from the National Science Foundation and some generous contributions of equipment and services from a number of software and telecommunications companies, the infrastructure of the GEM system was in place by the end of 1997. After governments in Europe and Japan agreed that a considerable amount of computing time on their supercomputers could be used for this purpose, the modeling component of the system was fully operational in June of 1998.

Permission to use data from earth-observing satellites operated by NASA and the European Space Agency was granted over the next two months. Links were also established to access data from ground-based observational systems outfitted with new sensors, such as hyperspectral and synthetic aperture radar devices. These high-quality data, which were processed with new information technologies such as data mining, multidimensional visualization, clustering, and machine inference, were entered into a network of supercomputers. The climate modeling software running on this network was constantly improved, and the vast amount of new high-quality data on environmental conditions and processes was consistently used to test predictions based on these models.

After GEM became fully operational in January of 2000, studies based on this system clearly indicated that large-scale human activities were massively disrupting major environmental systems. For example, a study on potable water disclosed that this resource is far more limited than previously imagined, and the study provided a detailed account of how much potable water will be available in the foreseeable future based on current trends in its conservation and use. The authors pointed out that only 2.5 percent of the water on this planet is fresh, the vast majority of which is frozen in glaciers and ice caps; that less than 0.3 percent (three-tenths of 1%) of the planet's store of freshwater is contained in lakes and rivers; and that much of this supply is threatened by poor management, pollution, and population growth. The study also estimated that global warming, which causes increased incidence of drought and extreme storms, has been responsible for 20 percent of the recent decline in the overall amount of potable water.

The authors made a convincing case that the average supply of water per person would decrease over the next twenty years by one-third in virtually all regions of the globe and that the shortages would be particularly severe in poorer countries. The study also pointed out that the expansion of the global economy, particularly attempts by developing countries to increase their GNP by promoting the rapid growth of highly polluting and poorly regulated industries, was a massive cause of these shortages. Another concern was that much of the 2 million tons of waste generated each day by the global economy is dumped into the world's rivers and lakes and that the amount of polluted water on the planet is more than the contents of the ten largest river basins. The study also warned that if current projections are correct and over half of the global population is living in cities in fifteen years, this could result in large increases in the amount of water consumed in cities and large decreases in the amount of water available for agriculture, which now accounts for about 70 percent of overall human consumption.

Simulations generated by the GEM system also provided a clearer picture of how competition for potable water can occasion conflicts between nation-states and where these conflicts are likely to occur. For example, 260 river basins are shared by at least two countries, and 40 percent of the global population is living in countries that will be competing for access to freshwater very soon if current practices continue. In the past five years, disagreements about which nation-state has the right to shared water resources have occasioned thirty-seven violent conflicts, and the incidence of such conflicts is projected to increase exponentially over the next ten years. In the Middle East, for example, most of the rainfall that replenishes the Mountain Aquifer that lies beneath the West Bank falls within Palestinian territory, but Israel appropriates about 85 percent of the annual yield for its own use. Since potable water is scare in this region, the Israelis and Palestinians have been fighting over access to water in this aquifer for years, and this issue is a major source of disagreement in efforts to negotiate terms for a peaceful settlement to the Arab-Israeli conflict. Relationships between the United States and Mexico have been soured by disagreements over the use of water from the Rio Grande, and Turkey's decision to dam the upper reaches of the Euphrates has occasioned growing hostility with neighboring countries that are also dependent on its waters.[3]

In a computer simulation of the impacts of human population growth on the global environment, GEM scientists assumed that the population would level off at 10 billion by 2050 and that this entire population would enjoy the same level of material prosperity as the middle classes of North America, western Europe, and Japan. The formulas used to assess the environmental impacts correlated population size, per capita affluence (consumption), and the amount of energy that must be consumed to achieve this level of affluence.[4] One result here was startling. If all the 6.4 billion people currently on this planet consumed the same amount of environmental resources per person as the average citizen of the United States, this would require two additional planet Earths.[5]

The study also pointed out that about 11 percent of the world's land surface is already under cultivation and the remaining 89 percent has either marginal agricultural value or no use at all. A computer simulation revealed that a marginal increase in agricultural production could be achieved by clearing and planting in tropical rain forests and savannas. However, the simulation also showed that this would occasion a catastrophic loss of species diversity and undermine the ability of the biosphere to maintain the relative abundance of atmospheric gases that maintain Earth temperature at levels suitable for life. Another simulation, in which deserts and nonarable croplands were irrigated, showed that this would result in the rapid depletion of potable water in regions where there are already too many people competing for too little water.

The authors also demonstrated that the aquifers of the world, which are critical to crop growth in drier regions, are already being drained of water faster than their reserves can be replaced by rainfall and runoff. The Ogallala aquifer, a principal source of water in the central United States, dropped 3 meters in a fifth of its area in the 1980s and is now half depleted in Kansas, Texas, and New Mexico. Even more dramatic, the water table under Beijing fell 37 meters from 1965 to 1995, and the groundwater reserves in the Arabian Peninsula are expected to be exhausted by 2050. Equally alarming, another study demonstrated that all seventeen of the world's oceanic fisheries have been harvested beyond capacity and that some fisheries, such as those in the Atlantic banks and Black Sea, have suffered a commercial collapse.[6]

A study on global warming predicted that the planet's average surface temperature would rise by 12 degrees Celsius over the next hundred years, a figure 60 percent higher than was estimated six years ago.[7] The computer simulations indicated that this rise in temperature would cause brutal droughts, massive floods, and violent storms around the planet. These simulations also showed that the breakup and melting of the Antarctic and Greenland ice shelves would cause sea levels to rise by as much as 86 centimeters and that the impacts on human populations would be disastrous. Tens of millions would be displaced in low-lying regions in China, Bangladesh, and Egypt, and some coastal nations, such as Kiritimati and the Marshall Islands and the small atoll countries in the western Pacific, would be completely underwater. The study also predicted that there will be large increases in precipitation patterns in North Africa, in the temperate regions of Eurasia and North America, and in Southeast Asia and the Pacific coast of South America. The amount of precipitation in Australia, most of South America, and southern Africa was projected to drop correspondingly with disastrous consequences for people living in these regions.

Computer simulations also indicated that a rise in marine water temperature above 26 degrees Celsius in areas where clouds and storms are generated would dramatically increase the frequency of tropical cyclones. Those living in the highly populated region of the eastern seaboard of the United States would experience more heat waves in the spring and more hurricanes in summer. Tundra ecosystems, which are vital aspects of the global ecosystem, could disappear entirely, and projected decreases in agricultural production would affect many more people in developing countries than in industrialized northern countries. These simulations also revealed that many species of microorganisms, plants, and animals would be unable to adapt to changes in their environment or to emigrate to more habitable areas and that this would occasion the extinction of large numbers of species and a dramatic decline in species diversity.

A computer simulation of the spread of agriculture from ten thousand years ago to the present showed that human activity has destroyed about half of the planet's forest cover, which reached its maximum extent six to eight thousand years ago following the retreat of continental glaciers. At present over 60 percent of temperate hardwood and mixed forests, 30 percent of conifer forests, 45 percent of tropical rain forests, and 70 percent of tropical dry forests have been lost, and the remainders are being cut at an accelerating rate.[8] Although the precise rate of extinction caused by the wholesale destruction of species habitats is not known, GEM scientists concluded that it is somewhere between one thousand and ten thousand times higher than the rate before human activities began to exert significant pressure on the global environment.[9]

A study on environmental conditions in the least developed countries revealed that extreme poverty in forty-nine of these countries doubled over the last thirty years and that the resulting living conditions massively contributed to environmental degradation. If current trends persist, the scientists predicted that the number of people living on less than $1 a day will increase from the current figure of 307 million to 420 million by 2015. Even more sobering, the authors concluded that most of these countries are trapped in a cycle of poverty that they cannot escape and that the usual dynamics of international markets will not relieve the terrible suffering of the hundreds of millions that live within their borders.[10]

These are merely a few examples of studies published by scientists working on the GEM project, and all of them demonstrate that the damage being done to the global environment by human activities has reached crisis proportions. The results of these studies were immediately published, and summaries of the conclusions were communicated to editors in print and electronic media, to the appropriate government officials in virtually all countries, to corporate officials and officers in most national and international corporations, and to representatives of international organizations, such as the World Bank, the regional development banks, and the International Monetary Fund.

In the United States, editors of newspapers and magazines made occasional passing mentions of these studies on their back pages, and two major television networks, CNN and Fox, commented on some of the more dramatic conclusions in sound bites on news programs. Most major environmental organizations did their best to make the public aware by featuring them on their Web sites, and four of these organizations funded a series of three programs on the crisis in the global environment that were shown on most PBS stations. In Canada, Europe, and Japan, there was marginally more coverage in print and electronic media. Three European countries, Germany, Sweden, and Denmark, created commissions to evaluate potential impacts on their national economies, but there was virtually no response from the governments of other counties. Some insurance companies took the studies seriously in calculating future risks and liabilities, but the economic decision makers in most major corporations worldwide went about business as usual and seemed quite unconcerned. This lack of concern was also apparent in the decision making of global economic planners at the World Bank, the regional development banks, and the International Monetary Fund.

Those who understood what the studies were actually saying about the human future were utterly amazed that so many seemingly well-educated, concerned, and responsible people either did not comprehend the implications or chose to ignore them. In their view, the best scientific research had revealed that the existence of humanity will be imperiled if we do not begin very soon to coordinate large-scale human activities very differently. And yet the reaction of the world to this news was roughly equivalent to rearranging a few chairs on the deck of the *Titanic*.

THE MAKING OF THE GODGAME

It was in this context that two of the original designers of the GEM system, physicists Jim Lothar and Robert Gray of the University of California at Berkeley, conceived of the prospect of creating a computer game for social scientists that would interface with the GEM system. Lothar first began thinking about this prospect after he played a commercial computer game with his son called SimEarth. In this game, players earn points by efficiently managing scarce planetary resources, and the goal is to prevent the untimely destruction of these resources.

As his son made adjustments in the use of one planetary resource, such as potable water, Lothar noticed that the impacts on other resources were far more complex than methodologies based on simple causality would allow. After playing the game himself for another thirty minutes, Lothar realized that these interactions seemed to be premised on a fairly sophisticated understanding of dynamical systems theory, which includes chaos theory and the theory of fractals. Given that few people outside the scientific community fully understand this theory, the fact that it had somehow influenced the makers of a commercial computer game was amazing. But what made this discovery particularly interesting for Lothar was that dynamical systems theory had served as the conceptual foundation for virtually all his work in environmental science.

Lothar soon learned that the designer of the SimEarth game was Will Wright, the trained anthropologist and bookish intellectual who was also responsible for creating SimCity, SimAnt, the SIMs, and, more recently, SimsOnline. Using the Google search engine, Lothar learned more about Wright and his company, Electronic Arts, and found an article published in *Wired Magazine* that described at some length Wright's interest in dynamical systems theory.[11] The article said that Wright developed SimCity after reading Jan Forrester's pioneering work on the uses of dynamical systems theory in the study of the limits of urban growth, that he was inspired to create SimEarth by reading books by James Lovelock and Lynn Margulis on emergent phenomena in the nonlinear system of life, and that SimAnt was based on ideas contained in a book by E. O. Wilson on the nonlinear dynamics of complex ecosystems.

During lunch the following Monday on the Berkeley campus, Lothar told Gray that he had been up much of the night thinking about a "far-out idea." The idea was to create a vastly more complex version of SimEarth that could facilitate the efforts of social scientists to better understand and more effectively deal with the crisis in the global environment, a game

SPRING CREEK CAMPUS
WITHDRAWN

that would interface with the GEM system. Over the next three weeks, the physicists developed a rough description of a user interface and various game methodologies, visual images, graphics designs, and interactive capabilities that might make the game an effective learning tool for social scientists. The physicists also made an initial assessment of the technological challenges that would have to be overcome to develop and implement this system and concluded that these challenges could be met if sufficient resources were available.

Lothar and Gray soon decided that the only designer of computer games with the background, talent, technical capabilities, and financial resources required to develop the game component of this system was Will Wright. In a series of e-mails and phone calls, Lothar and Gray briefly described the game to Wright and explained why it could be a vitally important tool in efforts to resolve the crisis in the global environment. After Wright indicated that he was very interested in the project, Lothar and Gray arranged a series of meetings with Wright in their offices on the Berkeley campus.

In spite of his growing enthusiasm, Wright was concerned that the successful completion of this project would require the development of software many orders of magnitude more complex than that used in any existing computer games, including those developed for training purposes in the U.S. military. As he became more familiar with the technical challenges over the next four months and began to arrive at more realistic estimates of development costs, there were many occasions when he was tempted to abandon the effort. When I asked Wright in a recent interview why he had not given in to this temptation, this was his response: "After a number of meetings with scientists working on the GEM project, I became really frightened. It suddenly became clear to me that these folks were not exaggerating anything. They had lots of good evidence that human beings are destroying life everywhere on the planet. And if we don't do things very differently very soon, the conditions that sustain human life will be threatened." Later in this conversation, Wright said that this revelation obliged him to come to a sobering conclusion: "I felt morally obligated to do everything in my power to develop the game software and to ensure that the interface with the GEM system is transparent and free of glitches."

MAINLY THE TRUTH

At the beginning of Mark Twains' *Adventures of Huckleberry Finn*, Huck makes the comment used as the epigraph to this chapter. Speaking about the author of *The Adventures of Tom Sawyer,* he says: "There was things he stretched, but mainly he told the truth. That is nothing. I never seen anybody but lied, one time or another." The same could be said about the pages you have read so far in this chapter. The material on the state of the global environment presented in the narratives about the Godgame and the GEM system is the truth as we know it in scientific terms. But the narratives within which these scientific truths are communicated are lies or, as I prefer to call them, useful fictions.

My rationale for including these fictions was to entice readers into thinking seriously about two scientific truths that most people, including very well educated people, routinely dismiss or ignore. The first of these truths is that the crisis in the global environment is menacingly real and must be resolved with all deliberate speed. And the second is that there is only one way in which we can hope to resolve this crisis prior to the point where large-scale changes in the global climate system endanger the lives of billions of people: the international community must begin with all deliberate speed to develop and implement institutional frameworks and processes capable of coordinating large-scale human activities in ways that will allow for the emergence of sustainable conditions in the global ecosystem.

This book promises to provide a reasonable, coherent account of what will be required to accomplish this feat. For the moment, however, allow me to distinguish between the truths and the untruths in this chapter and to comment on what the "stretched" truths, or useful fictions, were intended to reveal about the manner in which we are now attempting to resolve the environmental crisis. The names mentioned in the accounts of the Godgame and GEM systems are not those of real people, with one exception. Will Wright is an actual person, and everything said here about his background, interests, and accomplishments is, to the best of my knowledge, true. "The World Scientists' Warning to Humanity" is an actual document signed by a representative group of world-class scientists in 1992, and the account of the circumstances surrounding its publication and reception is also accurate.

All the observation systems, computer-based technologies, and telecommunications equipment described in the narrative are real, and there is no reason why such systems as the Godgame and GEM could not be created if sufficient amounts of resources were available. Details about how the Godgame might be played were derived from "Complex Environmental Systems," a report that members of the National Science Foundation (NSF) Advisory Committee for Environmental Research and

Education worked on for over three years.[12] Published by NSF in January of 2003, this document outlines a long list of ambitious, interdisciplinary computer-based research programs that NSF would like to pursue over the next ten years. In the introduction, the authors warn that the "footprint of human activity continues to expand to the point that it is having a significant impact on nearly all of Earth's environmental system" and that the ability of this system to "support all life, including human economic and social systems," is being threatened. They then argue that resolving this crisis will require a much-improved understanding of the complex interactions between global human activities and conditions in the global environment "across spatial, temporal and organizational scales."

This improved understanding of the complex interactions between "people, ecosystems, and the biosphere" will require, say the authors, an "integrated synthesis across disciplines" of research in "physical, chemical, biological and social sciences, mathematics and engineering." They then argue that the success of this research project will depend on the creation of a vast integrated network of personal computers, supercomputers, grid computers, high-speed telecommunications links, digital libraries, Web-based materials, and state-of-the-art software with a broad range of applications. And as the word "complex" in the title of the NSF document suggests, complexity theory, or, as it is more formally known, dynamical systems theory, is the theoretical foundation for all the proposed research programs.[13]

Such an integrated cluster of research programs would resemble the Godgame in many respects, but there is little or no prospect at this point in time that they will be funded by the U.S. Congress or approved by the Bush administration. There is no question that this ten-year research effort proposed by NSF could be crucial to our efforts to resolve the crisis in the global environment, and one can hope that the U.S. electorate will realize this and make its will known in the political process. But for reasons that will soon become obvious, even in the unlikely event that the NSF proposal is approved and funded, this will not in itself contribute in any substantive way to the timely resolution of the crisis in the global environment. And this would also be the case even if the vastly more ambitious research program described in the narratives about the Godgame and the GEM system actually existed.

The truths about the environmental crisis that will be explored in the remainder of this book are not widely recognized as truths for two reasons. They pose some very direct threats to our sense of safety and security, and they oblige us to call into question some fundamental assumptions about the terms of our existence in the natural world. The most menacing of these truths is that we are now engaged in the process of playing a very real godgame that is fast becoming a zero-sum endgame in which the winners or losers could be all of humanity. The next chapter will provide substantive validity to this large claim by examining some actual godgames now being played by strategic military planners at the U.S. Department of Defense.

2

GODGAMES AT THE PENTAGON
The New Terms of Human Survival

We've known for some time that we have to worry about the impacts of climate change on our children's and grandchildren's generations. But now we have to worry about ourselves as well.

— MARGARET BECKETT, BRITISH SECRETARY OF STATE FOR THE ENVIRONMENT

Our house is burning down and we've been blind to it. . . . The earth and mankind are in danger and we are all responsible. . . . We cannot say that we did not know! Climate warming is still reversible. Heavy will be the responsibility of those who refused to fight it.

— JACQUES CHIRAC, PRESIDENT OF FRANCE

It is well known that strategic planners at the Pentagon use some of the most sophisticated computer systems in the world to play war games. These interactive games, which are similar in design and function to the God-game described in the previous chapter, simulate armed conflicts between sovereign nation-states. The challenge to the players is to minimize threats to the national security of the United States with a well-orchestrated series of moves ranging from diplomatic initiatives to armed intervention. But what is not widely known is that researchers at the Pentagon also use these computer-based simulations to study potential threats to national security that could be occasioned by abrupt large-scale changes in the global environment.

Until recently, few people outside the inner circle of high-level military strategists and political planners knew about these godgames, because the results of previous reports on them were classified. For reasons that have yet to be determined, however, a copy of the latest report, "An Abrupt Climate Change Scenario and Its Implications for United States National

Security," was given to a journalist at *Fortune Magazine,* and the contents were summarized in an article published on January 26, 2004.[1] A copy of this document was made available two weeks later in electronic form on the Pentagon Web site.[2]

In the introduction, the authors warn that the assumption in the minds of "most people" that climate change will be gradual "may be a dangerous act of self-deception," because "recent evidence suggests that . . . a more dire climate scenario may actually be unfolding."[3] They then state that the dire scenario described in the report is plausible for the following reason: "Ocean, land, and atmosphere scientists at some of the world's most prestigious organizations have uncovered new evidence over the past decade suggesting that the plausibility of severe and rapid change is higher than most of the scientific community and perhaps all of the political community is prepared for."[4] Even more disturbing, the authors claim that such abrupt climate change is not only more plausible but also appears more imminent than previously believed: "some recent scientific findings suggest that we could be on the cusp of such an event."[5]

In this scenario, global warming causes additional melting of the Arctic glaciers and increased rainfall, sending massive amounts of freshwater into the oceans; this lowers the salinity of the waters in the North Atlantic, which results, in 2010, in the collapse of a massive current that flows north from the tropics known as the "global thermohaline conveyor." The circulation pattern of the Gulf Stream, the northern arm of this conveyor that now carries warm water into northern latitudes, shifts dramatically over the next ten years. The collapse of this massive current also causes other large-scale changes in the global environment and these changes create conditions that vastly increase tensions and conflicts between nation-states.

At the end of this ten-year period, in 2020, the average temperature in Asia, North America, and Europe has decreased by 5 to 6 degrees Fahrenheit, and the average temperature in Australia, South America, and southern Africa has increased by about 5 degrees Fahrenheit. Drought afflicts most agricultural regions, and there are severe shortages of potable water in most population centers, including those in Europe and eastern North America. In 2020, the climate in northern Europe, where annual rainfall has declined by 30 percent, resembles that in present-day Siberia. Conditions are so extreme in Scandinavian countries that large numbers of people in this region are migrating to warmer and more habitable climes in southern Europe. In western Europe, winter storms intensify, and the destructive impacts of these storms are amplified by strong westerly winds in the North Pacific. In Africa, climate change causes widespread famine and disease; large numbers of starving immigrants from this region attempt to enter countries in southern Europe, and these countries secure their borders in an effort to stem the tide of unwanted immigrants.

Unpredictable monsoons in China cause devastating floods in areas where vegetation has virtually disappeared because of droughts, and longer, colder winters and hotter summers create severe energy and water shortages. Similar problems exist in parts of Asia and in East Africa, and tensions between countries in this region of Africa occasion a series of cross-border military conflicts. Violent storms are increasingly common virtually everywhere on the planet, the lives of millions of people are threatened by floods, and most of Bangladesh is uninhabitable because of the rising sea level and contaminated water supplies. Rising ocean water from one of these storms breaks through levees in the Netherlands, making coastal cities such as The Hague unlivable.

In the United States, storms breach the delta island levees in the Sacramento River; saltwater can no longer be kept out of the aqueduct system that carries potable water to large populations in southern California during the dry season; and this massively disrupts the supply of freshwater to this region. Colder, windier, and dryer weather in northeastern states makes growing seasons shorter, and longer dryer conditions in southern and southwestern states dramatically reduce agricultural production in these regions as well. High winds and reduced rainfall in virtually all agricultural areas in the United States result in soil loss and reduced moisture in the soil, and this contributes to additional declines in food production.

Cooler temperatures in the Northern Hemisphere drive up the consumption of oil, and many industrialized countries respond to the large increases in the price of oil by greatly increasing their reliance on nuclear energy. As conflicts between nation-states over access to scarce environmental resources escalate, Japan, South Korea, and Germany use the spent fuel from their nuclear plants to develop nuclear weapons. Japan, menaced by flooded coastal cities and contaminated water supplies, and lacking sufficient oil and gas reserves to power its massive desalination plants and energy-intensive agricultural system, develops plans to gain access to Russian oil and gas reserves with the use of military force. If that occurs, the authors of the Pentagon report predict that the resulting conflict might easily escalate to the point where one of these countries elects to use nuclear weapons. In another scenario, a series of cross-border conflicts between Pakistan, India, and China escalates to the point that an exchange of nuclear weapons becomes highly probable.

In this geopolitical climate, say the authors, "Nations with the re-sources to do so may build virtual fortresses around their countries," and the primary concern of these countries will be to secure "resources for survival" as opposed to defending "religion, ideology, or national honor."[6] In their conclusion, the authors describe some ways in which the United States could build a virtual fortress around itself and some "unlikely al-liances" that may be required to secure the resources necessary to sustain the national economy. For example, "borders could be strengthened around the country to hold back unwanted starving immigrants from Caribbean islands (an especially severe problem), Mexico, and South America." Fill-ing the nation's energy requirements would require "expensive (economi-cally, politically, and morally) alternatives such as nuclear, hydrogen, and Middle Eastern contracts." Even so, the United States' diverse climate and abundant resources would leave it well positioned—"compared to others."[7]

One problem with this optimistic conclusion is obvious. The large-scale changes in the global environment described in the report could eas-ily occasion the collapse of the global economy and a breakdown of the rule of law on both the national and the international levels. If that hap-pens, it is very doubtful that any nation-state, including the last remain-ing superpower, will be able to protect its citizens, much less sustain a growth economy, under such chaotic conditions. However, the primary reason why this conclusion is fundamentally flawed is that the large-scale environmental changes would not be confined to a single decade. The col-lapse of the global thermohaline system would trigger a cascade of other large-scale, irreversible changes that would have disastrous environmen-tal impacts on every region or territory on the planet for a very long time.

LARGE-SCALE CHANGES IN THE GLOBAL ENVIRONMENT

After the release of the Pentagon report, spokespersons for the U.S. Department of Defense said on numerous occasions that the scenario de-scribed in the report was "extremely unlikely," and the clear message was that Americans should not be concerned that abrupt large-scale changes in the global environment could occur anytime soon. But what these in-dividuals failed to mention is that the vast majority of environmental sci-entists are very concerned about this prospect and some of them are quite convinced that we could be "on the cusp of such an event." Because most people, including most well-educated people, seem to be blissfully un-aware that massive changes in the global environment like those de-scribed in the Pentagon report can occur, let us briefly consider why most environmental scientists have concluded that this is very real possibility that we simply cannot afford to ignore.

Numerous scientific studies have demonstrated that the dynamics of environmental systems are such that small changes may produce small effects for an extended period of time. When, however, a system reaches a state known as "far-from-equilibrium," small changes can trigger very large effects, and these effects can cause other environmental systems to become less stable by moving them further away from equilibrium. For example, the loss of habitats in a particular ecological niche can proceed for several generations with only a gradual increase in the rate of species extinction and loss of biological diversity. But if this process continues, the entire ecological system eventually reaches a point where even very marginal losses in habitat result in sudden and massive changes, such as a dramatic increase in extinction rates and a huge loss of biological diversity.

Because such systems interact strongly with other systems in the region, these systems also tend to move toward a far-from-equilibrium state where similar large-scale changes can occur. When we consider that particular environmental systems are embedded in a seamless web of interactions with other systems, including the climate system, this leads to another imposing conclusion. None of the parts (ecological systems) can be isolated from the whole (biosphere or ecosystem), and the movement of progressively larger numbers of these parts to a state that is further from equilibrium can easily result in large-scale changes in the whole.

Much of the recent research on the global environment indicates that massive changes can occur very quickly and that the resulting conditions would constitute a major threat to human life. One of the most disturbing scenarios resembles that described in the Pentagon report. In this scenario, the melting of the ice in the Arctic Ocean, which covers a large area of Earth's surface and reflects sunlight back into space, creates a massive open sea that absorbs heat and accelerates the process of global warming. Oleg Anisimov, widely recognized as one of the leading experts on such phenomena, is convinced that this disastrous change is already in process. He points out that the snow and ice cover in the Arctic has decreased by 10 percent since 1970, and that the same melting process on land has increased the flow of rivers in Siberia. Equally alarming, higher temperatures in Siberia are thawing the permafrost, and large amounts of greenhouse gases trapped in this frozen soil are being released into the atmosphere.[8] Scientists have also determined that the glaciers in Alaska and the Alps have been in retreat for decades and that those in the high Andes and the Hindu Kush could vanish in the next twenty years.

A number of recent studies have also demonstrated that global warming is affecting large numbers of species and their environments and that this process could be moving the entire biosphere toward conditions of extreme disequilibrium. For example, a group of scientists recently conducted a systematic review of 143 studies on 1,473 species of plants and animals and concluded that a rapid rise in Earth temperature could easily result in massive changes in the entire biosphere. The scientists reported that birds are now laying eggs sooner than usual, plants are flowering earlier in the spring, and mammals are hibernating at different times. They also found that over 81 percent of the species surveyed had already experienced biological changes that are consistent with computer-based models on the impact of climate change, and these models indicate that more rapid global warming would increase these trends dramatically.[9] In a recent study published in the journal *Nature,* the authors reported that the range of species is shifting toward the poles at about four miles per decade and that laying of eggs and flowering of trees is occurring 2.3 days earlier than a decade ago.[10]

Even more alarming, another recent study published in *Nature* revealed that from 15 to 27 percent of all species in six critically important regions of diversity that represent about 20 percent of Earth's landmass could be threatened with extinction by 2050 in the absence of dramatic reductions in greenhouse gas emissions. The authors used data from sophisticated computer models that simulated the movement and interactions of 1,103 species in response to changes in temperature and climatic conditions. Based on careful extrapolations from these data, the researchers concluded that the global extinction of currently existing species by 2050 could range from 24 percent on the low end to 35 percent on the high end.[11]

Given that human beings exist in embedded and interactive relationships with the global environment, it should come as no surprise that climate change and environmental degradation have also already had large impacts on human populations. About 25 million people have been forced to abandon their lands over the last decade because of flooding, drought, soil erosion, deforestation, nuclear accidents, and toxic spills, and it is estimated that the numbers of environmental refugees are increasing by 5,000 a day. When we factor into this picture how human populations could be affected by projected large-scale changes in the global environment, it is easy to appreciate why experts are convinced that the numbers of environmental refugees may soon be increasing exponentially.

If sea levels rise by 1 meter as a result of global warming, as the scientists at the U.N. Intergovernmental Panel on Climate Change (IPCC) predict, this will result in massive flooding in countries as diverse as Bangladesh and Denmark, and most of the rice-growing regions in Thailand, Indonesia, and India will be destroyed. These scientists warn that most of the forests in Mexico, the Ivory Coast, and the Philippines, and much of the farmland topsoil in Ethiopia, El Salvador, and Nepal, could be lost over the next forty years. In twenty years, one in three people on the planet could face acute water shortages and the most severe shortages would be in poorer countries, such as Jordan, Egypt, and Pakistan. This means that tens of millions of people of all ages who are now living in these regions could soon be migrating over barren landscapes in a desperate attempt to find the water and foodstuffs required to sustain their existence. Another related problem is that 97 percent of global population growth is projected to occur in countries where food and water supplies are already stretched to the limit and migrants from the countryside are already flooding into huge cities that lack the environmental resources to sustain the existing population. According to scientists working with the U.N. Environment Programme, the numbers of environmental refugees could be 50 million in eight years and 150 million in forty-seven years.[12]

Some recent studies on global warming also suggest that Earth's surface temperature is increasing more rapidly than previous studies indicated. The IPCC projected in 2001 that global warming could increase Earth's temperature by as much as 6 degrees Centigrade. However, many of the leading atmospheric scientists who attended an international conference in Berlin in July of 2003 were convinced that the increase, if present trends continue, will be from 7 to 10 degrees Centigrade. A number of recent scientific studies have also shown that although climate change may be gradual for extended periods of time, the change tends to be very rapid when feedbacks from far-from-equilibrium systems begin to multiply. In a report by the National Academy of Sciences titled "Abrupt Change: Inevitable Surprises," the authors summarized the results of studies on transitions from ice age regimes to warm eras and concluded that they typically occur over a period of a few years. For example, studies of ice cores from Greenland dating from 11,500 years ago indicate that the mean temperature of Earth's surface increased 14 degrees Centigrade in just over ten years.[13]

There is another disturbing prospect that we should consider. The computer models that we now use to predict increases in Earth's temperature do not as yet factor in the potential impacts of a partial melting of the vast quantities of methane hydrate, a form of methane frozen in ice, around the fringes of the polar seas. This would release vast quantities of methane, a potent greenhouse gas. When these potential impacts are included in the computer simulations, it is very probable that the results will indicate that the increases in Earth temperature could occur in a much shorter period of time than previous simulations indicated.

The bad news about the state of the global environment was the subject of a report released in January 2005 by an international task force made up of senior politicians, scientists, and business leaders. This task force was established in March 2004 by the Institute for Public Policy Research, the Centre for American Progress, and the Australian Institute, and the fourteen members of this group included representatives from both developed and developing countries. In an interview on the day this report was released, Stephen Byers, a British member of Parliament who cochaired the task force with U.S. senator Olympia Stowe, said, "Our planet is at risk. With climate change, there is an ecological time-bomb ticking away, and people are becoming increasingly concerned about the changes and the extreme weather events they are already seeing."[14]

The report warned that global warming is approaching a critical point of no return where "abrupt, accelerated, or runaway climate change" will occur. One scenario described in this report was the same as that which served as the basis for assessing potential threats to the national security of the United States in the Pentagon report—rapid melting of the Greenland and West Antarctic ice sheets triggers the collapse of the global thermohaline system, and large-scale irreversible changes in the global climate system occur over a period of about ten years. The intent of this report was to prevent such changes by articulating initiatives that would allow the international community to coordinate large-scale human activities in environmentally responsible ways. For example, the report called on the eight leading industrial nations to dramatically reduce their emissions of carbon dioxide, to double their research spending on green technology, and to make every effort to include India and China in future agreements on global warming. But the hard truth here is that there is little or no prospect at this time that any of the recommendations made by this task force will be implemented. The next portion of this discussion will explain why this is the case.

THE USUAL SUSPECTS

Most of the commentary on the failure of the international community to deal effectively with the crisis in the global environment puts the blame on the usual suspects—the greed of international corporations, the inability of rich countries to empathize with the plight of poor countries, the refusal of first world nations to accept any changes in the global balance of power, and the attempt by the last remaining superpower to achieve political and economic hegemony. But the principal conceptual barrier to the resolution of this crisis is not any of the usual suspects. It is the failure to realize that arbitrary assumptions about the relationships between parts (sovereign nation-states and national economies) and wholes (international government and the global economy) in the present system of international government and in the economic theory that we now use to coordinate virtually all large-scale human activities are categorically different from and wholly incompatible with the actual dynamics of part-whole relationships in the global ecosystem.

This may seem like an esoteric problem with no real-world consequences, but that is anything but the case. The fundamental disjunction between arbitrary assumptions and actual dynamics not only explains why all previous efforts in the international community to resolve the environmental crisis have been hugely ineffectual. It also explains why there is no basis in the present system of international government and mainstream economic theory for coordinating the relationships between human systems and environmental systems in ways that could allow for the emergence of sustainable conditions in the global environment.

The understanding in the Pentagon report of the relationship between parts and wholes in geopolitical reality is predicated on the construct of the sovereign nation-state, and this construct is foundational to the present system of international government. In this system, the part (sovereign nation-state) is the sole source of political power, and the whole (international government) does not in itself have any political power.[15] The primary obligation of each part, as the Pentagon report nicely illustrates, is to protect and enhance its own interests. And this invariably results in a fundamental and irreconcilable conflict with the secondary obligation to serve the interests of the whole—all human beings and the state of the global environment.

The understanding of economic reality in the Pentagon report is predicated on assumptions about parts and wholes in neoclassical economic theory. In this theory, the part is defined as an economic actor or firm and the whole as a closed market system. Interactions between the parts are allegedly determined by "lawful" or "lawlike" mechanisms associated with the "natural laws of economics," and it is assumed that these mechanisms operate in a domain of reality that is separate and distinct from other domains, including political reality. It is also assumed that these mechanisms will, if left alone, necessarily result in the growth and expansion of closed market systems and that any attempt by government or any other external or "exogenous" agency to regulate or control economic activities will interfere with the proper functioning of these mechanisms. Because the mechanisms allegedly operate only within market systems, environmental resources that exist outside these systems have no market value, and the only market value that can be assigned to these resources within the systems is a function of the mechanisms. In the Pentagon report, these assumptions are implicit in the commentary on how the United States could use its military power and economic might to secure the natural resources required to sustain the national economy.

For reasons that will be examined later, assumptions about part-whole relationships in political and economic narratives like the Pentagon report are derived from, or were massively conditioned by, classical or Newtonian physics. In this physics, a part is a separable piece that has functional characteristics that contribute to the operation of a whole, and the whole is the sum of its constituent parts. Wholes in this scientific paradigm exist as separate and discrete entities in space and time, the external connections between smaller wholes account for the functional existence of larger wholes, and the condition of larger wholes is determined by the interactions of the smaller wholes that constitute its separable parts.

All these assumptions about part-whole relationships were completely undermined by the new physics, beginning with Einstein's special theory of relativity in 1905, and they have also been thoroughly discredited over the last three decades in the biological sciences. What is most important for our purposes is that assumptions about the relationship between parts (large-scale human activities) and whole (the global environment) in classical or Newtonian physics completely distort the real or actual character of those relationships. The large problem here is that most people, including most very well educated people, continue to believe that these assumptions are scientific. One reason why this is the case is that most textbooks studied in introductory courses in physics, chemistry, the earth sciences, and the biological sciences are still predicated on these scientifically outmoded assumptions.

For example, organisms are still described in the biology textbooks used in high schools and in most introductory biology courses in colleges as a collection of separable parts, and the parts in diagrams of these organisms appear to exist in fixed and static relationship to each other. This understanding of part-whole relationships is also apparent in these textbooks in graphic depictions of ecosystems that wrongly suggest that the state or condition of these systems is determined by internal interactions between separate and distinct parts and external interactions with other systems. In this view, the whole of the ecosystem is the sum of its discrete and separable parts, and the state of this whole is allegedly determined by external interactions between these parts.

This outmoded, mechanistic view of part-whole relationships in biological reality also functions as a frame tale in descriptions of environmental problems in print and electronic media. There are typically no suggestions in these accounts that the survival of a group of people living in one region on the globe is intimately connected with the survival of other groups of people living in geographically distant regions. Consequently, people living in prosperous countries—which are located almost exclusively in areas where overpopulation has not massively disrupted environmental systems, where potable water and foodstuffs are readily available, and where the natural environment "seems" robust and healthy—are largely unaware of the fact that our commonsense view of the relationship between distant peoples on the planet makes no sense at all in scientific or ecological terms.

The stark differences between the arbitrary assumptions about part-whole relationships in current political and economic narratives and the actual dynamics of these relationships in the global environment can be illustrated by comparing planet Earth as it is imaged on a typical globe with the satellite images of this planet that scientists use to study conditions in the global environment. On the globe, boundaries between nation-states are marked with dark lines, and the regions or territories governed by particular nation-states are painted different colors. The companies that create these globes reconfigure and rename the parts to reflect changes in our constructions of geopolitical reality, such as the dissolution of the Soviet Union. But Earth as it is imaged in this geopolitical landscape is static, the whole is represented as a collection of discrete and separate parts, landmasses and oceans are depicted as disconnected lumps of corrugated and smooth surfaces, and there is nothing to suggest that any of these parts are emergent from and embedded in the global environment.

The relationship between parts and wholes in the satellite images that environmental scientists use to study the complex web of interactions in the global environment are utterly different. In these images, it is quite obvious that Earth is a dynamic living system, that all aspects of this system are interdependent and interactive, and that the activities of human beings are embedded in and inseparably connected with this whole. The scientists who study these images are very much aware that the environmental impacts of all large-scale human activities, such as emissions of greenhouse gases in the United States, the destruction of the rain forest in Brazil, and the deteriorating conditions of the coral reefs off Australia, are not separate and discrete phenomena. They are enmeshed in a seamless web of interactive environmental systems and must be viewed as such in any successful effort to resolve the crisis in the global environment. Equally important, there are no overt indications in these images that nation-states, as separate and discrete entities, even exist.

Later in this discussion, it should become clear that all parts in the global environment or ecosystem, including human activities, are embedded in and inseparably connected with a whole that is greater than the sum of its parts. The stability of this whole is regulated and sustained by an intricate network of emergent regularities that mediate the interactions of the interdependent parts. Everything in this system is quite literally connected to everything else, there is no such thing as an isolated region or territory, and all human activities are enmeshed in a web of interactions with environmental systems and processes.

PARTS AND WHOLES IN GEOPOLITICAL REALITY

Perhaps the most radical conclusion that will be drawn in this book, an insight that is conspicuously missing from virtually all the literature on the crisis in the global environment, is that assumptions about part-whole relationships in the present system of international government and in neoclassical economic theory are predicated on metaphysical assumptions. The construct of the sovereign nation-state emerged in western Europe from the eleventh to the sixteenth centuries and became the basis for a new system of international government in the Peace of Westphalia in 1648. This treaty brought to a close eighty years of religious wars between Protestant and Catholic forces and established new rules of international law that eventually became foundational to the modern state system. The most fundamental of these rules is that a sovereign nation-state should not intervene in the internal affairs of another sovereign nation-state for any reason, including the most laudable humanitarian reasons.

For our purposes, what is most important about the Peace of Westphalia is that it essentially transferred metaphysically based assumptions about the sovereign power of absolute monarchs to the construct of the sovereign nation-state. Strangely enough, these assumptions remained essentially unchanged and eventually became foundational to the present system of international government. The origins and transformations of the construct of the sovereign nation-state have been exhaustively described by many scholars, and there is no space here to include this complex history.[16] However, we will examine the manner in which this construct was transformed in the eighteenth century by philosophers and political theorists in western Europe and the United States who authored new narratives about democratic systems of government.

Assumptions about part-whole relationships in the economic narrative that now serves as the basis for coordinating virtually all large-scale economic activities, neoclassical economic theory, were articulated by eighteenth-century philosophers who were attempting to understand new economic conditions that were altering the balance of power between sovereign nation-states. Markets as a means of exchanging goods had existed from the beginnings of recorded history, but the idea of a market system as a means of maintaining an entire society did not emerge until the seventeenth century. The philosophers who attempted to define the structure of this system lived during a period in which new national economies were increasingly dependent on industrial production and international trade. This was a time when the old economic order, premised on custom and command, gave way to a new economic order that was sensitively dependent on the actions of profit-seeking individuals operating within the contexts of national market systems.[17]

Since the complex web of institutions, laws, policies, and processes that sustain and regulate production and exchange in modern markets did not exist, the new economic order more closely resembled a buzzing confusion than a rational process. The philosophers involved in the creation of classical economics believed that order lay beneath this chaos and that the ideal model for disclosing this order was Newtonian physics. In this physics, a universal force, gravity, acts outside or between parts (irreducible mass points or atoms), the collection of parts constitutes wholes, and physical systems are presumed to exist in separate and discrete dimensions in space and time.

The creators of classical economics (Adam Smith, Thomas Malthus, and David Ricardo) posited the existence of a new set of laws, the natural laws of economics, and they viewed these laws as similar to and in some sense the same as the laws of classical physics. They assumed that these laws act, like the universal force of gravity, in a causal and linear fashion between or outside atomized parts (economic actors) to maintain the stability of wholes (markets). This strategy allowed the classical economists to argue that the natural laws manifest themselves as forces that govern the behavior of parts (economic actors) and perpetuate the orderly existence of wholes (markets) even if the parts are completely unaware that this is a consequence of their actions.

Adam Smith imaged the collective action of these forces as an "invisible hand," and this construct became the central legitimating principle in mainstream economics. As economists Kenneth Arrow and Hans Hahn put it, the "notion that a social system moved by independent actors in pursuit of different values is consistent with a final coherent state of balance . . . is surely the most important intellectual contribution that economic thought has made to the general understanding of social processes."[18] In *The Wealth of Nations*, Smith described the invisible hand as follows: "As every individual, therefore, endeavors as much as he can to employ his capital in the support of domestic industry, and so to direct that industry that its produce may be of the greatest value; every individual necessarily labours to render the annual revenue of the society as great as he can. He generally, indeed, neither intends to promote the public interest, nor knows how much he is promoting it . . . and by directing that industry in such a manner as its produce may be of the greatest value, he intends only his own gain, and he is in this, as in many other cases, led by the invisible hand to promote an end which was no part of his intention."[19]

Smith argued that his invisible hand is analogous to the invisible force that causes a pendulum to oscillate around its center and move toward equilibrium or a liquid to flow between connecting chambers and find its own level. Based on this analogy, he claimed that the hand in economic reality is the force that moves independent actors in pursuit of different values toward the equalization of rates of return and that accounts for the tendency of markets to move from low to high returns. Obviously, Smith's invisible hand has no physical content and is an emblem for something postulated but completely unproven and unknown. Later in this discussion, it will be easy to appreciate why this is the case. Smith's invisible hand is premised on metaphysical assumptions, and his belief in its existence was an article of faith.

In textbooks on economics, the creators of neoclassical economics (Stanley Jevons, Leon Walras, Maria Edgeworth, and Vilfredo Pareto) are credited with transforming the study of economics into a rigorous scientific discipline with the use of higher mathematics. There are, however, no mentions in these textbooks—or in all but a few books on the history of economic thought—of a rather salient fact. The progenitors of neo-classical economics, all of whom were trained as engineers, developed their theories by substituting economic variables for physical variables in the equations of a mid-nineteenth-century physical theory.[20]

A number of well-known mid-nineteenth-century mathematicians and physicists convincingly demonstrated that the economic variables are utterly different from the physical variables and that there is no way in which one can correctly assume that they are in any sense comparable. However, the economists refused or, more probably, failed to comprehend how devastating these arguments were and continued to claim that they had transformed economics into a science with much the same epistemological authority as the physical sciences. Eventually, the presumption that neoclassical economics is a science like the physical sciences was almost universally accepted, and this explains why we now award a Nobel Memorial Prize in economics that is widely and wrongly viewed as comparable to those in physics and chemistry.

The legacy of this strange misalliance between economic theory and mid-nineteenth-century physics is a view of market systems and processes that features the following assumptions:

- The market is a closed circular flow between production and consumption with no inlets or outlets.
- Market systems exist in a domain that is separate and distinct from the external environment.
- The natural laws of economics act causally on economic actors within closed market systems, and these actors obey fixed decision-making rules.
- The natural laws of economics will, if left alone, ensure that closed market systems will perpetually grow and expand.
- The natural laws of economics will, if left alone, ensure that the global economy will perpetually expand.
- Environmental problems result from market failures or incomplete markets.
- The natural laws of economics can, if left alone, resolve most environmental problems via price mechanisms and more efficient technologies and production processes.
- Inputs of raw materials into the closed market system from the external environment are "free" unless or until costs associated with their use are internalized within the system.

- The external resources of nature are largely inexhaustible, and those that are not can be replaced by other resources or by technologies that minimize the use of the exhaustible resources or rely on other resources.
- The external environment is a bottomless sink for waste materials and pollutants.
- The costs of damage to the environment by economic activities must be treated as costs that lie outside the closed market system or as costs that are not included in the pricing mechanisms that operate within the market systems.
- These costs can be internalized in the closed market system with the use of shadow pricing and the establishment of property rights for environmental resources and amenities.
- There are no biophysical limits to the growth of market systems.

The large problem here is that all these assumptions are fundamentally wrong in scientific or ecological terms. In these terms, markets are open systems that exist in embedded and interactive relationship to the global environment, and there is a very definite relationship between economic activities and large-scale damage to this environment. Natural resources, particularly nonrenewable resources, are exhaustible, and our overreliance on some of these resources, particularly fossil fuels, is causing what may soon become irreparable damage to the ecosystem. The natural environment is not separate from economic processes, and wastes and pollutants from these processes are already at levels that threaten the stability and sustainability of ecosystems. Last but not least, the limits to the growth of the global economy in biophysical terms are real and inescapable, and the idea that market systems can perpetually expand and consume more scarce and nonrenewable natural resources is utterly false.[21]

THE GODGAME IN THE INTERNATIONAL COMMUNITY

In the international community, the godgame is played within a system of international government predicated on the construct of the sovereign nation-state, and proposed solutions to the crisis in the global environment are massively conditioned by neoclassical economic theory. To my knowledge, a sovereign nation-state has never endorsed an agreement that privileges the goal of achieving a sustainable global environment over its own interests, and it is easy to understand why this is the case. If a nation-state elected to take this unprecedented step at a meeting at the United

Nations or another international organization, this would severely compromise its ability to defend its interests, and the resulting power vacuum could be exploited by other states.

The unfortunate result is that most proposals that could potentially reduce the destructive environmental impacts of large-scale human activities are never formally considered. If a proposal survives the negotiation process, the final agreement almost invariably makes a mockery of the original intent by failing to coordinate large-scale human activities in ways that can improve conditions in the global environment. Even more alarming, virtually all these agreements have sanctioned overall increases in both the scope and the scale of destructive environmental impacts by covertly or overtly allowing for the growth and expansion of the economic activities largely responsible for these impacts.

For example, Norway, Japan, and Greece, which have large shipping industries, blocked agreements on marine pollution from oil tankers, but Germany, Italy, the Netherlands, and Sweden were more flexible in these negotiations because their economies are much less dependent on these industries. Norway violated an agreement designed to prevent the extinction of whales and defended this action before the international community.[22] The United States, in contrast, had no difficulty taking the leading role in the passage of this agreement, because it no longer had a whaling industry and did not wish to offend the growing numbers of Americans associated with the "save the whales" movement. Thirty-two small island nation-states, along with those with densely populated coastal plains, such as Bangladesh, Egypt, and the Netherlands, actively supported initiatives to reduce carbon dioxide emissions to curb global warming because rising sea levels will imperil a significant percentage of their populations. But the representatives of economically prosperous industrialized states massively resisted these initiatives because they were convinced that the reductions in emissions would retard the growth and expansion of their economies.

In the standard model for forging these agreements, the first step is to negotiate a "general framework convention" that defines the environmental problem and the broad policy issues involved. If negotiations do not break down at this stage, the framework convention can be implemented in a "regime." A regime is an evolving system that defines the problem in more specific terms, the action-oriented "protocols" that could solve the problem, and the procedures and rules that should be followed. One of the major reasons why the agreements that survive this process have been hugely ineffectual is that the legal principle of state sovereignty ensures that governments can protect their own interests at every stage of the negotiations.

This largely explains why the Framework Convention on Climate Change (1992) failed to protect the climate system, the Convention on Biodiversity Preservation (1992) did not even begin to reduce losses in biodiversity, and the Convention to Combat Desertification (1994) did not slow, much less reverse, this process. The Convention on the Law of the Sea (1982) and a host of other international agreements that were intended to reduce ocean pollution, to prevent overfishing, and to protect endangered species failed to meet any of these objectives. Nonbinding principles that could serve as the basis for the sustainable management of forests were agreed to at the Earth Summit (1992), but negotiations broke down prior to the point where a general framework convention could be articulated. A Convention on the Non-Navigable Uses of International Watercourses has been negotiated but has not gone into effect, because some sovereign nation-states perceive this agreement as a threat to their national interests.[23]

Those who believe that a system of international government premised on the construct of the sovereign nation-state is capable of resolving the environmental crisis typically refer to the 1997 Montreal Protocol as the prime example of what can be accomplished when the international community is more committed to the realization of a particular goal. The Montreal agreement is viewed as remarkably successful because it resulted in dramatic reductions in the emissions of ozone-depleting chlorofluorocarbons (CFCs). But according to Mostafa Tolba, the executive director of the U.N. Environment Programme, "The difficulties in negotiating the Montreal Protocol had nothing to do with whether the environment was damaged or not. . . . It was who was going to get the edge over whom."[24]

The United States, which was developing viable substitutes for CFCs, joined Canada and the Nordic states in promoting the ban on these chemicals in the early 1980s. However, western European countries and Japan rejected this proposal because they lagged behind the United States in this development effort. During 1986–1987, the Soviet Union refused to endorse the ban, because its leaders were concerned that it would not be possible to develop an economically viable substitute prior to the time when the limits on the production of CFCs would take effect. China and India, which were gearing up for major increases in the production of CFCs, were also opposed to the ban because they feared that a transition to ozone-safe chemicals would be too costly or that the additional costs of production would price them out of the market.

Negotiations would have completely broken down at this point in the absence of two developments. First, it became clear that substitutes could be produced at commercially viable costs. And second, the so-called Multilateral Fund was created to provide developing countries with the capital required to rapidly shift production to these substitutes. However, negotiations began to break down once again because of disagreements over rules for implementing the protocol and over monitoring and assessment procedures. Apparently, the only reason why the protocol was finally approved is that the holes in the ozone layer had become so large that the potentially disastrous impacts on human populations in all nation-states were quite obvious and could no longer be ignored.

It is also important to note that this particular environmental problem could be understood, wrongly to be sure, within the context of the classical or Newtonian paradigm. In this instance, it was possible to view the holes in the ozone layer as isolated and discrete phenomena that resulted from a single initial condition, the CFC emissions, and to posit a solution that changed this condition by adjusting a single variable—the overall levels of these emissions. Also keep in mind that the prediction that the ozone layer will recover by 2050 is predicated on the now tenuous assumption that developing countries will reduce their CFC emissions to levels called for in the agreement.

Another major reason why such international agreements are incapable of making substantive contributions to the resolution of the crisis in the global environment is that assumptions about part-whole relationships in the political and economic narratives that serve as the basis for the negotiations effectively eliminate the possibility of implementing scientifically valid solutions to environmental problems. The essential problem here is that scientifically valid solutions, which recognize the embedded and interactive relationships between human systems and environmental systems, are categorically different from and completely incompatible with assumptions about the relationships between parts (sovereign nation-states and national economies) and wholes (the international system of government and the global market system) in current political and economic narratives. In these narratives, large-scale human activities are presumed to exist within the discrete and separate regions or territories governed by sovereign nation-states, and the expansion of these activities is closely associated with the perceived self-interests of these states.

Scientific evidence may play a supportive and enabling role in some negotiations, but only as a minimum condition for serious consideration of an environmental issue. For example, numerous scientific studies on the damage done to European forests by sulfur dioxide emissions led to an agreement in 1985 that reduced these emissions to 30 percent of 1980 levels. Similarly, the scientific evidence presented in the Second Assessment Report of the Intergovernmental Panel on Climate Change was partly responsible for the passage in 1997 of the Kyoto Protocol to the Framework Convention on Climate Change. But what is not widely known is that these agreements made a mockery of the scientifically based solutions. In the vast majority of negotiations on a great range of issues, such as commercial whaling, hazardous waste trade, the melting of ice sheets in Antarctica, and ocean dumping of radioactive waste, the scientific evidence was not given serious consideration. When this evidence was perceived as a direct threat to the perceived vested interests of particular nation-states, it was either systematically ignored or explicitly rejected by the representatives of these states.[25]

A BRIEF HISTORY OF THE ENVIRONMENTAL GODGAME

This book contains numerous demonstrations that there is no basis in the present system of international government and neoclassical economic theory for positing, much less implementing, viable solutions to the crisis in the global environment. Perhaps the easiest way to briefly illustrate why this is the case is to consider how the governments of sovereign nation-states have dealt with a number of global problems. In the initial phase of activity, the focus was on local problems, such as oil spills or the dumping of hazardous wastes. Attempts to deal with these problems at the regional level resulted in the Stockholm Conference in 1972 and the creation of the United Nations Environment Programme (UNEP) several years later.

The focus shifted to global problems after scientists disclosed in 1987 that emissions of CFCs had created a large hole in the stratospheric ozone layer and the U.N.-sponsored Bruntland Commission Report, *Our Common Future,* was published. The authors of this report summarized the results of recent scientific studies on longer-term and potentially irreversible problems, such as global warming and loss of species diversity, and argued that a resolution of these problems would require unprecedented levels of cooperation between nation-states. By the end of 1988, concerns about the crisis in the global environment were so widespread that *Time* magazine named Earth "Planet of the Year" and the international community began to take this crisis seriously for the first time.

The crisis was discussed at length in the U.N. General Assembly and in international meetings, such as the 1988 Toronto Conference, the 1989 Hague and Noordwijk conferences, the 1990 Second World Conference, and the 1992 United Nations Conference on Environment and Development in Rio de Janeiro. When more than one hundred heads of state arrived at the Rio conference, which was also known as the Earth Summit, environmentalists had high hopes that the outcomes would be positive. But shortly after the conference began, members of the U.S. delegation demanded that all references to production processes and levels of consumption in developed industrial economies be deleted from proposals. The delegates also indicated that the United States would not sign the global warming convention on greenhouse gas emissions unless it was purely voluntary and would not sign the biodiversity convention in any event, because this would compromise the intellectual property rights of American biotechnology companies.

A major dilemma at the Earth Summit was that the industrialized nations of the north were unwilling to accept proposals that reduced levels of consumption while the nations of the south, where widespread poverty exists, were unwilling to limit economic growth. The buzz phrase designed to appeal to nations in both the north and the south was "sustainable development," an idea that first came to international attention when *Our Common Future* was published in 1987. In this volume, sustainable development was defined as economic behavior that "meets the needs of the present without compromising the ability of the future generations to meet their own needs."[26] Because what sustainable development actually meant, for present or future generations, was not defined, the construct was vague enough to allow all parties to accept it in principle.

When the Earth Summit was over, delegates had approved two treaties, the Framework Convention on Climate Change and the Framework Convention on Biodiversity Preservation, and three nonbinding statements of principle—the Rio Declaration, Agenda 21, and a set of Forest Principles. Although the budget approved by the conference was woefully inadequate, the paucity of funds made little difference because the treaties were badly flawed and the statements of principle were nonbinding. During a conference held five years later to evaluate what had occurred since the Earth Summit, it was determined that some progress had been made in dealing with the population problem but that other environmental problems were larger and less tractable than ever. For example, scientists at the U.N.-sponsored Intergovernmental Panel on Climate Change (IPCC) reported that global warming was a much more menacing problem than had been previously thought and that a 50–70 percent reduction in global emissions of greenhouse gases was required if Earth temperatures were to remain at something like the current levels.

Prior to the Kyoto Conference on Climate Change in 1997, President Clinton agreed that global warming was a serious problem and proposed that the Annex 1 countries, which include the industrialized nations of Europe, North America, Japan, and the former Soviet bloc, reduce greenhouse gas emissions to 1990 levels by 2012. Clinton indicated that the proposal, in contrast with earlier proposals made by the United States, would be binding. However, the proposed reductions were not only much more modest than the 50–70 percent reductions that the IPCC scientists said would be required to deal with the problem of global warming. They would also ensure that this problem would become much more difficult to resolve, because the proposal would delay the process of reducing overall emissions twelve years longer than the scientists had recommended.

During the Kyoto Conference, the U.S. delegation argued that dramatic reductions in greenhouse gases would slow the growth of the global economy. Fearing this prospect, industrialized nations pledged to reduce greenhouse gas emissions by 5.2 percent below 1990 levels by 2012. But even this very small and wholly inadequate decrease in emissions was not acceptable to delegations from the third world, and the proposal was tabled until a follow-up meeting in Buenos Aires in 1998. Another proposal passed at the conference allowed the industrialized nations to maintain current levels of emissions of greenhouse gases by buying emissions rights from former USSR countries such as Russia and the Ukraine. The presumption was that these countries had rights to sell because previous levels of industrial output had been greatly reduced when their economies collapsed following the breakup of the Soviet Union.

In this scheme, emissions are treated as commodities, and the sale of the excess commodities to other industrialized nations by Russia and the Ukraine was intended to generate revenue that would allow these countries to grow their economies. This proposal was particularly attractive to the Annex 1 countries because it would effectively eliminate the obligation to reduce greenhouse emissions to the level called for in the Clinton proposal. If the sale of emissions rights worked as planned, the 5.2 percent target by 2012 would be reduced to less than 1 percent.

In November of 2000, delegates from 175 countries gathered in The Hague to consider environmental and economic policies that would oblige 38 industrial nations to reduce greenhouse emissions to the levels specified in the Kyoto Treaty. At the beginning of this meeting, IPCC scientists declared, for the first time in the twelve-year period that this group had been in existence, that the results of their research had "proven" that the crisis in the global environment was directly attributable to human activities.

In the face of what should have been a stark reminder that the industrial nations must make good on the commitments made in Kyoto, the U.S. delegation made a proposal that would effectively eliminate the economic burden of those commitments on the U.S. economy. The proposal contained another scheme for trading in emissions credits and a scheme for granting credit for planting forests and crops. After representatives of the European Union rejected this proposal on the grounds that it would provide the United States with an unfair economic advantage, negotiations broke down and nothing of substance was accomplished.

When President Bush announced in March of 2001 that the United States was unwilling to meet the modest reductions in greenhouse gas emissions provided in the Kyoto Treaty, representatives of the European Union were outraged. During an emergency visit to Washington a few days later, the E.U. representatives made their case to Christine Todd Whitman, the administrator of the Environmental Protection Agency. Whitman said that she told the representatives she was as "optimistic as the President that, working constructively with our friends and allies through international processes, we can develop technologies, market-based incentives and other innovative approaches to global climate change."[27]

The U.S. decision to withdraw from the Kyoto Treaty was also a central point of contention in a meeting between President Bush and the chancellor of Germany, Gerhard Schröder, held a day earlier. When asked to comment on the meeting, Bush said, "We will not do anything that harms our economy, because first things first are the people who live in America."[28] This comment provoked an interesting response from the president of the E.U. Commission, former Italian prime minister Romano Prodi: "If one wants to be a world leader, one must know how to look after the entire earth and not only American Industry."[29] The refusal of the Bush administration to approve the Kyoto accords became even more egregious after President Putin indicated in May of 2004 that Russia would ratify the treaty in exchange for European support for its efforts to join the World Trade Organization.[30]

As for what science has to say about how the crisis in the global environment can be resolved, the answer is obvious, and there is no room for debate—the international community must begin very soon to develop and implement institutional frameworks and processes capable of coordinating large-scale human activities in ways that can allow for the emergence of sustainable conditions in the global environment. However, the case will be made here that the success of this formidable enterprise will be entirely dependent on two very extraordinary and historically unprecedented developments: (1) the fairly rapid creation of a supranational system of federal government that will displace the present system of international government; and (2) the simultaneous development and implementation of an environmentally responsible economic theory that can realistically assess the costs of environmental impacts of economic activities and internalize those costs in pricing systems.

According to the biologist and ecologist Paul Ehrlich, "Those who claim to have simple solutions to complex problems are most often wrong, but nonetheless the search for broad generalities is necessary. We'll never deal with the devils in the details unless we see the big picture."[31] The solutions to the complex problem of resolving the environmental crisis described in this book are oversimplified, and they are wrong in the sense that they are not sufficiently nuanced or detailed to accomplish this goal. However, the broad generalities in this discussion that allow us to see the big picture and deal with the devils in the details are absolutely right in the sense that these generalities must be foundational to any successful attempt to develop and implement viable solutions.

It also seems clear that the United States, which was not so long ago the leader in the effort to resolve environmental problems, must assume that role once again and that this will not occur unless concerns about the environmental crisis and the manner in which it can be resolved rise to the top of the U.S. political agenda. Like any revolution in thought on a national scale, this one will be a bottom-up phenomenon. But if this revolution is to occur, the citizens of this country must realize that the terms of human survival are such that the winners of the godgame that is rapidly becoming a zero-sum endgame must play by rules that do not now exist for military strategists at the Pentagon or for political leaders and economic planners of sovereign nation-states.

3

A NEW VIEW OF NATURE
Parts and Wholes in Biological Reality

We are Nature, long have we been absent, but now we will return.

— WALT WHITMAN

Imagine that a computer game like the Godgame described in the first chapter is available for home use. Assume that the players of this game can view interactions between human and environmental systems from the same godlike perspective in outer space and can zoom in and out at will to observe these interactions from the global to local levels. If a user zooms in on urban environments, human systems appear as extensive networks of highways and tracks that resemble the circulation system of some giant organism. Products from distant factories, farms, and coastal ports are flowing through the arteries of this system to energy-hungry urban centers, and raw materials are flowing to processing and manufacturing plants. The weblike connections between electric power plants, transformers, cables, power lines, phones, radios, televisions, and computers resemble the spine and branches of a central nervous system, and the centers of production, distribution, and exchange can be likened to tissues and organs. If a player zooms out and traces the threadlike connections between these systems over the horizon and around the planet, this might conjure up the image of a superorganism that is growing at an alarming rate.

Obviously, the players will not assume that this global technological system is a superorganism in any literal sense. On the other hand, they cannot fail to notice that this system consumes vast amounts of natural resources, massively damages and disrupts environmental systems from the tropics to the poles, and does resemble, in ecological terms at least, a superorganism that feeds off the living system of the planet and extends

its bodily organization into every ecological niche. The more astute players will also realize that if this system continues to grow at the present
rate, using existing technologies and energy resources, such growth can
easily undermine the capacity of the system of life to sustain human life.

If we must begin very soon to coordinate large-scale human activities
in ways that will allow for the emergence of sustainable conditions in the
global environment, this will obviously require some understanding of how
the interactions between human and environmental systems are viewed in
environmental science. Fortunately, acquiring a working knowledge of
this real-world view is not very difficult. The real challenge is to use this
knowledge to posit viable solutions to the environmental crisis.

One of the major reasons why we have failed to resolve this crisis is
that scientifically outmoded assumptions about part-whole relationships
in Newtonian or classical physics massively condition our understanding
of the causes of environmental problems and the manner in which they
can be resolved. These scientifically outmoded assumptions emerged during the first scientific revolution of the seventeenth century and can be
briefly summarized as follows: (1) the fundamental unit in physical reality
is a discrete and separate part (mass point or atom); (2) the interactions between these parts are completely determined by universal physical laws;
(3) these interactions result in wholes (physical systems or processes) that
can be reduced to and explained in terms of the sum of their constituent
parts; (4) the nature and function of a whole can be understood in terms
of the interactions "between" constituent parts; and (5) the future of any
physical system or process can eventually be known and described in exhaustive detail by physical theories if all the initial conditions are known.

All the assumptions about part-whole relationships in Newtonian or
classical physics were undermined during the second scientific revolution
in the twentieth century beginning with the publication of Einstein's special theory of relativity in 1905. Classical or Newtonian physics is now
viewed as a higher-level approximation of physical processes that is useful in situations where the speed of light and the quantum of action can
be conveniently ignored for practical purposes. But for most of the twentieth century, many physicists assumed, wrongly as it turned out, that
quantum physics was the most complete description of physical reality on
the microlevel and that classical physics was the most complete description on the macrolevel. For our purposes, this seemingly esoteric issue is
important because most teachers of introductory biology courses still presume that this two-domain distinction is scientific.

This explains why most introductory textbooks in biology make no mention of the fact that Darwin predicated his theory of evolution on out-moded assumptions about part-whole relationships in Newtonian physics. And it also explains why this theory is still taught in something like its original form in most introductory courses in biology on the high school level and in many courses on the college level. Although Darwin's insights into the dynamics of evolution were remarkably prescient, there is no basis in his mechanistic view of part-whole relationships in biological reality for understanding the complex interactions between human systems and environmental systems in ecological terms. The large problem here is that the vast majority of students in the American educational system have taken introductory biology courses in which they were taught that this mechanistic view is scientific. One of the unfortunate consequences is that most of the commentaries on environmental problems in both print and electronic media are written by people who still believe that Darwinian assumptions about part-whole relationships in biological reality are sci-entific. Another is that the vast majority of political leaders and economic planners also presume that this is the case, and this massively frustrates their ability to understand what environmental scientists are saying about the causes of the crisis in the global environment and the manner in which it can be resolved.

PARTS AND WHOLES IN DARWINIAN THEORY

Charles Darwin was a great admirer of the work of Isaac Newton, and his theory of evolution is predicated on a conception of the relationship between parts (organisms) and wholes (species) that mirrors the relation-ship between parts (mass points or atoms) and wholes (physical systems) in Newtonian physics. Darwin made his theory public for the first time in a paper delivered to the Linnaean Society in 1858. The paper begins, "All nature is at war, one organism with another, or with external nature."[1] In *The Origin of Species,* Darwin is more specific about the character of this war: "There must be in every case a struggle for existence, either one in-dividual with another of the same species, or with the individuals of dis-tinct species, or with the physical conditions of life."[2]

Based on the assumption that the study of variation in domestic animals and plants "afforded the best and safest clue" to understanding evolu-tion, Darwin concluded that nature could, by crossbreeding and selection of traits, produce new species. His explanation of the mechanism that re-sults in new species took the form of the following argument: (1) the prin-ciple of geometric increase in population indicates that more individuals in each species will be produced than can survive; (2) the struggle for existence occurs owing to shortage of resources; (3) in this struggle for existence, slight variations, if they prove advantageous, will accumulate in interbreeding groups, and this can result in new species. In analogy with the animal breeder's artificial selection of traits, Darwin termed the elimination of the disadvantaged organisms and the promotion of the advantaged "natural selection."

In Darwin's view, the "struggle for existence" occurs *between* an individual organism and other individual organisms in the "same species," *between* an individual organism of one species and that of a "different species," or *between* an individual organism and the "physical conditions of life." The whole as Darwin conceived it is the collection of all individual parts (organisms), and the struggle for survival occurs *between* or *outside* the parts. Natural selection occurs, says Darwin, when variations "useful to each being's own welfare," or useful to the welfare of an individual organism, provide a survival advantage and the organism produces "offspring similarly characterized."

Because Darwin assumed that the force responsible for selection operates outside the parts, he described the whole in terms of "relations" between the parts. For example, the "infinite complexity of relations of all organic beings to each other and to their conditions of life" refers to relations between parts, and the "infinite diversity in structure, constitution, habits" refers to "advantageous" traits within the parts. The individual organisms or parts in Darwin's theory resemble classical atoms, and the force that drives the interactions of the parts, the "struggle for life," resembles Newton's force of universal gravity. Darwin may have parted company with classical determinism in the claim that changes, or mutations, within organisms occurred randomly, but his view of the relationship between parts and wholes was essentially Newtonian.

Although Darwin's speculation that mutations were random was later shown to be correct, he could not say anything about the mechanisms involved, because the concept of genes was not known to him. A contemporary of Darwin, the monk Gregor Mendel, introduced the concept of genes in a paper published in an obscure Austrian journal in 1865. But it was not until about 1910 that scientists began to realize that genes could be the basic unit of evolution and that a better understanding of gene transmission could put the theory of evolution on firmer scientific foundations. During the 1940s, Theodosius Dobzhansky, Ernst Mayr, and others synthesized Darwin's idea that organisms and populations gradually change with Mendel's concept of genetic inheritance in what came to be known as the Modern Synthesis. One aspect of the Modern Synthesis, the concept of emergence, eventually became foundational to the new understanding of part-whole relationships in the new biology. Emergence refers to new properties that emerge from wholes or systems that cannot be explained by interactions between discrete components or parts.

EMERGENCE IN BIOLOGICAL REALITY

Research in the new biology challenged the Darwinian assumption that evolution is a process in which natural selection acts outside or between parts (organisms). It did so by disclosing that a scientifically valid understanding of the function of these parts requires an examination of the manner in which new wholes emerge that cannot be reduced to or explained in terms of their constituent parts. As Ernst Mayr put it, living systems "almost always have the peculiarity that the characteristics of the whole cannot (not even in theory) be deduced from the most complete knowledge of components, taken separately or in other partial combinations. This appearance of new characteristics in wholes has been designated emergence."[3]

The concept of emergence essentially recognizes that an assemblage of parts in successive levels of organization in nature can result in wholes that display new or novel properties. As P. B. and J. S. Medawar put it, "Each higher-level subject contains ideas and conceptions peculiar to itself. These are the 'emergent' properties."[4] From this perspective, organisms are not mixtures or compounds of inorganic parts but new wholes with emergent properties that are embedded in and intimately related to more complex wholes with their own emergent properties.

Over the last three decades, new mathematical tools and techniques have been developed in an effort to better understand living systems as self-organizing networks, where self-organization is defined as the spontaneous emergence of a globally coherent pattern out of local interactions. This new theory of self-organization and adaptation makes extensive use of the mathematics of dynamical systems theory, which is also known as systems dynamics, complex dynamics, and nonlinear dynamics. Scientists use dynamical systems theory to study the "hidden" dynamics of nonlinear systems that result in the emergence of new structures or behavior that cannot be explained in terms of the sum of the properties of their constituent parts. However, dynamical systems theory is not a theory as that term is normally used in science. It is a mathematical theory predicated on concepts and techniques that apply to a broad range of phenomena, and the same is true for two important branches of this theory, chaos theory and the theory of fractals.

Scientists now use dynamical systems theory to study the self-organizing dynamics of the system of life on every level—from molecules to genes to cells to embryological development to complex adaptive behavior. These studies have revealed that all biological systems display emergent properties that are embedded in a complex web of dynamic interconnections with their environments in a state or condition known as "far-from-equilibrium." For those not familiar with this concept, a physical system is in equilibrium when its energy is distributed in the most statistically probable way, or when the forces, influences, reactions, and so on balance each other out and there is no change. If the universe existed in this state, there would be no complexity or novelty, and life would not exist.

In nonlinear systems, there are typically large numbers of initial conditions and many degrees of freedom, or directions in which the systems can develop or evolve, and the future of these systems can be predicted only within a range of probabilities. Until recently, scientists avoided the study of nonlinear systems because of their seemingly chaotic nature and the fact that nonlinear equations are usually too difficult to solve. Rather than deal with nature in its full complexity, scientists routinely described nonlinear processes by using linear approximations that could be represented in formulas and solved analytically. The term "linear" in the phrase "linear equations" refers to the fact that when the movement of a system described by these equations is plotted on a graph, the trajectory is a straight line.

Some efforts were made to solve nonlinear equations numerically by using various combinations for the variables until some approximation fit the nonlinear equations. For most nonlinear equations, however, this is a very cumbersome and time-consuming process that yields only very approximate solutions. This situation changed dramatically with the availability of powerful computers that can compute the large numbers of values that satisfy the nonlinear equations and provide solutions represented graphically as a curve or set of curves.

In the 1960s, Nobel laureate Ilya Prigogine used dynamical systems theory and the new mathematics of complexity to develop a nonlinear dynamics for the study of far-from-equilibrium systems. He demonstrated that the ability of these systems to display spontaneous self-organization is associated with feedback loops and that the equations that described these loops were nonlinear. Prigogine also discovered a correlation between the level of complexity in these systems and the degree of nonlinearity in the mathematical equations describing the feedback loops. This allowed him to answer a very puzzling question—how do small changes in nonlinear systems produce large effects? The answer was that the initial effects in these systems are amplified by self-reinforcing feedback loops.

A feedback loop is essentially a series of causally connected elements in which an initial element causes effects on other elements that propagate around a loop and "feed back" into the original element. In other words, an original input affects the last output in repeated cycles, and each input is modified or changed by the previous cycle. A feedback loop is called positive if recurrent inputs amplify the initial change and move the system in a particular direction, and negative if these inputs counteract or suppress the initial change and move the system back toward its original state. Positive feedbacks can occasion large changes in biological systems that can result in novel structures and behavior, and negative feedbacks can stabilize these systems by preventing the changes from occurring in a runaway or explosive manner. In mathematical terms, the loops are represented in a special kind of nonlinear process, called iteration, in which a function operates repeatedly on itself.

In Prigogine's theory, there is usually more than one possible solution to a set of equations describing a nonlinear system, and the number of solutions increases in proportion to the degree of nonlinearity. When a nonlinear system arrives at a bifurcation point, or the point where new structures or behavior may suddenly emerge, there are typically a number of paths or branches that can be followed. Equally interesting, the path or branch that is followed is unique for each system and cannot be predicted with any degree of certainty. This means that there is an irreducibly random element in nonlinear systems and that the behavior of a particular system can be predicted with a fair degree of accuracy for only a short period of time. For example, the essential indeterminacy in the nonlinear system of the atmosphere is such that we can never hope to make accurate predictions about weather conditions on both regional and global levels beyond a limited time period. The current estimate is ten days or less.

The most startling aspect of Prigogine's theory is a new view of the role played by irreversibility. In classical thermodynamics, irreversibility is associated with energy losses and increased entropy or disorder. These dynamics were used to explain the existence of the "arrow of time," or the progression of events in a fixed direction from past to future. Because the entropy law, or the second law of thermodynamics, clearly implied that all the order in the universe would eventually be displaced by disorder, some intellectuals, such as Henry Adams in *The Education of Henry Adams,* concluded that this view of the cosmic future was a cause for despair. Prigogine did not undermine this scientific understanding of the ultimate fate of the cosmos, but he did demonstrate that irreversibility can play a constructive role and lead to higher levels of order. As he put it, "Irreversibility is the mechanism that brings order out of chaos."[5]

Prigogine showed that far-from-equilibrium systems are open systems, meaning that energy and matter flow through them from the outside, and that this condition allows new structures or patterns to spontaneously emerge in the absence of any external agency that imposes these structures or patterns. Because this increase in order correlates with a reduction in entropy or disorder, and because this process is irreversible in the sense that it cannot run backward to its original state, irreversibility in these terms is "the mechanism that brings order out of chaos." However, this appearance of order out of chaos does not violate the second law of thermodynamics. The evolution of more and more complex forms of life on Earth may seem to reverse the law of increasing entropy. But since the energy that flows through these living systems comes primarily from the sun and the sun necessarily becomes more disordered or more entropic in the process of generating this energy, the overall amount of entropy in the universe increases, and the second law is not violated in this larger context.

Prigogine's work is merely one example of the manner in which dynamical systems theory has led to dramatic new insights into the self-organizing and self-regulating dynamics of life. For example, Stuart Kauffman used the new mathematics of this theory to study the development of organisms and ecosystems in computer simulations. These simulations model networks of mutually interacting or inhibiting genes that result in differentiation between organs and tissues during embryological development.[6] Kauffman argues that the dynamics of these self-organizing networks are essential aspects of evolution that should be viewed as complementary to the dynamics of Darwinian selection.

Similarly, John Holland has developed computer simulations in which genetic algorithms are used to model the mechanisms that allow biological organisms to adapt to changing conditions in their environments.[7] These algorithms mimic the dynamics of mutation and natural selection in a virtual reality in which the most fit new combinations of genes result in organisms that survive and reproduce. Holland has also extended his model to study entire ecological systems in which interactions between relatively simple organisms result in the emergence of complex systems with several hierarchical levels of organization. Even more ambitious, Chris Langton and others have developed computer programs in a new discipline called "artificial life" that mimic the dynamics associated with reproduction, sexuality, the coevolution of organisms, and predator-prey relationships.[8]

Research based on dynamical systems theory has demonstrated that complex adaptive systems in biological reality reside on the edge of chaos, or in a narrow domain between relative equilibrium or stability and turbulent chaotic activity. Per Bak has labeled the mechanisms by which these systems maintain themselves in this domain "self-organized criticality."[9] These mechanisms typically obey a "power law," which essentially says that large changes in ecosystems are possible but much less probable than small changes. Another hallmark of complex adaptive systems is that they feature many levels of organizations where interactions between agents at one level allow for the emergence of different structures and processes at another level.

For example, feedback loops between proteins, lipids, and nucleic acids allow for the emergence of a cell, and feedback loops between cells allow for the emergence of a tissue. This process further unfolds as feedback loops at progressively higher levels of self-organization allow for the emergence of organs, whole organisms, and ecosystems. Feedback loops also modify the structures and functions of complex adaptive systems in response to changing conditions in environmental niches. This process is roughly analogous to the manner in which feedback loops between neurons and neuronal patterns in the human brain are strengthened or weakened in response to external stimuli.

Research based on dynamical systems theory has also shown that complex adaptive systems tend to be fairly stable, robust, and resilient because the mechanisms that result in emergent order are distributed over the entire system. Because the feedback loops are widely distributed and redundant, nondamaged regions in ecosystems can often restore damaged regions over a relatively short period of time. But if large-scale human activities disrupt the complex web of feedback loops in ecosystems to the point where the self-regulating and self-sustaining mechanisms in these far-from-equilibrium systems are disabled, large-scale changes in the whole of the global environment can occur over a few years.

What is most important about dynamical systems theory for our purposes is that research based on this theory will be critically important in the effort to resolve the crisis in the global environment. As we saw in the first chapter, this research has gifted us with a reasonable scientific basis for coordinating large-scale human activities in ways that can allow for the emergence of sustainable conditions in the global environment. It is also capable of predicting within an increasingly narrower range of statistical probabilities when large-scale changes in global environmental conditions are likely to occur. But since macrolevel indeterminacy is an indelible feature of biological life, there is a limit on our ability to precisely determine conditions of sustainability in the global environment or to make precise predictions about when large-scale changes in this environment will occur.[10]

PARTS AND WHOLES IN THE SYSTEM OF LIFE

We now know that the process of emergence has resulted in increasingly more complex life-forms during the entire history of life on Earth. This process began with one self-replicating molecule that was the ancestor of DNA, and all the organisms that have existed on this planet are the direct descendants of a single life-form.[11] During the first 2 billion years of life on Earth, prokaryotes, or organisms composed of cells with no nucleus, were the sole inhabitants, and the emergence of more complex life-forms resulted from networking and symbiosis. Over the course of these 2 billion years, feedback loops between prokaryotes transformed Earth's surface and atmosphere and allowed for the emergence of the processes of fermentation, photosynthesis, and oxygen breathing.

One of the reasons why the interactions between these simple organisms could result in such complex processes is that the absence of a nucleus with a surrounding membrane in bacteria allowed bits of genetic material within bacteria to be routinely and rapidly transferred to other bacteria. Consequently, an individual bacterium had the use of accessory genes, often from very different strains, that could perform functions not performed by its own DNA. Some of this genetic material was incorporated into the DNA of a bacterium and passed on to other bacteria. What this picture suggests, as Lynn Margulis and Dorian Sagan put it, is that "all the world's bacteria have access to a single gene pool and hence to the adaptive mechanisms of the entire bacterial kingdom."[12]

Because an individual bacterium can access genes in large numbers of other bacteria, the speed of genetic recombination is much greater than that allowed by mutation in organisms with a nucleus or by random changes inside these organisms. This explains why bacteria can adapt to a change in the global environment in a few years. If the only mechanism at work were random genetic mutations inside organisms, much longer periods of time would be required for bacteria to adapt to a global change in the conditions for survival. "By constantly and rapidly adapting to environmental conditions," write Margulis and Sagan, "the organisms of the microcosm support the entire biota, their global exchange network ultimately affecting every living plant and animal."[13]

The discovery of symbiotic alliances between different organisms that become permanent in new organisms is another aspect of our new under-standing of evolution that is not in accord with the assumption that natu-ral selection can act only outside or between individual organisms. In the cells of higher organisms, there are several organelles that have double membranes, and it is now believed that these organelles were originally independent organisms that evolved symbiotic relationships with other organisms. For example, the mitochondria found in the cytoplasm of modern animal cells allow these animal cells to utilize oxygen and to exist in an oxygen-rich environment. Given that mitochondria have their own genes composed of DNA, reproduce by simple division, and do so at times different from divisions in the rest of the cell, they resemble discrete or separate organisms in spite of the fact that they perform integral and essential functions in the life of the cell.

The explanation for this extraordinary alliance between mitochondria and the rest of the cell is that oxygen-requiring prokaryotes in primeval seas combined with other organisms. These ancestors of modern mitochon-dria entered other organisms and provided waste disposal and oxygen-derived energy in exchange for food and shelter, and the previously separate organisms evolved together into more complex forms of oxygen-requiring life. Similarly, the ancestors of the chloroplasts inside the cells of all green plants were also originally separate organisms that evolved the capacity to convert carbon dioxide and water into oxygen and sugar in the process of photosynthesis. Like the ancestors of the mitochondria, these organ-isms also combined with other organisms, and a new life-form emerged as a result of this symbiotic relationship. What is most remarkable here is that the emergent new organisms displayed behavior that could not be reduced to or explained in terms of the sum of their symbiotic parts.[14]

A great deal of evidence also suggests that the biosphere displays emer-gent properties that maintain conditions suitable for life, and some of these properties are associated with feedback loops between the evolved inter-actions of organisms. For example, it now seems clear that the temperature of Earth's surface and the composition of the air have been continuously regulated by the entire biota. Although the complex network responsible for this feat is not well understood, the evidence suggests that emergent dynamics in the entire biota are responsible.

THE WHOLE WITHIN THE PARTS

In the system of life, the whole within the parts (organisms) is DNA, and a complete strand of DNA exists in the nucleus of each cell. DNA codes for the production of enzymes in a complex network of feedback loops that determine which enzymes are produced. Cell types differ from one another not merely because they contain particular genes, but also because different sequences in these genes are activated in specific cellular environments. After the discovery of the structure of DNA, many molecular biologists assumed that genes were merely a set of instructions on how to make a body and organisms based on initial inputs. We now know that this is not the case.

The genetic information in DNA that codes for an initial protein is a necessary but not sufficient cause in the process of creating an organism because a protein typically changes its form and function via a complex network of feedback loops with other proteins. Each of the estimated thirty thousand genes in human DNA codes for the production of a single protein, but this initial input does not determine the function of this protein in a causal, linear fashion. One reason why this is the case is that subsequent interactions with other proteins typically result in smaller sequences that are recombined to form about ten other proteins that perform specialized functions. Another is that a large repertoire of regulatory mechanisms modifies human proteins to perform specialized functions on a moment-to-moment basis, and these mechanisms respond to a wide range of environmental stimuli. It has also been discovered recently that RNA, after being transcribed from the nucleotide sequence in DNA, can feed back and modify the genome, and that these modifications can be inherited through cell divisions and influence development.[15] This means that an organism cannot be reduced to or explained in terms of the sum of its initial computable parts, because the whole organism displays unique and complex emergent behaviors that result from interactions within and between parts.

Organisms are still compared in biology textbooks with factories or machines, and this mechanistic view of part-whole relationships is pervasive in public debates about the crisis in the global environment and in descriptions of environmental problems in the media. But a machine is a unity of order and not of substance, and the order that exists in a machine exists outside or between the parts. A machine is constructed from without, the whole is the assemblage of its constituent parts, and the interactions between the parts define the function of the whole. Parts of machines can be separated and reassembled and the machine will run normally. But if we separate a living organism into its component parts, the emergent properties of life vanish.[16] Our fondness for mechanistic explanations also explains why models of DNA, which resemble futuristic Tinkertoy machines, wrongly suggest that the building blocks of life exist in fixed and static relationship to one another in a rigid spiral staircase. In reality, the base pairs in this molecule are always moving and vibrating, electrons are constantly migrating, and nothing remains the same for more than for a few milliseconds.[17]

Recent studies in biology have also revealed that feedback loops in evolved interactions between organisms in a particular ecology or ecosystem typically result in a web of interactions that sustains biological diversity. Organisms in the same habitat often display adaptive behavior that involves the division of the habitat into ecological niches, whereby the presence of one species does not compromise the existence of another, similar species in the same habitat. For example, the zebra, wildebeest, and gazelle are common prey to five carnivores—lion, leopard, cheetah, hyena, and wild dog. These predators coexist, however, because they developed five different ways of living off the three prey species that do not directly compete with one another. As the ethologist James Gould explains: "Cheetahs are unique in their high-speed chase strategy, but as a consequence must specialize on small gazelle. Only the leopard uses an ambush strategy, which seems to play no favorites in the prey it chooses. Hyenas and wild dogs are similar, but hunt at different times. And the lion exploits the brute-force niche, depending alternately on short, powerful rushes and strong-arm robbery."[18]

Herbivores also display evolved behavior that minimizes competition for scarce resources in the interests of sustaining other life-forms in the environment. Paul Colinvaux has studied such behavior on the African savanna: "Zebras take the long dry stems of grasses for which their horsy incisor teeth are nicely suited. Wildebeest take the side-shoot grasses, gathering with their tongues in the bovine way and tearing off the food against their single set of incisors. Thompson's gazelles graze where others have been before, picking out ground-hugging plants and other tidbits."[19]

Similarly, three species of yellow weaverbirds in central Africa live on the same shore of a lake without struggle because one species eats only hard black seeds, another soft green seeds, and the third only insects.[20] In North America, twenty different insects feed on the same white pine, but five eat only foliage, three live off birds, three on twigs, two on wood, two on roots, one on bark, and four on cambium.[21] A newly hatched garter snake pursues worm scent over cricket scent, and a newly hatched green snake in the same environment displays the opposite preference. Yet both species of snake could eat the same prey.[22] The point is that emergent cooperative behaviors within parts (organisms) that maintain sustainable conditions suitable for life in the whole (environment or ecosystem) are everywhere present in nature.

PARTS AND WHOLES IN PUBLIC POLICY

If life could be understood as a system in which distinct and separate organisms interact in accordance with completely deterministic laws, we could reasonably expect that the future state of the global environment could be predicted with a high level of certainty. However, this expectation is not reasonable or even rational, because life is a nonlinear system that maintains and reconstitutes itself via a vast web of indeterminate feedback loops. Predictions based on improved computer-based models may provide more accurate assessments of the impacts of large-scale human activities on the global environment within an increasingly narrow range of statistical probabilities. But there is no prospect that these predictions will ever be accurate to a degree demanded by those who believe that we live in a Newtonian universe.

In public debates about environmental problems, this is a large and menacing problem. For example, when scientists testify before committees in the U.S. Congress and describe future conditions in the global environment in terms of a range of statistical probabilities, this testimony is almost invariably dismissed by one or more committee members on the grounds that the less than precise predictions indicate that the scientists do not really understand the problems. Those who make this claim typically argue that we should not implement any proposed solutions to environmental problems in the absence of a "proper" scientific understanding of those problems. Clearly, this response is utterly irresponsible for a now obvious reason—the future of the nonlinear system of life cannot, in principle, be predicted with a high degree of accuracy, and the levels of uncertainty increase in direct proportion to the amount of time involved.

The only reasonable, not to mention morally responsible, way to deal with the uncertainties in the scientific predictions is to systematically appeal to the precautionary principle. This principle essentially states that in dealing with uncertainties about future environmental changes that would potentially have disastrous impacts on human populations, we should err on the side of caution. According to Charles Perrins, "The class of problems for which the precautionary principle is advocated as an alternative to conventional decision-making models is that for which the level of uncertainty and the potential costs of current activities are both high." In these situations, writes Perrins, "The optimal policy is then the one that minimizes the maximum environmental costs over variation in the unobserved part of the history of the system."[23]

The precautionary principle in various forms has been written into every international agreement on the global environment since the Earth Summit at Rio de Janeiro in 1992. In the Rio declaration, the principle is stated as follows: "When there are threats of serious or irreversible damage, lack of full scientific certainty shall not be used as a reason for postponing cost-effective measures to prevent environmental degradation." The suggestion that "full scientific certainty" is possible and the qualification that the measures taken must be "cost-effective," as this concept is defined in neoclassical economic theory, were included in the Rio declaration to satisfy the concerns of representatives from economically prosperous industrialized countries. Nevertheless, the fact that the precautionary principle in some form was included is a step in the right direction.

In the next chapter, we will consider what science has to say about the emergence from the system of life of a species that evolved the capacity to acquire and use fully complex language systems about sixty-five thousand years ago. One of the chapter's objectives is to explain how this species, among the millions that have existed, managed to massively disrupt the self-regulating and self-perpetuating dynamics of life on an entire planet. The other is to demonstrate that when we enlarge the framework of human history to include what science has to say about this history, it becomes clear that the causes of the crisis in the global environment and the manner in which it can be resolved are the same.

This crisis exists because fully modern humans could organize their collective activities based on themes and narratives and could externalize ideas as artifacts. And the fundamental challenge at this critical point in human history is to use this extraordinary ability to accomplish two formidable objectives. The first is to articulate institutional frameworks and processes capable of coordinating large-scale human activities in environmentally responsible ways on a planetary scale. And the second related objective is to develop and implement technologies on this scale that have relatively benign environmental impacts. The barriers to the success of this grand enterprise are formidable. But as the next chapter will demonstrate, the prospects of resolving the environmental crisis can be greatly enhanced by viewing human history through the conceptual lenses of modern science.

4

THE AMAZING GIFT OF LANGUAGE
The Emergence of Fully Conscious Humans

Never doubt that a small group of thoughtful, committed citizens can change the world. Indeed, it is the only thing that ever has.

— MARGARET MEAD

Suppose that you are still playing the Godgame described at the beginning of the previous chapter on your home computer and the following question appears on the screen: "What adaptive trait allowed one species among the millions that have existed on this planet to live in environments that were not species-specific, increase its numbers to 6.4 billion individuals, appropriate roughly 90 percent of the planetary biomass for its own use, and create global technological systems that are rapidly undermining the capacity of the system of life to sustain its existence?" Assuming that you have access to the relevant scientific material, it would not take long to realize that there is one fundamental reason why fully modern humans were capable of accomplishing these feats—the evolution of the bodies and brains of our ancestors resulted in the capacity to acquire and use fully complex language systems.

In an effort to put this utterly amazing and hugely improbable development in perspective, let us consider the question of whether fully conscious and self-aware life-forms exist on other planets. A great deal of evidence suggests that the chemical compounds that allowed biological life to emerge on this planet may be present in the universe at large, and laboratory experiments have demonstrated that some of the necessary ingredients, amino acids, can spontaneously emerge under suitable conditions. In order for life to arise from these compounds on other planets, a delicate balance between many other factors, such as temperature, atmospheric pressure, and water content, would be required. But since galaxies number in the billions and an average galaxy contains hundreds of billions of stars, many planets with conditions suitable for life could circle their own sun in our galaxy or in neighboring galaxies. If we assume that biological life has arisen on millions of these planets, it is conceivable that the process of evolution on some of these planets resulted in the emergence of intelligent life-forms and that some have developed advanced civilizations.

The most ardent promoters of this thesis tend to be physicists and molecular biologists, and public acceptance of their views resulted in the creation of the Search for Extraterrestrial Intelligence (SETI) project. The intent of those involved in this project, as many Americans learned for the first time after seeing a movie based on the late Carl Sagan's book *Cosmos,* is to intercept intragalactic or intergalactic communications between advanced civilizations on other planets. But what the book and movie failed to mention is that many scientists, most of whom are evolutionary biologists, are convinced that the odds that advanced civilizations exist anywhere else in the vast cosmos are slim to none. And one of them, Ernst Mayr, has made a rather convincing case that SETI was a deplorable waste of taxpayers' money.[1]

The skeptics point out that even if we assume that life has arisen numerous times on other planets, we must then imagine an evolutionary pathway that results in the emergence of a species that has the capacity to acquire and use a complex communication system, such as the human language system. Because mutations are random and the course of evolution cannot be predicted, the skeptics claim that there is no basis for assuming that life on other planets would necessarily result in a fully conscious and self-aware life-form. During billions of years of evolution on this planet, 99 percent of existing species became extinct, and only a small percentage of mammals, the anthropoid apes, emerged via innumerable indeterminate branch points with an intelligence that surpasses that of other mammals. During the 25 million years in which these apes have existed, there were probably hundreds of branching points and independently evolving lines, and only one became the lineage that evolved into modern humans.

When we consider the myriad number of mutations that eventually allowed fully modern humans to image and manipulate a world in the symbolic space of the mind, it is not difficult to appreciate why increasing numbers of scientists have become skeptical about the prospect that intelligent life exists on other planets. From their perspective, it could well be that Earth is the only planet on which fully conscious beings exist. The scientific jury is still out on this question, and this will probably remain the case for a very long time. But if the skeptics are correct, the question of whether the intelligent life-forms on this planet will resolve the crisis in the global environment takes on a much larger significance. If we fail and our species becomes extinct, this would be a tragedy of cosmic proportions because consciousness as an emergent property of a universe that has been evolving toward higher levels of complexity for over 13 billion years would cease to exist. In these terms, the universe itself would no longer be aware of its own awareness, and nothing in the vast reaches of interstellar space would have any meaning beyond the brute fact of existence.

THE GREAT LEAP FORWARD

We will never know in any exhaustive detail how our hominid ancestors evolved the capacity to acquire and use complex language systems. We do know with some certainty, however, that this capacity evolved over a period of about 2 million years. Each of the incremental changes in the brains and bodies of our ancestors that culminated in this dramatic result enhanced the prospect that those who possessed these traits would survive and pass their genes on to subsequent generations. It now appears, however, that this process did not begin to result in survival advantages any greater than those of other existing species of hominids until about 200,000 years ago. During this period, a relatively small number of mutations in the bodies and brains of a group of modern humans living in present-day Ethiopia, Kenya, and Tanzania apparently allowed for a much higher level of integration between a myriad number of previously evolved functions and processes.

A number of evolutionary biologists have speculated that this group was isolated for an extended period of time and that the mutations that resulted in the capacity to acquire and use fully complex language systems made them utterly different from other surviving groups of hominids. What is most remarkable here is that recent studies in genetics indicate that all of the 6.4 billion people alive today are the direct descendants of about two thousand individuals in the small lineage of hominids that became fully modern humans.[2] The other groups of hominids that existed during this period, including an earlier lineage of our own species, did not evolve the capacity to acquire and use fully complex language systems and all of them are now extinct.

Prior to 70,000 years ago, when our ancestors had not yet migrated out of Africa, their stone tools were primitive. Those found in the fossil remains display little innovation and are similar to tools used by Neanderthals.

There were apparently no unequivocal compound tools, such as a wooden handle with an axe-like blade, and no variations in toolmaking in different geographical locations. But about 40,000 years ago a group of fully modern humans living in France and Spain were capable of inventing cultural artifacts that grandly testify to their creativity and intelligence. Compound tools, standardized bone and antler tools, and tools that fall into distinct categories or functions, such as mortars and pestles, needles, rope, and fishhooks, appear in the fossil remains. Also found in these remains are weapons designed to kill large animals at a distance—darts, barbed harpoons, bows and arrows, and spear throwers. Other artifacts suggest that human life had become more than a brutal struggle to survive. Rock paintings, necklaces, pendants, fired-clay ceramic sculptures, flutes, and rattles are indicative of profound aesthetic preoccupations and religious impulses. Equally interesting, the cultures of people living in geographically disparate places become after this point in time increasingly disparate.

Why did complex human societies appear in just a few thousand years in Africa, western Asia, and Europe after a 2-million-year period in which our hominid ancestors lived in extremely primitive conditions and human life was virtually static? The most reasonable explanation is that a series of mutations in one small lineage of hominids resulted in a reorganization of neuronal patterns, pathways, and feedback loops that occasioned a phase change in cognition that culminated in the ability to acquire and use a fully complex language system about 65,000 years ago. Some experts argue that this brain reorganization occurred over something like one hundred generations during a period in which selection pressures due to climatic stress were very high and fortuitous mutations that dramatically enhanced language abilities provided a distinct survival advantage.[3] This hypothesis has been reinforced by convincing evidence that all extant human languages have a common origin in a single language system that existed about 50,000 years ago.[4]

But even if the evolution of the capacity to acquire and use fully complex language systems was more gradual, the result was utterly amazing. A lineage of hominids that had previously seemed dull, slow, and destined for extinction became a community of individuals that was capable of inhabiting a language-based symbolic universe. In this universe, experience could be represented and organized in themes and narratives, and the terms of survival could be altered and manipulated with complex social behavior and ideas externalized as artifacts. Our hominid ancestors may have been very similar to other species of hominids prior to their emergence from the system of life as fully conscious modern humans. But after this momentous event (from our point of view) occurred, the difference between our species and other life-forms, including our primate cousins, became a yawning chasm.

If it were possible for any human being alive today to create a family tree that moved back through all the generations of forebears to the first small group of ancestors who were capable of acquiring and using a complex language system, this would demonstrate that the claim that all humans are part of one extended family is not an artifact of some idealistic conception of universal humanity. It is simply a statement of fact.[5] The descendants of the first group of fully modern humans were able to migrate over time to very diverse regions of the globe because they had the capacity to create new narratives that could more effectively organize their collective activities in diverse ecological niches, and because they were able to invent new technologies more suitable for exploiting local resources.

The first migration out of East Africa, beginning about 45,000 years ago, was apparently north along the Nile Valley and across the Sinai Peninsula into the Middle East, the Near East, southeastern Europe, and southwestern Europe. The branch of this family that crossed over the Asian mainland into Australia and New Guinea between 40,000 to 30,000 years ago apparently made use of some form of watercraft. Other members of this extended family moved along the coastlines of India and southeastern Asia, and some of their descendants crossed the land bridge that joined Siberia and Alaska into North and South America about 12,000 years ago.

As various branches of our extended family migrated over the course of many generations to more distant regions, minor mutations occurred that enhanced survival under disparate climatic conditions. For those living in equatorial regions, where ultraviolet rays from the sun are intense, dark skin helped to prevent skin cancer and severe sunburn, which can result in serious infections. But in regions where these rays were less intense, dark skin was a liability because it did not allow enough ultraviolet light to penetrate the skin and synthesize a sufficient amount of vitamin D to prevent the painful and disfiguring disease of rickets. In this situation, minor mutations in the genes of people who lived in these regions resulted in lighter skin.[6]

Other minor mutations in the genes of members of our extended family who eked out their existence for many generations in the Siberian snowfield resulted in the epicanthic fold over their eyes that enhanced vision in cold winds and reduced the glare of the sun. Similarly, the Pygmies of equatorial Africa have smaller bodies because mutations that reduced body mass were conducive to survival in sweltering rain forests, and Africans and aboriginal Australians have frizzy hair and broad noses because mutations that resulted in these features enhanced the prospects of survival in hot climates.

The group of our forebears who first evolved the capacity to acquire and use complex language systems lived as hunter-gatherer tribes in the same region of Africa, spoke the same language, and had no difficulty communicating with one another. But after their descendants split off into groups that migrated to disparate parts of the globe, each group invented new words and developed alternate ways of inflecting words and arranging sequences of words in grammatical and syntactical terms. If two of these groups came into contact after only a few generations, they would have been able to understand each other without much difficulty. However, this would not have been the case if these groups were separated for about a thousand years, because the languages spoken by each would have changed so much that there would be no basis for meaningful communication. But if a professional linguist could study the two languages, he or she would have no difficulty concluding that they were related and could be traced back to a single source.[7]

THE EMERGENCE OF COMPLEX SOCIAL SYSTEMS

Prior to the point where fully modern humans evolved the capacity to acquire and use fully complex language systems, the dynamics involved in the evolution of our species were no different from those involved in the evolution of other species. But after this momentous event occurred, a new complex adaptive system emerged, the human mind, which profoundly altered the terms of the relationship with other complex adaptive systems. The now obvious reason why this was the case is that fully modern humans had the extraordinary and utterly unique ability to coordinate their collective activities based on themes and narratives and to externalize ideas as artifacts.

But after the human mind emerged, the world that previous generations of hominids perceived as single and entire became two worlds—an inner world, in which the self that is aware of its own awareness exists, and an outer world, in which this self seeks to gratify its needs and establish a meaningful sense of connection with other selves. One of the large compulsions in this linguistically constructed symbolic universe was to code and recode experience, to translate everything into representation, and to seek out the deeper hidden logic that might eliminate inconsistencies and ambiguities. However, the most fundamental impulse in the storied lives of the inhabitants of this universe is now and always has been to close the gap between the inner and outer worlds by integrating all seemingly discordant parts into a meaningful and coherent whole.

We now know that the innate capacity of the brain of a normal human infant to acquire and use complex language systems is the initial condition that allows for the emergence of the human mind. It is also clear, however, that this capacity cannot be realized without prolonged exposure to a complex linguistic environment in which this brain is transformed into a mind through fairly incessant interactions with other minds. This transformation process is an intensely communal activity in which the web of linguistically constructed reality that emerges from the interactions between individual minds functions as a culture, or what will be termed here the "extended mind."

The social dimension of human consciousness has been rather systematically ignored by scientists, and almost all the current theories on cognition implicitly assume that the appropriate unit of analysis is the body and brain of the individual.[8] This bias has been reinforced of late by the availability of computer-based imaging systems that allow scientists to study single, isolated brains, and that disallow the prospect of studying the interactions between brains required to transmit and construct human reality. This view of cognition is flawed for two reasons. A human brain in isolation cannot become a human mind, and the study of a human mind in isolation reveals nothing about the process of constructing reality in its complex social and psychological dimensions and provides only limited insight into the full range of human cognitive processes.

The more realistic view is that the individual mind emerges from the complex web of interactive relationships with the extended mind and the cultural transmission process perpetuates the existence of the extended mind in individual minds. The human reality that emerges in the interactions between individual minds and the extended mind is more than the sum of its parts and cannot be reduced to, or explained in terms of, the cognitive processes that exist in the individual parts. It also seems clear that the relationship between the extended mind and the individual mind is complementary and that both aspects must be taken into account to achieve an understanding of the total reality.

The capacity of the extended mind to generate new narratives and to externalize ideas as artifacts was greatly enhanced after some members of our extended family settled in an area of the Middle East known as the Fertile Crescent about 12,000 years ago. This region featured a large range of altitudes and a great diversity of climatic conditions, and the mild, wet winters and hot, dry summers favored the evolution of a variety of plants with large seeds that could survive the dry season and readily sprout when the rainy season began. Thirty-six of the fifty-six species of wild grasses on this planet that are suitable for domestication because of their large seeds grew in concentrated abundance in the Fertile Crescent. Other species existed in regions with similar climates, but they were far fewer in number, scattered over larger territories, and less suitable for domestication.

The ecology of the Fertile Crescent, particularly the abundance of wild grasses with large seeds, was also conducive to the evolution of four large group-living grazing mammals—the goat, sheep, pig, and cow. These animals were passive, social, and amenable to human manipulation and control. Over a period of several thousand years, the fully modern humans that settled in this region began to raise these animals in captivity and to modify their appearance and behavior by breeding them and taking control over their food supply. Other large mammals existed in areas with similar climates, such as California, Chile, southwestern Australia, and South Africa, but none were as suitable for domestication.

In the initial phase of the process of creating a system of agriculture in the Fertile Crescent, the members of our extended human family living in this region collected large quantities of naturally growing wild cereals when the seeds were ripe and stored them for use later in the year. Eventually, they took the seeds from the hillsides, where rain was unpredictable, and planted them in flood plains, where the growth of the plants was less dependent on water supplied by intermittent rain. Over a period of several thousand years, feedbacks between biological and cultural processes resulted in the emergence of social organizations in which the plants were systematically grown in fields and the animals were used for fertilizer, milk, wool, plowing, and transport. These feedbacks culminated in a system for intensive food production comprised of three cereals that were the main source of carbohydrates, four pulses that provided some protein, and four domestic animals that were the principal sources of protein. The first societies that were entirely dependent on crops and domesticated animals for their survival appeared in the Fertile Crescent about 8,000 years ago.

The capacity of the extended mind to externalize ideas as artifacts was greatly amplified in the Fertile Crescent because increasing numbers of people were living in settled communities and working together to harvest, husk, and store large amounts of grain. The list of these new artifacts includes sickles to cut grain stalks, baskets to transport grain, mortars, pestles, and grinding slabs to remove the husks, and underground storage pits that were plastered to make them waterproof. Large-scale organized food production required special skills, training, and functions, and this resulted in the emergence of narratives that were capable of organizing human activities in increasingly more complex ways.

Contrast these developments with what occurred in Mesoamerica. In this ecology, there were only two small animals that could be domesticated for meat, the turkey and the dog, and the meat produced by these animals was much lower in quantity than that produced by cows, sheep, goats, and pigs. The only stable source of grain was corn, a plant that was difficult to domesticate and slow to develop, and other plants in the region were either much more difficult to domesticate or not suitable for domestication. Consequently, the members of our extended family living in Mesoamerica did not begin the transition from a hunter-gatherer society to an agricultural society until 5,500 years ago, and this transition was not complete until 3,500 years ago.[9]

FEEDBACKS TO THE BIOSPHERE

The emergence of complex agricultural societies represented the first phase of a process in which feedbacks between biological and cultural processes would eventually transform the entire biosphere. The biosphere, which is approximately twenty-three miles thick, extends from the depths of the ocean to the top of the troposphere. The mutual interactions of all organisms in the biosphere mediate the growth and metabolism of organisms and modulate the temperature, alkalinity, and atmospheric composition of the system of life. If Earth could be reduced to the size of a basketball, the biosphere would be thinner than the finest paper.

In the initial stage of the human transformation of the biosphere, the wild plants in the Fertile Crescent initially cultivated as crops (wheat, barley, and peas) were already edible, existed in abundance in the wild, and could be easily sown and harvested within a few months. These plants were self-pollinating, produced seeds that could be stored for later consumption, and all that was required to make them more suitable as crops was to plant the seeds of mutated plants that had more desirable characteristics. For example, the seeds of mutated wheat plants that had non-shattering stalks were used to grow more wheat, and these mutated plants became the ancestors of the domesticated plants that produced all crops of wheat.

During the next stage, which began about 4000 B.C., fruit and nut trees in the Fertile Crescent that could be grown by simply planting cuttings or seeds were domesticated to produce olives, figs, dates, and pomegranates. Given that these crops did not yield food until at least three years after they were planted and did not reach full productive capacity for about a decade, they could be grown only by people in settled villages who were capable of long-range planning. The third stage involved the domestication of trees that produced apples, pears, plums, and cherries, which could not be grown from cuttings and tended to yield highly variable and often worthless fruit when grown from seeds. The cultivation of these trees required the invention of the difficult technique of grafting, and this could not have occurred in the absence of conscious experimentation over a fairly extended period of time. The degree of expertise in the extended mind required to domesticate these trees largely explains why they were not cultivated until the beginning of the classical period in Greece. Other plants domesticated during this period, such as rye, oats, turnips, radishes, beets, leeks, and lettuce, initially appeared as weeds in fields of cultivated crops.

Many of the plants domesticated later, such as those that produce lima beans, watermelons, potatoes, eggplants, and cabbages, had wild ancestors that were bitter and often poisonous. But after the seeds of mutated plants that yielded edible food were replanted over many generations, these plants greatly increased in number and eventually became important crops in the expanding agriculture system. Other mutant plants that had seeds that did not have to be pollinated were also eventually incorporated into the system to produce seedless bananas, grapes, oranges, and pineapples.

These feedbacks between biological and cultural processes seem innocent enough until we realize that only a few thousand of the roughly 200,000 wild plants are consumed by humans and only a few hundred of these are grown as domesticated crops. Most of these crops produce food that merely supplements the human diet, and over 80 percent of the annual tonnage of all crops comes from a mere twelve species—the cereals wheat, corn, rice, barley, and sorghum; the pulse soybean; the tubers potato, manioc, and sweet potato; the sugar-producing sugarcane and sugar beet; and the fruit banana. Three of these species, the cereals wheat, rice, and corn, account for more than half of the human intake from all plants. Virtually all of these crops were cultivated by Roman times, and not one new major food plant has been domesticated in modern times.[10]

Similarly, there are 148 large surviving species of wild mammalian herbivores or omnivores that weigh over a hundred pounds, but only nine were domesticated in limited regions (Arabian camel, Bactrian camel, llama/

alpaca, donkey, reindeer, water buffalo, yak, banteng, and gaur), and only five (cow, sheep, goat, pig, and horse) had characteristics that made them suitable for domestication on a global scale. Four of the five large mammals that eventually became foundational to a global agricultural system were domesticated in the Fertile Crescent by about 4000 B.C., and the fifth, the horse, was domesticated about the same time by nomadic peoples living in the Ukrainian steppes north of the Black and Caspian seas.[11]

Obviously, these were not the only species with characteristics that made them candidates for domestication. Birds (the chicken in China, various species of duck and goose in Eurasia, turkeys in Mesoamerica, the guinea fowl in Africa, and the Muscovy duck in South America) were domesticated for meat, eggs, and feathers. Several small mammals (the rabbit in Europe and the guinea pig in the Andes) were domesticated for meat, and some insects were domesticated to produce honey (honeybees in Eurasia) and silk (the silkworm moth in China). But these inputs into the emergent global agricultural system were quite meager in comparison with the meat, milk products, fertilizer, land transport, leather, plow traction, and wool provided by the five large mammals.

The domesticated plants and animals that became the basis for the agricultural system that eventually became a global system originally constituted a small fraction of the total biomass of the planet. But as agriculture made our species increasingly more immune to the usual dynamics of evolution that regulate population growth, the domesticated plants and animals also increased in numbers well beyond the limit that the natural course of evolution would have allowed. One large problem here is that the vast majority of the biomass in the global agricultural system is composed of a very limited number of plants and animals, and the world's food supply, As E. O. Wilson puts it, "hangs by a slender thread of biodiversity."[12] If the plants in any species in this system were greatly reduced in number as a result of disease or large-scale changes in the global climate system, this could easily occasion massive starvation, and the repercussions in economic and political terms would be staggering.

FEEDBACKS FROM HUMAN POPULATION GROWTH

Following the emergence of agriculturally based societies, human population growth was fairly constant. Each period of rapid growth was occasioned by positive feedbacks between biological and cultural processes that resulted in the emergence of larger and more complex social systems and increased inputs of energy into these systems. There is, however, no such thing as a free lunch in nature, because the price that must be paid for the consumption of matter-energy in any form, including plants and animals, is an increase in entropy. Virtually all the energy that allows the system of life to become less entropic, or to evolve toward higher levels of complexity, comes from the sun, and this energy is stored in plants and animals. As noted earlier, entropy is essentially a measure of disorder in a system—the higher the entropy, the greater the disorder. The energy in the system of life is a limited resource, and the inputs of increasingly larger amounts of matter-energy into human subsystems have contributed to an increase in the overall entropy in the system.

The population explosion between 8,000 B.C. and 3,000 B.C. from about 5 million to 100 million was fueled by more systematic exploitation of the energy contained in the seed plants and domesticated large mammals in the Fertile Crescent. These plants and animals eventually became the foundation for bulk flow systems for the transport of energy, which made it possible for people to live in greater population densities in villages and cities. After about 4,000 B.C., the increase in the number of people living at higher population densities could be sustained only by new technologies that allowed more energy to be stored and transferred in bulk flow systems. The list of these technologies includes baskets, pottery, wheeled vehicles, irrigation systems, horse collars, sails, and rudders.

These bulk flow systems also promoted trade between urban centers. The camel caravans that traveled over trade routes on the Silk Road and around the Indian Ocean from 100 B.C. to A.D. 1400 brought civilizations in Rome, the eastern Mediterranean, East Africa, the Near East, India, Southeast Asia, China, and Japan into contact with one another. During this period, the agricultural system that first emerged in the Fertile Crescent greatly expanded, and the human diseases that resulted from living in close proximity to the domesticated animals in this system traveled over the trade routes to infect distant populations.

After 1492, the transfer of plants, animals, and diseases between Europe and the Americas resulted in feedbacks between biological and cultural processes that dramatically altered the global distribution of organisms to a degree that had not been witnessed since the end of the last Ice Age.[13] The introduction of European crops (wheat, rice, sugar, coffee) and animals (cattle, horses, pigs, sheep) in conjunction with the widespread dissemination of European farming practices that destroyed old-growth forests and wetlands massively transformed the natural environment throughout North and South America.[14]

Europeans did not settle in the Americas in great numbers for another three hundred years after the Columbian Exchange began, but they did import during this period large numbers of African slaves. This hideous trade in human beings was deemed necessary because the crops grown in the Americas for sale in Europe required an enormous amount of human labor and this labor was not available in the New World because European diseases had decimated much of the indigenous population.[15] Two key food staples from the Americas, corn and potatoes, fueled the growth of the European population prior to the Industrial Revolution and massively contributed to its success by vastly increasing the pool of cheap labor.[16] But the overall rate of increase in the global human population prior to this revolution, from about 250 million in A.D. 100 to 800 million in A.D. 1800, was modest owing to the lethality of crowd diseases such as measles, smallpox, and influenza and the limited amount of energy that could be extracted from Earth's biomass by human labor, draft animals, windmills, and waterwheels.

What is most important to appreciate here is that growth in the human population has correlated positively with humans' consumption of more matter-energy, and this consumption increased exponentially as new technologies made it possible to extract the energy contained in the ancient biomass of Earth as fossil fuels. During the nineteenth century, coal-powered steam engines extended the agricultural system that supplied foodstuffs to cities by several orders of magnitude and set in motion positive feedback loops that increased the populations of cities and the levels of their productivity and consumption. After 1860, three feedbacks between biological and cultural processes made it increasingly possible to feed the burgeoning populations of industrial cities, and all of them involved exponential increases in the use of oil.

First, a billion acres of new land was incorporated into an increasingly global food production system in the Corn Belt of the United States, in southern Russia, and in the pampas of Argentina, Australia, and South Africa. Second, the mechanization of agriculture, including the massive use of chemical fertilizers, pesticides, and herbicides, resulted in large increases in agricultural productivity while simultaneously reducing labor costs. And third, new food preservation technologies and a rapidly expanding fossil-fuel-based transportation system vastly increased the amount of foodstuffs that could be grown in the Southern Hemisphere and consumed in Europe and North America.[17]

As increasing numbers of people began to live in large cities, biological feedbacks in the form of the crowd diseases carried by domesticated animals infected more humans, and the number of infections increased in almost direct proportion to urban population growth. Until the beginning of the twentieth century, death rates in cities exceeded birthrates owing to the lethality of crowd diseases and environmentally induced illness, such as heart and lung disease. During this period, cities were viewed as death traps, and population growth in cities required a constant influx of healthy peasants from the countryside.[18] In 1800, when the global population was approximately 800 million, about 24 million people lived in cities, and no city had more than a million inhabitants. In 1900, when the world's population was roughly 1.6 billion, some 600 million lived in cities, and nine cities had populations greater than one million.[19]

During the twentieth century, the global population increased to over 6 billion, about 3 billion people eventually lived in cities, and twenty-one of these cities now house populations in excess of 10 million. This exponential increase in the numbers of people living in cities could not have occurred in the absence of an increasingly global agricultural production system and a food transportation network that consumed increasingly larger amounts of fossil fuels. There were, however, two other developments that massively contributed to this trend—improvements in and increased use of sanitation and water treatment facilities reduced the numbers of deaths from transmitted viral and bacterial infections, and drugs and medical procedures extended the average life span.[20]

Since 1960, the rapid emergence of a worldwide telecommunications network allowed systems of production, distribution, and exchange to be linked together into a web of interconnections that allowed for the emergence of a truly global economy. Most of the products that now exist in abundance in retail stores in industrialized countries are assembled at sites around the globe from component parts made in other, distant locations, and foodstuffs and other products in grocery stores in these countries travel on average about two thousand miles prior to purchase.[21] The components of the global economic system (capital, labor, energy resources, raw materials, component parts, finished products, and waste materials) now move through the system with minimal resistance from tariff barriers, transport costs, local markets, and cultural differences.

FEEDBACKS FROM THE ENERGY REGIME OF OIL

Obviously, myriad feedbacks between biological and cultural processes contributed to the emergence of the global market system, but the feedbacks in this process that had the most destructive environmental impacts involved the use of enormous amounts of oil. Lobbyists for the petroleum industry are quick to point out that the energy regime of oil provided enormous economic benefits to roughly one billion people in advanced industrial societies and generated much of the capital required to create the new global economy.[22] But what these individuals are very reluctant to talk about is that the largest single cause of the crisis in the global environment is a global market system that is entirely dependent in virtually all its operations on large supplies of oil.

Global demand for oil increased so significantly in the twentieth century that at any time after 1970 about five gallons of oil were in transit on large seagoing tankers for every man, woman, and child on the face of the earth. This prodigious flow of oil spurred the phenomenal growth of industrialization worldwide and allowed for the exponential expansion of the petrochemical industry, which was producing by 1999 over a billion tons of organic chemicals annually.[23] This industry replaced degradable materials, such as wood and paper, with new nondegradable materials, particularly plastics. One unfortunate result was that landfills, rivers, streams, and ocean beds became increasingly saturated with the remains of these unwanted but very durable products. The industry also manufactured prodigious amounts of chemical fertilizers, herbicides, and pesticides that contributed, along with the heavy use of farm equipment powered by gasoline and diesel engines, to the widespread mechanization and industrialization of agriculture in countries where arable land was plentiful and labor costs were low.

By the 1990s, the new mechanized system had transformed agricultural practices in Europe, North America, Japan, Australia, and New Zealand, and this resulted in a new set of feedbacks between biological and cultural processes. Farmers in these countries now specialize in single crops that plant geneticists have bred for responsiveness to chemical fertilizers, resistance to chemical pesticides, and compatibility with mechanized harvesting. The dependence of this new agricultural system on oil was greatly amplified after patchwork quilt farms were displaced with vast fields dedicated to monoculture. Because monoculture crops are more vulnerable to insects and other pests, a vast increase in the use of chemical pesticides was required to grow them. And because these crops also deplete specific nutrients in the soil much faster, farmers were obliged to vastly increase their use of chemical fertilizers as well.

The foodstuffs produced in this global market and the packaged goods and other products made from materials produced on farms are transported over great distances by another system that owes its existence to prodigious supplies of oil—a vast network of barges, ships, cargo vessels, railroads, and trucks. Foodstuffs are typically transported thousands of miles on this system from fields to processing centers to markets, and it is not unusual for those who grow the crops to consume products made from those same crops that have traveled thousands of miles back over this system to local wholesalers and retailers.

Oil also fuels another transportation system of roughly a billion cars, buses, small trucks, and motorbikes that travel along a network of roads that covers roughly 10 percent of the land surface in North America, Europe, and Japan and about 2 percent of the land surface worldwide.[24] The average American car, assuming that it actually gets the federally mandated 27.5 mile per gallon, travels approximately 100,000 miles in its lifetime and emits around 35 tons of carbon dioxide or monoxide. The over 500 million cars in use worldwide generate about 25 percent of global greenhouse gas emissions, and the U.N. Population Fund projects that by 2025 cars in developing countries will be emitting four times as much carbon dioxide as the industrialized countries emit today.[25] Also consider that the process of manufacturing a car generates on average about as much air pollution as driving a car for ten years and produces approximately 29 tons of waste.[26]

In the absence of these transportation systems and other systems dependent on abundant supplies of cheap oil, such as electric power plants, the massive increase worldwide in the numbers and sizes of cities would not have occurred. Over half the population of countries throughout the world will soon be living in oil-hungry cities, and most of these cities will not have adequate sewage disposal systems, wastewater treatment facilities, and supplies of potable water.[27] Because cities generate large amounts of waste and pollutants and require enormous inputs of energy, this mode of organizing large-scale human activities has dramatically increased our environmentally destructive impacts on a global scale.

GLOBAL SYSTEMS AND THE EMERGENT ECOLOGICAL MIND

This brief account of how feedbacks between biological and cultural processes in human history can be viewed through the conceptual lenses of dynamical systems theory does not even begin to deal with all of the complex dynamics involved. But it does illustrate that these feedbacks played a large and seminal role throughout this history and that any narrative about human history that fails to recognize this fact can no longer be viewed as realistic, objective, and free of ideological or cultural biases. Some historians have already begun to revise traditional accounts of human history to include these feedbacks, and there are some indications that this may soon become a standard practice among professional historians. This is an extremely important development because those who read these new accounts will be obliged to confront two scientific truths that must be better understood and appreciated by a significant percentage of the global human population in any successful attempt to resolve the crisis in the global environment. The first truth is that the descendants of the small lineage of hominids that evolved the capacity to acquire and use complex language systems are now and have always been embedded in and interactive with the system of life. And the second is that our best scientific understanding of the dynamics involved in feedbacks between biological and cultural processes must be foundational to any successful attempt to coordinate large-scale human activities in ways that will allow for the emergence of sustainable conditions in the global environment.

Equally important, this understanding of human history can also serve us well by enhancing the prospect that the international community can achieve the level of cooperation required to develop and implement viable solutions to the environmental crisis. The now obvious reason why this is the case is that these new historical narratives are premised on the scientifically valid assumption that all of the 6.4 billion people on this planet are members of one extended family and very similar to one another in genetic, cognitive, emotional, and behavioral terms. It is naïve to assume that groups of people who organize their experience in diverse linguistic and cultural contexts will suddenly realize that all human beings are part of one extended family merely because science has demonstrated that this is the case. On the other hand, any realistic and pragmatic assessment of the manner in which the crisis in the global environment can be resolved during the time frame in which a resolution is possible clearly indicates that an enlarged sense of our shared humanity will be a critically important aspect of this process.

There is, however, another lesson to be learned by enlarging the framework of historical narratives to include feedbacks between biological and cultural processes. From this perspective, it is quite clear that the extended mind has expanded throughout the course of human history in almost direct proportion to the increased numbers of people living in larger and more complex social systems. This was the case because efforts to coordinate collective human activities within these larger systems occasioned the emergence of new narratives that enlarged the bases for mutual recognition and cooperation between people who were not members of the same kinship groups.

The philosopher Peter Singer makes a compelling argument that the ability of fully modern humans to include those outside their immediate kinship groups within what he terms the "expanding moral circle" has become progressively more pronounced over the course of human history. He claims that this circle has moved outward from family, clan, tribe, state, and nation-state, and may soon include all of humanity. The force that drives this process, says Singer, is "cultural evolution," which he views as similar to, and in some sense the same as, natural evolution. Equally remarkable, he argues that this force is now resulting in the emergence of a universal set of moral principles or a global ethic or ethos.[28]

If Singer is correct, cultural evolution may account for the abolition of despotism, slavery, feudalism, and racial segregation in most of the world and more recent attempts to secure the rights and guarantee the freedoms of women and minorities. It may also be responsible for the general decline in violence in Western democracies over the last fifty years, which is apparent in the overall decrease in the numbers of deadly ethnic riots, civil wars, and wars of aggression between nation-states.[29] Similarly, the U.N. Universal Declaration of Human Rights may, as Singer suggests, signal that human consciousness is evolving toward a universal set of moral principles or a global ethic or ethos that will soon be embraced by all of humanity.

From a scientific point of view, however, there are two basic flaws in Singer's argument. First, there is no basis for assuming that cultural evolution is similar to and in some sense the same as natural evolution. Natural evolution does not evolve in any fixed direction, because random mutations are a fundamental aspect of this process and feedback loops in the nonlinear system of life are highly indeterminate. Second, feedbacks between cultural and biological processes are also highly indeterminate and cannot be reduced to or explained in terms of linear causal influences or connections. It is, however, possible to argue in scientific terms that the expanding moral circle is a real or actual dynamic in human history.

This argument is premised on the assumption that the expansion of the moral circle is a pronounced tendency in this history that can be explained in terms of feedbacks between biological and cultural processes that result in the emergence of new narratives that coordinate collective human activities in increasingly larger and more complex social systems. If one can accept this assumption, the expansion of the moral circle can be viewed as a "natural" phenomenon. In this view, the evolved capacity of our species to invent new narratives capable of organizing complex collective activities in progressively larger social organizations is a natural human response to conditions that threaten human survival.

Because the vast majority of the present generation of humans live their lives in a vast network of global systems and organize their experience in terms of narratives that coordinate activities within these systems, it is not surprising that a document recently appeared, the Universal Declaration of Human Rights, that is intended to enlarge the bases for mutual recognition and cooperation between all human beings. It is also worth noting that this document is premised on an assumption that is consistent with the scientific truth that all of the direct descendants of the small lineage of hominids that evolved the capacity to acquire and use complex language systems are very similar. The assumption is that all of the 6.4 billion people on this planet have the same basic needs and aspirations and should be afforded the same basic human rights.

The progressive emergence over the last few decades of more democratic systems of government and free-market systems can also be explained in these terms. Given that the basic needs and desires of all the existing members of the extended human family are very similar, the fact that increasing numbers of people in diverse linguistic and cultural contexts wish to enjoy greater degrees of freedom and autonomy in political reality and the opportunity to consume more goods and commodities by hard work and personal initiative in economic reality is not mysterious in the least. Another reason why this trend has become more pronounced over the last two decades is that the vast majority of people living outside of economically prosperous democratic countries are rather constantly reminded of the benefits of living in those countries.

The products of industrialized countries flow through the global market system to even the most remote villages and towns, and there are few people on this planet who have not been exposed to advertising campaigns that associate the consumption of these products with the benefits of living in affluent consumer societies. Narratives about the freedoms and opportunities enjoyed by people who live in these societies travel around the planet through the global telecommunications system at the speed of light, and it is very difficult, as cultural anthropologists have discovered, to find any human population that has not been massively transformed by these narratives.

Obviously, this does not mean that political and economic narratives that can serve as the basis for creating the institutional frameworks and processes capable of coordinating large-scale human activities in environmentally responsible ways on a global scale will spontaneously appear. But it does mean that narratives that describe the causes of the crisis in the global environment and the manner in which it can be solved can now be communicated to large numbers of individual minds very rapidly through the global telecommunications and market systems. It is, therefore, not unreasonable to assume that if sufficient numbers of these narratives were circulating through these systems, this could occasion the fairly rapid emergence of an extended "ecological mind" that would enlarge the bases for achieving the level of cooperation in the international community required to resolve the environmental crisis.

In the next chapter, we will examine how an eighteenth-century dialogue between the truths of religion and science resulted in the emergence of new political narratives about democratic systems of government and a new economic narrative about free-market systems. The authors of these seminally important narratives were attempting to make religious truths in the Judeo-Christian tradition consistent with scientific truths in Newtonian physics. In an effort to reconcile the differences between these two kinds of truths, these authors posited the existence of "natural laws," which were assumed to be equivalent to and in some sense the same as the laws of classical physics. They then argued that the putative natural laws govern the movement and interaction of people in political and economic reality in much the same way that the laws of Newtonian physics govern the movement and interaction of material bodies.

This frequently ignored and often misunderstood chapter in human history is critically important for our purposes because the contemporary versions of these narratives are not only predicated on a belief in the real or actual existence of these nonexistent natural laws. They are also premised on the same assumptions about part-whole relationships that the original authors of these narratives derived from Newtonian physics. One unfortunate consequence is that there is no basis in the political and economic narratives that now serve as the basis for coordinating virtually all large-scale human activities for positing, much less implementing, viable solutions to the crisis in the global environment. The other is that unqualified belief in the real or actual existence of the natural laws of economics became foundational over the last few decades to a teleological view of the human future known as the Washington consensus or the market consensus.

For reasons that should become increasingly clear in the next three chapters, the true believers in this alleged consensus are unwittingly living in the service of false gods, and their vision of the human future functions in operative terms as a quasi-religious belief system. One of the more sobering conclusions that will be drawn here is that if we fail to realize this is the case, there will be no prospect of resolving the environmental crisis prior to the point when abrupt large-scale changes in the global climate system imperil the lives of billions of people.

THE GODS OF THE SOULLESS MACHINE
Newtonian Physics, Metaphysics, and Natural Laws

> . . . May God keep us
> From single Vision and Newton's sleep!
> – WILLIAM BLAKE

Let us now imagine that you have been playing the Godgame on your home computer for some time and have now have arrived at the phase of the game where the players are challenged to coordinate large-scale human activities in environmentally responsible ways on a global or planetary scale. At this point, another question appears on the screen: "What narratives define the institutional frameworks and processes that are primarily responsible for coordinating the relationship between parts (large-scale human activities) and whole (global environment or ecosystem)?" The obvious answer is the political narrative that coordinates the relationships between peoples and governments in the international community and the economic narrative that serves as the basis for coordinating virtually all large-scale economic activities.

When we think about how to resolve the crisis in the global environment in these terms, the solution seems rather obvious. The international community must begin very soon to develop and implement political and economic narratives that can serve as the basis for articulating institutional frameworks and processes that can coordinate large-scale human activities in ways that can allow for the emergence of sustainable conditions in the global environment. Equally obvious, this effort must be predicated on our best scientific understanding of the actual dynamics of the interactions between parts (large-scale human activities) and whole (sustainable global environment).

The principal reason why this community has failed to implement this obvious solution was discussed earlier—assumptions about the relationships between parts (sovereign nation-states and national economies) and wholes (the international system of government and the global market system) in the present system of international government and neoclassical economic theory are categorically different from and wholly incompatible with the actual dynamics of part-whole relationships in the system of life. There is, however, another, equally important reason why the international community has not given any serious consideration to this obvious solution.

Most political leaders and economic planners presume that neoclassical economic theory, the economic narrative that now serves as the basis for coordinating virtually all large-scale economic activities in the global market system, is scientific. For reasons that will soon become obvious, there is no basis for assuming that neoclassical economics is a rigorously mathematical discipline comparable to physics, and the claim that the theories used by neoclassical economists are scientific is bogus. However, the intent in this portion of the discussion is not to launch an ill-mannered attack on mainstream economists or to denigrate the virtues of the free-market system. It is to make the case that the only way in which we can hope to resolve the environmental crisis while simultaneously preserving the substantive benefits of free-market economies is to develop and implement an environmentally responsible economic theory with all deliberate speed.

The fundamental reason why the mathematical theories used by neoclassical economists cannot be viewed as scientific is that the natural laws that are foundational to these theories are predicated on metaphysical assumptions. In this chapter, one objective is to examine the origins of these assumptions in the work of some eighteenth-century philosophers who authored new narratives about free-market systems. The other is to demonstrate that this metaphysically based conception of natural laws was also foundational to the work of other seminally important eighteenth-century philosophers who created new narratives about democratic systems of government. The analysis has been extended to include this second set of narratives for the following reason—this background is required to understand why the market consensus or the Washington consensus, which massively conditions the manner in which political leaders and economic planners coordinate large-scale economic activities, functions in operative terms as a quasi-religious system.

THE CLOCKWORK UNIVERSE

The philosophers who articulated these natural laws lived in an era in which it was still possible to imagine that single individuals could integrate all human knowledge into a cohesive intellectual framework. John Locke, who knew Newton personally because they were both members of the same intellectual society in London, posited the existence of universal natural laws that could explain the workings of human reason. Following the principles of Bacon's "new learning," or methods of inductive reasoning that were designed to derive first principles from the concrete data of experience rather than a priori speculation, Locke examined human history in an effort to uncover the source of human ideas. In *An Essay Concerning Human Understanding,* he argued that the "ground of belief" is experience and that the raw material for human thought consists of information from the five senses that is imprinted on the tabula rasa, or blank slate, of the human brain:[1] "Let us suppose the mind to be, as we say, white paper void of all characters, without any ideas. How comes it to be furnished? . . . Whence has it all the materials of reason and knowledge? To this I answer, in my word, from experience."[2]

Locke concluded that "simple ideas" consist of sense data, which function as the basic units of human knowledge, and that complex ideas are generated from these units by mental mechanisms that operate in accordance with natural laws that govern the associative process. Locke claimed that these lawful or lawlike dynamics determine the similarities and differences between units of simple ideas and that this becomes the basis for abstract higher-level generalizations and more general truths. Assuming that the natural laws of reason are just as transcendent, immutable, and universal as the laws of Newtonian physics, Locke argued that the truth value of any human knowledge claim can be empirically assessed by examining sensory experience and the logical coherence of associations between basic units of simple ideas. In an effort to answer the question why some people are not rational, Locke said that irrationality results from erroneous associations between ideas that become fixed in childhood.

Locke did not provide a detailed account of how experience leads to learning or how sensations are transformed into ideas and concepts, and this project was undertaken later by the Scottish philosopher David Hume and the English philosopher-physician David Hartley. They argued that learning occurs when previously unrelated ideas are linked together in a chain of association in a mental field of force that closely resembles Newton's gravitational force. In this postulated field, Hume and Hartley claimed that the mind is attracted to ideas associated with pleasure and repelled by those associated with pain. Taken together, the theories of Locke, Hume, and Hartley constituted a mechanistic psychology in which natural laws determine the causal linkages between experience, ideas, and feelings in much the same way that Newton's universal laws of gravity determine the interactions between masses of material objects.

Jean d'Alembert, coauthor with Denis Diderot of the greatest of the eighteenth-century monuments to Enlightenment thought, the *Encylopédie,* said that Locke "reduced metaphysics to what it really ought to be: the experimental physics of the soul."[3] In retrospect, d'Alembert's comment was much more insightful than he could have known because Locke assumed that the natural laws that were foundational to his philosophical speculations emanated, like the laws of classical physics, from the perfect mind of the Creator. As an orthodox Christian, Locke insisted that God was active in the universe in "genuine" acts of revelation that were "above" but "not contrary to" reason.[4] However, most of the moral philosophers who embraced Locke's view of natural laws could not make this leap of faith. They reasoned that if everything that happens in physical reality is predetermined by the laws of Newtonian physics, and if human thought and behavior is largely determined by natural laws, the active intervention of God in this universe is not needed or required.

In *Two Treatises on Government,* Locke attempted to explain the origins of government in terms of the lawful or lawlike operations of natural laws. He began with the assumption that in a "state of nature," or prior to the time when human experience was organized in social systems, the natural laws operated without interference and ensured that all humans had "natural rights" to life, liberty, and property. Locke then argued that after the numbers of people living in social systems grew larger, an impartial judge was required to protect these natural rights.

After declaring that this judge did not exist in the state of nature, Locke argued that people mutually agreed to enter into a social contract with a nascent government. In this agreement, government was obligated to protect the natural rights of individuals provided that they behaved reasonably in their dealings with government. But if any government failed to meet this obligation or claimed absolute authority to legislate over these rights without the consent of the governed, a new government could be formed. Although government as Locke defined it was composed of landed aristocracy and their representatives in Parliament, his "social contract theory" was used in the eighteenth century to support demands for constitutional government, the rule of law, and the protection of individual rights.

Thomas Hobbes, who was a member of the intellectual society in London that included Newton and Locke, used the new learning methods of Bacon to examine human behavior in a state of nature and arrived at a very different conclusion. According to Hobbes, humans are driven by animalistic instincts in a ruthless struggle for self-preservation. "[D]uring the time men live without a common power to keep them all in awe," he wrote, "they are in that condition that is called war; and such a war as is of every man against every man." The resulting condition precludes the development of trade, industry, scholarship, and the arts. Most famously, he declared that the life of man without a sovereign is "solitary, poor, nasty, brutish, and short."[5] In Hobbes's view, this hellish state can be avoided only if people surrender their autonomy to the will of a sovereign monarch or to an assembly that derives its authority from such a monarch. His term for this centralized authority was the leviathan, a Hebrew word for the monstrous sea creature subdued by God at the dawn of creation.

THE FRENCH CONNECTION
Most of the eighteenth-century philosophers who embraced this conception of natural laws were French, and they are collectively known as the "philosophes." These thinkers were convinced that a set of immaterial natural laws govern the movement and interaction of atomized individuals much as the law of gravity governs the movement and interaction of mass points, or atoms, in Newtonian physics. Charles-Louis de Secondat, Baron de Montesquieu, appealed to this physics to create sociology, a new field of study premised on the idea that observation of empirical data could uncover natural laws that govern complex social phenomena.

In a study of the institutions of monarchy, republic, and despotism, Montesquieu argued that because equilibrium results from the operation of physical laws in Newtonian physics, it is reasonable to assume that equilibrium in social reality results from the operation of natural laws. In *The Spirit of the Laws*, Montesquieu claimed that natural laws in social realty can function properly and maintain equilibrium only in systems of government in which there is a separation of powers between executive, legislative, and judicial branches. As Robert Aron points out, "Montesquieu's essential idea is not the separation of powers in the judicial sense but what might be called the *equilibrium of social forces* as a condition of political freedom."[6]

A similar view of natural laws appears in the work of François Quesnay, the founder of the French Physiocratic movement. Quesnay was a physician who included among his patients Madame de Pompadour, mistress to

Louis XV. However, Quesnay's primary interest was to make rational sense out of the chaotic economic system of France in the years prior to the French revolution. He and his followers sought to disclose the existence of an order of nature, or "physiocracy," in which only land yields a surplus because machines merely reshape material taken from nature with no net increase in the amount of material.

Quesnay claimed that the natural laws that determine economic value, like the laws of Newtonian physics, are created by God and operate on atomized individuals to perpetuate and sustain the whole of human society in harmony. He wrote that both sets of laws, those that operate on the human intellect and those that govern the behavior of matter, constitute "the general order of the formation of the universe, where everything is foreseen and arranged by the Supreme Wisdom."[7] The order that results from the action of the natural laws is apparent, he claimed, in the continuous production and distribution of food and other goods essential to human survival. Quesnay was also convinced that these laws, like those of Newtonian physics, act with a precision that lends itself to description and analysis in geometrical and arithmetical terms: "The natural laws of the order of society, are precisely the physical laws of the perpetual reproduction of the goods necessary for man's subsistence, conservation and well-being."[8]

Quesnay's most celebrated attempt to disclose the existence of these putative natural laws took the form of the *Tableau économique,* which was intended to provide a rigorous calculation of the effects of measures taken by the "Sovereign" to ensure the economic well-being of the state. In the *Tableau,* hypothetical production and distribution figures for the national product are factored into an "arithmetical formula," and the resulting political arithmetic allegedly provides a basis for the correct administration of the national economy based on rigorous calculation and measurement of relevant quantities.[9] It is also worth noting that Quesnay was among the first of a long line of economic theorists who did not understand the physics that was foundational to his economic theory and the mathematics used in the *Tableau* was limited to arithmetic and geometry.

Anne-Robert-Jacques Turgot is recognized for articulating a view of a mechanistic economic system based on the metaphor of the circulation of blood. In this system, there is an alleged resemblance between the workings of a market and the dynamics of fluids. In contrast with the other Physiocrats, Turgot did not use mathematical formalism to develop a systematic treatment of the market. But he did manage to introduce the concept of equilibrium in a loose exposition in which the workings of the market economy are linked to the equilibrium of fluids in a system of interconnected vessels. The reciprocal influence of unequal products of capital, he wrote, will be the same as that "between two liquids of unequal gravity that communicate with one another at the bottom of a reversed siphon of which they occupy the two branches: they will not be on a level, but the height of one cannot increase without the other also rising in the opposite branch."[10] In a celebrated letter to David Hume, Turgot elaborated on his definition of the term "equilibrium." The term, he said, mirrors that in Newtonian physics and denotes levels of production, employment, and remuneration that tend to remain in equilibrium.

The Marquis de Condorcet, who died after spending several months in hiding as a fugitive from the Terror during the French Revolution, was a skilled mathematician who possessed a more refined understanding of Newtonian physics than his friend and mentor Turgot. Condorcet's formidable ambition was to create a *mathématique sociale* that would describe the lawful dynamics governing human choice with the use of probability calculus. After pointing out that careful observation and the collection of large amounts of empirical data had served as the basis for describing hidden lawful dynamics in astronomy, Condorcet argued that the same methods could be used to describe the hidden lawful dynamics of social and economic systems. He then declared, "Whoever reflects upon the nature of the moral sciences cannot, in fact, but see that, supported by factual observation like the physical sciences, they must follow the same method, acquire an equally precise language, and attain the same degree of certainty."[11]

Condorcet held that the mathematical tool that could yield results comparable to those in the physical sciences was the probability calculus invented by Newton and Leibniz, and he used this tool in an effort to uncover the hidden dynamics of social and political realities. In a study on the democratically elected assemblies, Condorcet examined the behavior of a voter as *homo suffragans*—an atomized participant in the electoral process. In the probability calculus that was intended to predict the results of elections, each voter is represented as the rough equivalent of the Newtonian constructs of the material point, the line without extension, and the frictionless surface. The resulting mathematical abstraction, a dimensionless material point, possesses only one real quantity—a mass expressed in completely formal and quantitative terms. Hence *homo suffragans* is a social atom that has been divested of all human qualities other than the social faculty of voting.[12] As we shall see, *homo economicus* in the mathematical theories used by mainstream economists is represented in much the same way.

THE DEISTS

John Toland, a contemporary of Locke, was probably the first moral philosopher to systematically challenge the assumption that God can actively intervene in a universe in which physical events are predetermined by physical laws and human thought and action are largely determined by natural laws. In *Christianity Not Mysterious,* Toland argued that a credible natural religion must display logical consistency even if this requires abandoning traditional Christian beliefs. He then discounted the possibility of miracles, or divine intervention in any form, and relegated God to the role of the Supreme Craftsman who had fashioned a clockwork universe that could run perfectly well in his absence.

This marked the beginnings of a religious and philosophical movement known as Deism. The God of the Deists, in spite of all their claims about benevolence and providential design, was an absentee landlord utterly removed from the everyday existence of human beings and completely indifferent to their petitions and concerns. However, the Deists were not merely concerned with religious issues, and they articulated a comprehensive worldview consistent with the belief that natural laws originated in the perfectly rational mind of a benevolent Creator. The attempts by some of the more intellectually gifted Deists to systematically disclose the operations of these laws resulted in conceptions of universal human rights and freedoms that became foundational to new systems of democratic government in the United States and Europe. And they also resulted in a conception of the natural laws of economics that became foundational to the economic theory that we now use to coordinate global economic activities.

In colonial North America, the Deists who articulated a new system of democratic government predicated on a belief in the existence of natural laws included such notables as Benjamin Franklin, Thomas Jefferson, Ethan Allan, Thomas Paine, Elihu Palmer, and Philip Freneau. Influenced by Locke and the French philosophes, the American Deists became staunch republicans and ardent defenders of a humanism that emphasized the fundamental importance of freedom of conscience and expression, separation of church and state, and universal public education. Franklin, an orthodox Christian, was somewhat ambivalent in his attitude toward the Deistic God, but his attempts to resolve the contradictions convinced him that religious toleration was one of the cornerstones of a democratic society. Jefferson frequently engaged in speculations about the implications of Deism in his voluminous correspondence with friends and family members. The projects that grew out of these speculations included legislation that promoted freedom of conscience and public education and an attempt to fashion a coherent ethical system that could ensure equality of treatment under the law for all citizens in a democracy.

Paine and Palmer openly appealed to Deism in their public condemnations of alliances between church and state, and Palmer, the more radical of the two, advocated the abolition of slavery, the emancipation of women, and the end of the brutal oppression of Native Americans. Ethan Allen, remembered today as the flamboyant leader of the Green Mountain Boys in his native Vermont, was also the author of the first systematic treatment of Deism by an American, *Reason the Only Oracle of Man*. Freneau, who expressed his Deistic sentiments in poetry, was preoccupied with freedom of conscience and the invidious roles played in society by superstition, religious intolerance, and social elitism.[13]

The authors of the founding documents of the new American republic derived virtually all of their most important ideas from treatises on natural law written by the British moral philosophers and the French philosophes. The understanding of human nature embedded in these American documents is an interesting combination of the optimistic vision of Locke and the tragic vision of Hobbes. Most of the framers were very much aware that government, as James Madison put it, is the "greatest of all reflections on human nature,"[14] and the tension between the disparate conceptions of human nature in the work of Locke and Hobbes is everywhere present in the Declaration of Independence, the Constitution, and the Bill of Rights.

Locke's vision of government as a social contract between people and government in which the people are endowed with universal and inalienable rights resonates in the language used by Jefferson in the opening sentences of the Declaration of Independence: "We hold these truths to be self-evident, that all men are created equal, that they are endowed by their Creator with inalienable Rights, that among these are Life, Liberty, and the pursuit of Happiness."

Many scholars have demonstrated that this language reflects the influence of Locke's social contract theory, but very little has been said about the fact that it also reflects the influence of Deism. The choice of the word "Creator," as opposed to the word God, implies that the "endowment" of "inalienable Rights" occurred at the first moment of creation. The unqualified assertion that "these truths" are "self-evident" suggests that the truths are associated with the operation of natural laws that govern the workings of social systems and that the truths are known by reason as opposed to revelation. In the next paragraph, Jefferson appeals once again to Locke's social contract theory: "That to secure these rights, Governments are instituted among Men, deriving their just powers from the consent of the governed. That whenever any Form of Government becomes destructive of these ends, it is the Right of the People to alter or abolish it, to institute a new Government, laying its foundation on such Principles and organizing its Powers in such form, as to them seem most likely to effect their Safety and Happiness."

Much has been written about the fact that this passage incorporates Locke's claim that the primary obligation of government is to secure and protect the inalienable natural rights of individuals and that the governed are empowered to transform government and even to create a new government if the existing government fails to meet this obligation. However, scant attention has been paid to the fact that the language used by Jefferson makes covert appeals to the God of the Deists. This language clearly indicates that the sole agency that has the "Right" to institute a government or to "alter" or "abolish" a government is human, and the implication is that the "Principles" upon which governments of the people are founded are associated with the operations of universal natural laws. The claim that the only agency imbued with the "powers" to create, alter, or abolish governments is the people suggests that natural laws are embedded in this process and are not dependent in their operations on divine intervention. What makes this language radical in an eighteenth-century context is that the agency that informs or gives form to government is natural laws, which serve as the foundation for natural rights, and not a God that actively organizes and directs human experience and demands obeisance to moral laws.

The influence of Hobbes's vision of human nature is most apparent in the manner in which the founders chose to organize the powers of government. The central concern here was to reconcile what the founders viewed as the innate human compulsion to dominate others in an effort to enhance self-esteem with the fact that officials of government are empowered to make decisions and to create and enforce laws. The Hobbesian view of human nature is apparent in virtually all discussions about this problem in letters written by the founders and in records of their public debates. For example, John Adams wrote, "The desire for the esteem of others is as real a want of nature as hunger. It is the principal end of government to regulate this passion."[15] As Alexander Hamilton put it, "The love of fame is the ruling passion of the noblest minds."[16] James Madison pithily described the problem as follows: "If men were angels, no government would be necessary. If angels were to govern men, neither external nor internal controls on government would be necessary."[17]

The system of checks and balances intended to curb these tendencies was premised on Montesquieu's assumption that the best way to ensure that natural laws will remain in equilibrium and guarantee political freedom is to create a political system in which political powers are separated between three branches of government—the executive, the legislative, and the judicial. The founders also appealed to this assumption to legitimate the idea that there should be a division of powers and decision-making authority between federal and state governments, that the legislative branch should be split into two houses, and that Congress, as opposed to the president, should have the power to declare war.

NATURAL LAWS AND THE ECONOMIC NARRATIVE OF ADAM SMITH

Some historians make passing mention of the fact that Adam Smith was a Deist, but the large role played by Deism in Smith's economic theory is systematically ignored in virtually all textbook accounts of the history of economics. Smith, who was notoriously absentminded, lectured much of his life on problems in moral philosophy at the University of Glasgow. The discipline of moral philosophy, which was much more broadly defined than it is today, covered natural philosophy, ethics, jurisprudence, and political economy.[18] It was on this broad canvas that Smith attempted to depict the inner workings of Newton's clockwork universe and the place of human beings within its systems, wheels, and chains. In the process, he developed an understanding of the lawful mechanisms of free-market systems that become foundational to the work of the neoclassical economists.

Understanding the work of Adam Smith as a whole is widely recognized as difficult because of what an earlier generation of German scholars termed "das Adam Smith Problem." The problem concerns the glaring contradiction between the themes in Smith's two books—self-interest in *The Wealth of Nations* (1776) and sympathy in *The Theory of Moral Sentiments* (1759). Some have argued that these contradictions result from some radical change in the worldview of Smith during the seventeen-year period between publication of the two books. The problem with this thesis is that both books were rather consistently revised and edited for five or more editions in Smith's lifetime and the final edition of *The Theory of*

Moral Sentiments was published in the year of his death (1790). More important, Smith viewed both books as part of a single corpus, and his reasons for doing so become clear when they are read in this way.

Most of those who have struggled with the Adam Smith problem have apparently failed to recognize that the problem can be resolved based on an improved understanding of the central role played by Deism in all of Smith's published work. Smith's lifelong preoccupation with Deism is most apparent in his extensive use of mechanical metaphors and analogies and his firm conviction that the orderly machinations of market systems are regulated and maintained by natural laws that are ontologically equivalent to the laws of Newtonian physics.

Although the construct of the invisible hand is the ghost in the machine in virtually all of Smith's writings, it is explicitly mentioned only three times in three very different theological contexts. In the essays, the invisible hand is that of Jupiter, and the construct is used to illustrate how primitive or "savage" people dealt with the irregular phenomena of nature. In *The Theory of Moral Sentiments,* the hand belongs to a Deistic providence, which ensures that the less fortunate are fed in spite of the greed of the rich. In *The Wealth of Nations,* the hand is the metaphor for the natural laws that act to maintain harmony and stability in market systems with the same impersonal force as the laws of physics. Taken together, the essays and *The Theory of Moral Sentiments* constitute a critique of the history, sociology, and psychology of religion. This critique is designed to demonstrate that during the course of civilization polytheism was replaced by theism and human beings eventually came to realize that nature is a system or machine that obeys both physical and natural laws.[19]

In the long essay on astronomy, the invisible hand of Jupiter symbolizes the "principles that lead and direct philosophical inquiries," which Smith defines as the passions of wonder, surprise, and admiration.[20] In the section titled "Of the Origin of Philosophy," he claims that polytheism originated among primitive people and was a product of the "vulgar superstition which ascribes all the irregular events of nature to the favour or displeasure of intelligent, though invisible beings, to gods, daemons, witches, genii, fairies."[21] These primitive people, who were not aware of the existence of nature's "hidden chains," were awed, says Smith, by "magnificent" irregularities, such as thunder, lightning and comets. He then mentions the invisible hand in an effort to explain why such people responded differently to regular and irregular phenomena: "It is the irregular events of nature only that are ascribed to the agency and power of the gods. Fire burns, and water refreshes; heavenly bodies descend, and lighter substances fly upwards, by the necessity of their own nature; nor was the invisible hand of Jupiter ever apprehended to be employed in those matters."[22] Smith argues that the reason why these savage people associated the activities of the gods with irregular events is that man was the only "designing" power that they knew and man "never acts but either to stop, or to alter the course, which natural events take, if left to themselves." He then claims that the fundamental problem with the "lowest and most pusillanimous superstition" of these savages is that it prevented them from realizing that "hidden chains" link all events to the invisible causes of physical and natural laws.

Smith frequently identifies nature with the way things operate on their own accord, and the goal of philosophy, he says, is to "lay open" the "invisible chains which bind together" the natural world.[23] It is, therefore, no accident that the argument for the system of natural liberty in *The Wealth of Nations* is designed to promote trust in the "natural course of things." This trust is warranted, says Smith, because the "hidden chains" of the invisible hand regulate the "system of natural liberty" and constrict the sphere of human "intention and foresight."[24] His argument for the existence of this system is premised on the assumption that "no human wisdom or knowledge could ever be sufficient" to provide the sovereign with the ability to effectively manage the "industry of private people" and direct it "toward the employments most suitable to the interests of society." Given that human beings, individually or collectively, cannot effectively manage market economies or predict their futures, the only alternative, argues Smith, is for each individual "to pursue his interests in his own way" within "the laws of justice."[25]

The usual interpretation of Smith's system of natural liberty is that it legitimates the idea that each of us should have the freedom to pursue our livelihood and self-interest in the absence of traditional political, religious, and moral constraints. Because this system requires that the role of government be limited, it is also widely assumed that Smith makes government the servant of individualism. The problem with these interpretations, which are typically used to support the claim that Smith was a libertarian, is that the system of natural liberty is embedded in larger systems and all of these systems obey natural laws.

In the section on education in *The Wealth of Nations,* Smith first endorses the idea from the ancient Greeks that philosophy should be divided into natural philosophy, which would later be called "physics," moral philosophy, and logic. He then argues that this division requires that the study of both the human mind and "the Deity" must fall under the province of physics, which investigates "the origin and the revolutions of the great system of the universe." Smith then concludes that the human mind and the Deity, "in whatever their essence might be supposed to consist," are "parts of the great system of the universe."[26]

In the physics essay, Smith criticizes those who attempt to explain nature's "seeming incoherence" by appealing "to the arbitrary will of some designing, though invisible beings, who produced it for some private and particular purposes." He then proceeds to fault the superstitious for their inability to conceive of the "idea of a universal mind, of a God of all, who originally formed the whole, and who governs the whole by general laws, directed to the conservation and prosperity of the whole, without regard to that of any private individual."[27] But as our ancestors progressed in knowledge, says Smith, they realized that nature is "a complete machine . . . a coherent system, governed by general laws, and directed to general ends, viz., its own preservation and prosperity."[28] Clearly, Smith believed that the universal mind of God served as a template for the creation of a world that is entirely governed following its creation by general laws. His phrase "general laws" refers to both physical and natural laws, and he implies that they have the same ontological status—both originate from the universal mind of a Deistic God, exist in a realm separate and discrete from the material world, and act on atomized parts to maintain the stability of the whole.

The special character of Smith's metaphysics allows us to answer a question that has perplexed most experts on the history of economic thought: Why does he appeal to God to legitimate the existence of the invisible hand in his other major work, *The Theory of Moral Sentiments,* and yet refrain from doing so in *The Wealth of Nations?* The answer is that the understanding of the character of natural laws in *The Wealth of Nations* is more narrowly predicated on the assumption that these laws have coequal status with the laws of Newtonian physics. The omission of any appeals to God not only serves to reinforce the seeming validity of this assumption. It also implies that the real existence of the natural laws is self-evident and, therefore, any appeal to metaphysics is ad hoc and unnecessary.

Smith's metaphysics also provides a basis for understanding why he had no difficulty arriving at the conclusion that would later impress Charles Darwin—natural laws act to preserve the whole (human population) without regard for the well-being of particular parts (individuals). In Smith's view, mind and nature are systems or machines that do not require any "personal" intervention, because the orderly relation between parts is governed and maintained by general laws. This also explains why the biblical God, who disrupts the orderly workings of nature by staging miracles and singles out individuals or groups for covenants, revelations, rewards and punishments, is conspicuously absent in virtually all of Smith's work. From his perspective, this God is a product of the frenzied imagination of those who did not realize that nature is "a complete machine" in which "hidden chains" govern the orderly interaction of parts to preserve the existence of the whole.

These views are apparent in Smith's descriptions of the workings of the invisible hand in *The Theory of Moral Sentiments*. Here the hand is part of the "regular" workings of nature and ensures that social benefits result as an unintended outcome of selfish actions. Smith argues, for example, that the invisible hand increases the fertility of the earth and benefits the whole of mankind despite inequality in capital resources and ownership of land. But since the landlord, writes Smith, can eat only a portion of the produce of his land, the remainder is consumed by those who provide him with luxuries.[29] Hence the rich, despite their "natural selfishness and rapacity," are led by an invisible hand to make nearly the same distribution of the necessities of life that would have been made had the earth been divided into equal portions among all its inhabitants; and thus without intending it, without knowing it, they advance the best interests of society, and afford means to the multiplication of the species.[30]

In *The Theory of Moral Sentiments,* Smith says that a "wise man does not look upon himself as a whole, separated and detached from every other part of nature, to be taken care of by itself and for itself." He rather considers himself as "an atom, a particle, of an immense and infinite system, which must and ought to be disposed of according to the convenience of the whole."[31] The basic argument here is that natural laws act outside or between the parts (atomized individuals) to enhance the welfare of the whole (human population) as a collection of parts, and the freedom of the parts is utterly constrained by these laws. In the "great machine of the universe" with its "secret wheels and springs,"[32] the system of natural liberty may allow the atomized individual to live with the illusion that his or her actions are freely taken. But as the wise man knows, this freedom does not exist, because the "connecting chains" of the invisible hand sustain the whole (economy) in the absence of conscious intervention by parts (economic actors).

It is this understanding of the part-whole relationships that informs Smith's commentary on the "prudent man" in *The Wealth of Nations*. The prudent man is praised for his "industry and frugality" and for "steadily sacrificing the ease and enjoyment of the present moment." The reward for this virtue, says Smith, is that the "situation" of this man grows "better and better every day."[33] In addition to celebrating the economic virtues of the prudent man, Smith also stresses his apolitical character. The prudent man "has no taste for that foolish importance which many people wish to derive from appearing to have some influence in the management" of public policy. Such a man prefers "that the public business were well managed by some other person" so that he is left to "the undisturbed enjoyment of secure tranquility."[34] The clear inference is that this tranquility derives from the recognition that public affairs are managed by natural laws in ways that sustain order and stability and that the actions of atomized individuals serve only to frustrate the proper functioning of these laws.

Smith's understanding of natural laws also explains why he consistently denigrates the power of human choice and alleges that human planning, intention, and foresight have had little or no impact on the course of history. Smith talks a great deal about great moments in history, but he never suggests that these moments are due to the actions of great men. The driving force that inexorably moves the whole of humanity toward greater wealth and progress with something like the precision of a linear equation results from the mechanisms associated with the natural laws. This view is apparent in *The Theory of Moral Sentiments* in the beginning of the paragraph on the invisible hand:

> And it is well that nature imposes upon us in this manner. It is this deception that rouses and keeps in continual motion the industry of mankind. It is this which first prompted them to cultivate the ground, to build houses, to found cities and commonwealths, and to invent and improve all the sciences and the arts, which ennoble and embellish human life; which have entirely changed the whole face of the globe, have turned the rude forests of nature into agreeable and fertile plains, and made the trackless and barren ocean a new fund of subsistence, and the great high road of communication to the different nations of the world. The earth by these labours of mankind has been obliged to redouble her natural fertility, and to maintain a greater multitude of inhabitants.[35]

According to Smith, the natural laws that impose on atomized human beings and keep them in motion are not dependent in their operation on the intelligence and creativity of individuals, even in the sciences and the arts. Even more interesting for our purposes, the laws that govern the ever-expanding market systems oblige "earth" to "redouble her natural fertility" to maintain the growing human population.

TIGHTENING THE CHAINS: THOMAS MALTHUS AND DAVID RICARDO

The other creators of the narrative that we now call classical economics, Thomas Malthus and David Ricardo, endorsed Smith's understanding of natural laws and attempted to tighten the "invisible chains" that "connect" parts in the machine of the market system in a more rigidly deterministic way. Malthus's *Essay on the Principle of Population as It Affects the Future Improvement of Society* was written in response to the views of a utopian thinker named William Godwin. In Godwin's teleological account of the human future, the sexual passions that lead to increases in birthrate will somehow diminish after a universal harmony in social and political reality is achieved. When that occurs, wrote Godwin, "there will be no war, no crime, no administration of justice, as it is called, and no government. Besides there will be no disease, anguish, melancholy, or resentment."[36]

Malthus's dissenting views were published anonymously in 1798. The usual interpretation of his principle of population is straightforward—since population increases geometrically and food supply increases arithmetically, there is a tendency for population growth to outrun the means of subsistence. Note, however, the manner in which this argument is actually made:

> I think I may fairly make two postulata.
>
> First, That food is necessary to the existence of man.
>
> Secondly, That the passion between the sexes is necessary and will remain nearly in its present state.
>
> These two laws, even since we have had any knowledge of mankind, appear to have been fixed laws of nature, and, as we have not hitherto seen any alteration of them, we have no right to conclude that they will ever cease to be what they now are, without an immediate act of power in that Being who first arranged the system of the universe, and for the advantage of his creatures, still executes, according to fixed laws, all its various operations.[37]

Although Malthus, an ordained clergyman, allows for the prospect that the "laws of nature" can be altered by an "immediate act of power in that Being who first arranged the system of the universe," his conception of this Being closely resembles the Deistic God of Smith. For example, the claim that "fixed natural laws," like the laws of physics, govern the "various operations" of the "system of the universe" in a causal and deterministic fashion clearly implies that the system does not need or require any intervention from God or any other "external" agency.

While Smith argued that the natural laws that determine the future of markets are essentially benevolent, Malthus concluded that the natural laws of population could potentially threaten the very existence of humanity:

> Assuming then, my postulata as granted, I say that the power of population is indefinitely greater than the power in the earth to produce subsistence for man.
>
> Population, when unchecked, increases in a geometrical ratio. Subsistence increases only in an arithmetical ratio. A slight acquaintance with numbers will show the immensity of the first power in comparison of the second.
>
> By that law of our nature which makes food necessary to the life of man, the effects of these two unequal powers must be kept equal.
>
> This implies a strong constantly operating check on population from the difficulty of subsistence. This difficulty must fall some where and must necessarily be severely felt by a large portion of mankind.[38]

Malthus concedes that the inequality between the "powers" associated with the mechanisms of the natural laws could potentially have disastrous consequences for all of mankind. But he also claims that this does not occur, because the interaction between the mechanisms results in "a strong constantly operating check" on population growth that affects only a "portion" of mankind. Assuming, like Smith, that impersonal and deterministic natural laws govern the interaction between parts (individuals) to perpetuate the existence of the whole (all human beings), Malthus concludes that we should not interfere with the operation of these laws. In his view, the death of large numbers of the working poor is the unfortunate but inevitable result of the lawful mechanisms of an essentially benevolent nature.

The natural laws of Smith may be more benevolent and less menacing than those of Malthus, but there is no difference between them in ontological terms. Natural laws as both Smith and Malthus conceived them are created by a God who withdraws from the universe after the first moment of creation; they exist in a realm prior to and separate from physical reality; and they act causally and deterministically on atomized parts to sustain the whole. Malthus's assumption that the "unseen chains" of the laws of population, like those of the natural laws that collectively constitute the invisible hand, cannot be broken served to reinforce the view that social and political problems do not lie within the domain of economic theory. This assumption allowed subsequent generations of economists to more effectively argue that the business of economists is to describe the lawful workings of the free-market system and not to concern themselves with problems that exist in "other" domains of reality.

David Ricardo was the son of a Jewish merchant-banker, and his expertise as a stockbroker allowed him to retire with a large fortune at the age of forty-two. The system or machine of the market in Ricardo's *On the Principles of Political Economy* (1817) is as abstract and unadorned as a linear equation, and the atomized entities within this system are "forced" to obey the "laws of behavior." Workers appear, as Robert Heilbroner puts it, as "undifferentiated units of economic energy, whose only human aspect is a hopeless addiction to what is euphemistically called 'the delights of domestic society.'" And capitalists are depicted as "a gray and uniform lot, whose entire purpose on earth is to accumulate—that is, to save profits and to reinvest them by hiring more men to work for them; and this they do with unvarying dependability."[39]

One of Ricardo's burning ambitions was to repeal a set of laws, passed by a Parliament largely controlled by large landowners, that were designed to prevent cheap grain from being imported into Britain. In Ricardo's view, these so-called Corn Laws were an obvious impediment to improving national welfare, and most of his economic theory is intended to demonstrate that this is the case. Like Smith, Ricardo believed that if the natural laws of economics are allowed to operate without interference, the market system will expand and new shops and factories will create more demand for labor. As the population increases, the increased demand for grain will, he said, result in higher prices and in the cultivation of more marginal land.

In an attempt to uncover the lawful dynamics of this process, Ricardo developed a theory of rents premised on the assumption of the Physiocrats that only land yields surplus value and capital investments do not increase this value. Ricardo argues, however, that while fertile land in earlier times was a gift of nature that existed in such abundance that it was regarded as free, progress has resulted in a situation in which fertile land is scarce and capital investment is required to increase production. He then argues that the cultivation of the more marginal land necessarily increases the overall costs of production and that this is reflected in higher prices for grain and increases in rent for the landlord who owns the best land.

Rent as Ricardo defines it is the difference in profits that results when the costs of growing crops on fecund land are less that those of growing crops on less fecund land. In both instances, landlords must pay the same wages and bear the same capital expenses, but the landlord who owns the more fertile land reaps more profits than his competitors. The problem with this picture, says Ricardo, is that the group that is responsible for this progress, the capitalists, are obliged to pay higher subsistence-level wages to workers while the rising aggregate of rents increases the profits of landlords.[40] What is significant here for our purposes is the assumption that the "laws" of supply and demand determine which resources of nature are free and which are included within the system of the market. This assumption survives in the mathematical theories used by mainstream economists, and this is one of the major reasons why there is no basis in this theory for realistically accounting for the costs of environmental resources.

Some historians of mainstream economics recognize that the French moral philosophers who influenced Smith's conception of natural laws made overt appeals to metaphysics to legitimate the existence of these laws. But most avoid confronting the Adam Smith problem by extracting well-known passages from *The Wealth of Nations* and treating them as pieces of revisionist history. Others seek to avoid the problem by arguing that *The Wealth of Nations,* given the absence of appeals to the Judeo-Christian God, is an entirely secular study of economic reality that is different in kind from Smith's other works. One large explanation for this failure to recognize that the invisible hand was and is a metaphysical construct is that these historians are viewing Smith's construct of the invisible hand through the conceptual lenses of neoclassical economic theory.[41]

In the next chapter, we will examine how the creators of neoclassical economics disguised the metaphysical foundations of Smith's natural laws of economics under the guise of a mathematical formalism borrowed wholesale from the equations of a badly conceived and soon to be outmoded mid-nineteenth-century physical theory. After substituting economic variables for the physical variables in the equations of this theory, these economists claimed that they had transformed the study of economics into a rigorously mathematical discipline comparable to the physical sciences. A number of scientists told the economists that there was absolutely no basis for making these substitutions, because the physical variables were completely different from the economic variables and the physical equations had nothing to do with the behavior of people in market systems. But the economists, all of whom were trained as engineers, apparently failed to understand the arguments of the scientists and continued to argue that their mathematical theories were scientific.

In what is surely one of the strangest chapters in intellectual history, the origins of neoclassical economic theory in mid-nineteenth-century physics were forgotten, subsequent generations of mainstream economists disguised the metaphysical foundations of the natural laws of economics under an increasingly more elaborate maze of mathematical formalism, and the totally unsubstantiated claim that this discipline was scientific was almost universally accepted. These developments are extremely important for our purposes because neoclassical economic theory is the narrative that coordinates large-scale human activities in the global market system and there is no basis in this narrative for internalizing the environmental costs of economic activities in pricing systems or for realistically accounting for these costs in monetary terms.

THE GOD WITH THE INVISIBLE HAND
Neoclassical Economics and Mid-Nineteenth-Century Physics

> One of the largest and most important questions facing the governments of the industrial countries is that the economics profession—I choose my words with care—is intellectually bankrupt. It might as well not exist.
>
> — JOHN KENNETH GALBRAITH

The causes of the crisis in the global environment may be staggeringly complex, but the most effective way to deal with it in economic terms seems rather obvious. We must use scientifically valid measures of the damage done to the global environment by large-scale economic activities as a basis for assessing the costs of this damage, and we must develop means and methods for including these costs in the economic system. If this could be accomplished within the framework of mainstream economics, we could begin rather quickly to posit viable economic solutions to environmental problems based on assumptions about the character of economic reality that are well known and almost universally accepted. The business of managing natural resources and developing more environmentally friendly technologies would be "business as usual," and global economic planners and environmental scientists could work together in harmony to fashion a global economic order that is both prosperous and secure. Unfortunately, this cannot and will not happen because metaphysically based assumptions about part-whole relationships in the neoclassical economic paradigm are categorically different from and entirely incompatible with the actual dynamics of part-whole relationships in the system of life.

These metaphysical assumptions became embedded in neoclassical economics as a result of the failed attempt by its creators to transform the study of economics into a rigorously mathematical scientific discipline by substituting economic variables for physical variables in the equations of a mid-nineteenth-century physical theory. For those interested in a more complete discussion of the manner in which the economists abused this physics, an earlier book of mine, *The Wealth of Nature: How Mainstream Economics Has Failed the Environment,* might be useful.[1] A more exhaustive discussion can be found in two books by Philip Mirowski, a professor of economics and a historian of science at Notre Dame.[2] Another must read for those who wish to explore this aspect of the history of economic thought in more detail is a book by Bruno Ingrao, a professor of economics at the University of Sassari, and Georgio Israel, a professor of mathematics at the University of Rome.[3]

The physics that the creators of neoclassical economics used as the template for their theories was developed from the 1840s to the 1860s. Responding to the inability of Newtonian mechanics to account for the phenomena of heat, light, and electricity, physicists during this period came up with a profusion of hypotheses about matter and forces. In 1847 Hermann-Ludwig Ferdinand von Helmholtz, one of the best-known and most widely respected physicists at this time, posited the existence of a vague and ill-defined energy that could unify these phenomena. This served as a catalyst for a movement in which physicists attempted to explain very diverse physical phenomena in terms of a unified and protean field of energy.

Because the physicists were unable to specify the actual character of this energy and could not be precise about what was being measured, their theories were not subject to repeatable experiments under controlled conditions. Obviously, this violated one of the cardinal rules of the scientific method—the predictions of any scientific theory must be testable and potentially falsifiable in repeatable experiments under controlled conditions. The amorphous character of energy in the physical theories also obliged the physicists to appeal to the law of the conservation of energy, which states that the sum of kinetic and potential energy in a closed system is conserved. This appeal was necessary because it was the only means of asserting that the vaguely defined system somehow remains the "same" as it undergoes changes and transformations.[4]

The creators of neoclassical economics (William Stanley Jevons, Léon Walras, Francis Ysidro Edgeworth, and Vilfredo Pareto) began with the assumption that a particle or mass point could be viewed as the equivalent of an atomized economic actor that moves along a path in accordance with the principle of least action. Aware that energy in the equations of mid-nineteenth-century physics is a force that pervades all space, the economists concluded that this space could also be filled by a postulated form of energy called utility. None of these figures appear to have seriously considered the fact that utility, defined as economic satisfaction and well-being, cannot be directly known or measured and is in no way comparable to energy as that term was used in mid-nineteenth-century physics. Equally remarkable, they also dismissed or rationalized away issues of integration and invariance that are critically important in the proper application of the conservation principle.

The strategy used by the economists was as simple as it was absurd—they took the equations from the mid-nineteenth-century physical theory and changed the names of the variables. Utility was substituted for energy, the sum of utility for potential energy, and expenditure for kinetic energy. Although there was no basis for claiming that the natural laws of economics are in any sense the equivalent of the physical variables, the strategy allowed utility to be treated as a field of vector potentials in which the sum of income and utility is conserved. None of these now famous people seemed to realize that the sum of income and utility in neoclassical economics, much less in economic reality, is not conserved and that the conservation principle is quite meaningless in any real economic process. Nevertheless, this blatantly unscientific assumption is now used to legitimate the existence of the invisible hand in its current form—constrained maximization in general equilibrium theory.

In the mathematical formalism that resulted from these substitutions, the minds of atomized economic actors are presumed to operate within a field of force identified, in both figurative and literal terms, with energy. The forces associated with this energy were represented as prices, and spatial coordinates described quantities of goods. Because utility-energy in this formalism is conserved, the first neoclassical economists were obliged to view production and consumption of goods and commodities as physically neutral processes that do not alter the sum of utility. They did so by arriving at a very strange interpretation of what was then regarded as a self-evident truth in the physical sciences—the law of the conservation of matter or the idea that matter cannot be created or destroyed. If matter, they argued, is immutable, then the production of goods and commodities cannot alter or change the stuff out of which goods or commodities are made. They then concluded that any value that accrues as a result of production can reside only in the mental space of economic actors. Similarly, they argued that if the immutable stuff out of which goods or commodities are made cannot be changed by consumption, any value associated with consumption must also reside in the minds of economic actors.

This strange view of substance in economic reality was used to interpret the meaning of the economic variables in the equations borrowed from mid-nineteenth-century physics. In the formalism of this theory, the atomized immaterial minds of economic actors are assumed to operate within a field of force (utility) in which the natural laws of economics legislate over the choices made by the actors. This became the basis for a fundamental assumption in neoclassical economics—the value assigned to all the immutable unchanging stuff that circulates in a closed loop from production to consumption in a market system results from the operation of the putative natural laws.

THE CREATORS OF NEOCLASSICAL ECONOMICS

William Stanley Jevons, after being encouraged by his father to become an engineer, studied chemistry and mathematics in London and attended some of Michael Faraday's lectures at the Royal Institution. In these lectures, Faraday demonstrated that magnetic forces did not obey the Newtonian force rule and argued that other forces must be present. Jevons was also familiar with the work of Thompson and Joule on the interconvertibility of heat and mechanical energy that laid the foundations for the law of the conservation of energy. But since Jevons was not a skilled mathematician, his understanding of scientific matters was crude at best and completely distorted at worst.

In order to appreciate why Jevons appeared to have no difficulty identifying mind or consciousness in economic reality with a point particle moving in a field of energy, consider the following passage from his major work, *The Principles of Science:* "Life seems to be nothing but a special form of energy which is manifested in heat and electricity and mechanical force. The time may come, it almost seems, when the tender mechanism of the brain will be traced out, and every thought reduced to the expenditure of a determinate weight of nitrogen and phosphorous. No apparent limit exists to the success of the scientific method in weighing and measuring, and reducing beneath the sway of law, the phenomena of matter and mind. . . . Must not the same inexorable reign of law which is apparent in the motions of brute matter be extended to the human heart?"[5]

Mind, says Jevons, is a manifestation of energy; the physical substrate of mind can be reduced to a measurable quantity, such as the "weight of nitrogen and phosphorous"; and the "phenomena" of mind are potentially explainable in terms of collections of particles subject to the "inexorable reign" of deterministic physical laws. If one actually believed, as Jevons apparently did, that this is the case, it would not require a great leap of faith to arrive at what is, in retrospect, a very strange conclusion. If mind in economic reality is a manifestation of energy that is similar to or the same as the protean field of amorphous energy described in mid-nineteenth-century physics, utility can be substituted for energy in the equations of this physics.

Jevons was quite convinced that his appropriation of the equations of mid-nineteenth-century physics had transformed economics into a science, but his understanding of the ontological status of the natural laws that allegedly act between or outside the parts (economic actors) to maintain the stability of the whole (market system) was the same as that of Adam Smith. Jevons also predicated the existence of these laws on the seventeenth-century assumption of metaphysical dualism and believed that natural laws had coequal status with physical laws. In the following passage from *Theory of Political Economy*, Jevons defends the claim that his theory is scientific: "The theory consists of applying differential calculus to the familiar notions of wealth, utility, value, demand, supply, capital, interest, labour, and all the other quantitative notions belonging to the daily operations of industry. . . .To me it seems that our science must be mathematical, simply because it deals in quantities. Whenever things treated are capable of being greater or less, there the laws and relations must be mathematical in nature."[6]

Jevons argues that because his theory deals in quantities that are subject to continuous variation, this justifies the translation of nebulous constructs in economic theory into well-defined quantities with the use of the differential calculus. In Newtonian physics, the differential calculus describes the movement of point particles in vector space in terms of continuous functions that result in infinitely small differentials in accordance with the classical laws of motion. Jevons, however, seems quite oblivious to the fact that economic actors cannot be described in this fashion. Also, one does not have to be a trained logician to appreciate the absurdity of this circular argument—the theory must be scientific because it is mathematical and the theory must be mathematical because it is scientific. This same argument would be used repeatedly by subsequent generations of mainstream economists to defend the claim that economics is a rigorously mathematical discipline comparable to physics.

Léon Walras, who was also encouraged by his father to study engineering, enrolled in the Ecole des Mines in 1845. Dissatisfied with the study of engineering, Walras read philosophy, history, literary criticism, and political economy. During this period, he also read a popular account of the philosophy of Kant and embraced a confused monism that was a synthesis of materialism and spiritualism.[7] In spite of his lack of training in either mathematics or physics, Walras viewed Newtonian astronomy and classical mechanics as the unequaled models of scientific knowledge, and his grand ambition was to use these models to create "the science of economic forces, analogous to the science of astronomical forces."[8]

Like Jevons, Walras posited an additive utility function in which the utility of a good is solely the function of the quantity of the good consumed. The additive utility function allows the utility of a bundle of goods to be expressed as the sum of the single utility functions that allegedly express the pleasure derived by the consumer in his or her consumption of each good in the bundle. Walras's *rareté*, which is the equivalent to Jevons's marginal utility, refers to the last increment of utility (pleasure) derived by a consumer from an infinitesimal increment in the consumption of a particular good. He also claimed that while the marginal utility of a good is positive, the added utility for the consumer of successive amounts of a particular good gradually diminishes. For example, the first piece of bread consumed by a hungry man will have the most added utility, and the amount of utility associated with consuming subsequent pieces will gradually diminish.

In *Elements of Pure Economics*, Walras makes a stark distinction between forces associated with the natural laws of economics and the force of free will: "Facts of the first category are found in nature, and that is why we call them natural phenomena. Facts of the second category are found in man, and that is why we call them human phenomena."[9] Walras claims that all natural forces that operate outside the atomized human mind are "blind and ineluctable," and he includes in these forces those associated with the natural laws of economics. Later in this same discussion, the distinction between the natural and the human becomes a distinction between things and persons, and this distinction becomes the basis for yet another distinction between the relations of persons and things in industry and the relations between persons and other persons in institutions. Walras then concludes, "The theory of industry is called applied science or art; the theory of institutions moral science or ethics."[10]

This categorical distinction between the domain of economics and all other human domains, including government, became one of the central dogmas of mainstream economics. But how does Walras justify its existence? He does so by claiming that there is only one natural phenomenon in economic reality—the single relation between two things represented by the value or price of a good. "Thus," he argues, "any value in exchange, once established, partakes of the character of a natural phenomenon, natural in origins, natural in its manifestations and natural in essence."[11]

Assuming that "natural" means "from or pertaining to nature," on what basis does Walras conclude that a value established in an exchange can be viewed as natural in its origins, manifestations, and essence? Markets are human inventions that have taken a wide range of different forms, the value of any commodity is normally a function of a staggering array of variables, and prices paid are invariably tied to individual tastes and preferences. For Walras, however, none of this matters, because he assumes that prices are governed by deterministic "natural" laws, and this allows him to argue that these prices are "natural" in origins, manifestations, and essence. When contemporary mainstream economists use the term natural, as in natural rates of unemployment, they rarely comment on its meaning. Their use of the word implies, however, that there is a natural, lawful order in market systems and that whatever is natural must be good. And this serves to reinforce the view that outside intervention by government or any other agency on closed market systems will disrupt the otherwise inevitable progress toward the good.

Although Walras's natural economic order is very rigid and highly mechanistic, he does not claim that human will has no influence on prices. But he does say that the forces that regulate comparative prices are comparable to the law of gravity, and this becomes the basis for the following argument. Just as the force of human will can resist the force of gravity, it can also resist the forces that regulate competitive prices. Yet one cannot, says Walras, fundamentally alter the manner in which economic forces govern the interaction of atomized economic actors any more that one can alter the manner in which gravity governs the interactions of point particles. Because the force of gravity in classical physics tends to move physical systems toward equilibrium, Walras concludes that economic forces tend to move competitive prices toward equilibrium. It is this more restricted view of determinism that allegedly legitimates his "theory of the determination of prices under a hypothetical regime of perfect competition."[12]

The fact that the neoclassical model in mainstream economics was derived from this incredibly inept manipulation of a soon to be outmoded physical theory would soon be forgotten. What survives, however, is the assumption that the usefulness of economic models in neoclassical economics is a form of scientific proof. Note how Walras exploits this idea in an attempt to reinforce his claim that economics is a science in the following commentary on the relationship between geometry and prices: "If the pure theory of economics or the theory of exchange and value in exchange, that is, the theory of social wealth considered by itself, is a physico-mathematical science like mechanics or hydrodynamics, then economists should not be afraid to use the methods and language of mathematics."[13]

In the same way that pure mathematics precedes applied science, Walras argues, pure economics should precede applied economics. The only basis for the claim that his economics is "pure" is that it represents vague economic concepts in the mathematical equations of mid-nineteenth-century physics. Yet this is the basis for his "proof" that the resulting economic theory "resembles the physico-mathematical sciences in every respect" and should be viewed as a science "like mechanics or hydrodynamics."

In the cryptic discussions of the origins of neoclassical economic theory found in most introductory economics textbooks, the claim is normally made that this theory was independently and simultaneously "discovered" in the 1870s by the Englishman Jevons, the Frenchman Walras, and the Austrian Carl Menger (1840–1921). The implication is that any theory that emerges independently and simultaneously in very different cultural contexts must be empirically valid. As Mirowski has demonstrated in exhaustive detail, however, this discovery was not simultaneous, and the inclusion of Menger in the pantheon of the first neoclassical economists was a historical accident.[14]

Menger did claim that he was one of the originators of neoclassical economic theory, but he rejected the unifying principle of the theory, the construct of utility, and made no use of the new mathematical techniques borrowed from mid-nineteenth-century physics. Mirowski agues that the primary reason why Menger's false claim was taken seriously is that one of his illustrious students, Friedrich von Wieser, managed to successfully promote it during a period in which the work of his former teacher was largely unavailable outside the German-speaking world. In any event, the argument that general equilibrium theory must reveal truths about economic reality because of the manner in which it was "discovered" is clearly bogus.

The other two economists who are recognized as the creators of neoclassical economic theory are Francis Ysidro Edgeworth and Vilfredo Pareto. Both embraced Walras's claim that utility was the equivalent of energy in the equations of mid-nineteenth-century physics along with his conclusion that economics had become a rigorously scientific discipline. As Edgeworth put it:

The application of mathematics to the world of the soul is countenanced by the hypothesis . . . that Pleasure is the concomitant of Energy. Energy may be regarded as the central idea of Mathematical Physics: maximum energy the object of the principle investigations in that science. . . . 'Mechanique Sociale' may one day take her place along with 'Mechanique Celeste,' throned each upon the double-sided height of one maximal principle, the supreme principle of moral as of physical science. As the movements of each particle, constrained or loose, in a material cosmos are continually subjugated to one maximum sub-total of accumulated energy, so the movements of each soul whether selfishly isolated or linked sympathetically, may continually be realizing the maximum of pleasure.[15]

Pareto was equally convinced that the equations borrowed from the physics had transformed the study of economics into a rigorously mathematical discipline like physics: "Strange disputes about predestination, about the efficacy of grace, etc., and in our own day incoherent ramblings on solidarity show that men have not freed themselves from these daydreams which have been gotten rid of in the physical sciences, but which still burden the social sciences." But this no longer applies, said Pareto, to the study of economics, because the "use of mathematics" in the new "theory of economic science" has all of the "rigor of rational mechanics."[16]

MORE RECENT DEVELOPMENTS IN NEOCLASSICAL ECONOMICS

Alfred Marshall, the dominant figure in mainstream economics from 1890 to the beginning of World War I, popularized neoclassical economic theory and altered some of the work he promoted. Many historians of economics have cited Marshall's claim that the "Mecca of the economist lies in economic biology" and concluded that he preferred the biological metaphor to the physics metaphor. In the next sentence, however, Marshall writes, "But biological conceptions are more complex that those of mechanics; a volume on Foundations must therefore give a relatively large place to mechanical analogies."[17] When Marshall made this comment, the physical theory used by the creators of neoclassical economics was outmoded, and yet he appears to have been completely unaware that this was the case.

John Maynard Keynes, a student of Marshall, wrote his most seminal work during a period in which the Great Depression was challenging neoclassical assumptions about the lawful mechanisms of market systems. In 1935, Keynes said the following in a letter to playwright George Bernard Shaw: "You have to know that I am writing a book on economic theory which will largely revolutionize—not as I suppose at once, but in the course of the next ten years—the way the world thinks about economic problems."[18] What is most radical about the book that Keynes felt would occasion this revolution, *The General Theory of Employment, Interest and Money,* is that it grounds economic processes in historical time, or in a more experiential sense of time in which the future cannot be known and the past cannot be changed.

As we have seen, the mathematical formalism of mid-nineteenth-century physics obliged Walras to view economic actors as imbued with prodigious knowledge of economic variables and existing in a wholly abstract realm where time in all its actual dimensions does not exist. Keynes's more recognizably human economic actor is quite different. He or she is motivated in part by "animal spirits" and irrational desires and inhabits an economic reality in which knowledge is always proximate and future outcomes are essentially indeterminate.

In *The General Theory,* Keynes first made the case that there is nothing inherent in the mechanisms of a free-market system to prevent a situation in which surplus saving does not result in lower interest rates and investment spending plummets owing to expectations of future low sales. In the absence of borrowing and investment spending, there is, said Keynes, no economic impetus to expand or grow the economy. As the worldwide depression in the 1930s had shown, these conditions could lead to some very unfortunate results—massive unemployment, a spiral of contraction due to lack of spending on capital equipment, and a climate of uncertainty in which private investment was not sufficient to reverse the economic decline. Keynes's well-known solution to this problem was that government should take up the slack by funding projects that would employ the unemployed. The monies earned by these individuals would, said Keynes, increase the buying power that fuels consumption and lead to resumption of private investment and business expansion.

There was much that was troubling, then and now, about *The General Theory* from the perspective of neoclassical economists. Keynes's claim that the unimpeded operations of the natural laws of economics can result in a situation in which an economy not only fails to grow but even contracts suggested that the laws of economics are fallible. Because the prescribed remedy for this situation is large-scale intervention by government, or by an agency "outside" the closed market system, this not only suggested that the system cannot under all conditions be viewed as closed. It also indicated that there are situations where the natural laws of economics, if left alone, cannot sustain the economic well-being of even the majority of economic actors.

The realization that led Keynes to develop a theory that would later be dubbed the "Keynesian heresy" is apparent a letter he wrote in 1934 to economist John Hicks: "I shall hope to convince you some day that Walras's theory and all the others along these lines are little better than nonsense."[19] If Keynes had been able to convince other neoclassical economists that Walrasian general equilibrium theory is "nonsense," then the revolution he had in mind might have actually occurred. This did not happen, however, because Keynes wed new assumptions about economic reality to a mathematical formalism that was essentially the same as that which Walras derived from mid-nineteenth-century physics.

Keynes's suggestion that the behavior of economic actors and firms cannot under certain conditions prevent the market system from moving toward a state of general equilibrium resulted in the development of macroeconomics. Based largely on the broadly homogeneous categories of economic activity developed by Keynes, macroeconomists attempt to study the whole of the economy by representing the economic behavior of economic actors and firms within these categories as lawfully determined based on deductions from general equilibrium theory. The resulting mathematical models are used to assess macroeconomic issues, such as the effects of government policies on inflation and unemployment, the impacts on stock markets of changes in the overnight interest rates by the central bank, and the overall costs associated with increases in the minimum wage. But since virtually all of these macroeconomic models are extensions of the means and methods of the microeconomic models in general equilibrium theory, they are predicated on the same assumptions about the relationships between parts (economic actors and firms) and wholes (market systems).

In the 1930s and 1940s, the foundations were laid for the axiomatization of general equilibrium theory, or for reformulating it within a framework of hypotheses perfectly delineated and rigorously expressed in mathematical language. The impulse toward axiomatization came from two gifted mathematicians, John von Neumann and Oskar Morgenstern, who were highly critical of the conversational and imprecise language used by neoclassical economists and their apparent unwillingness to develop more sophisticated mathematical models. In a conversation with Morgenstern on the state of this discipline at the end of the 1930s, von Neumann remarked, "You know, Oskar, if those books are unearthed sometime a hundred years hence, people will not believe they were written in our time. Rather they will think that they are contemporary with Newton, so primitive is their mathematics."[20] Morgenstern was similarly disdainful of the state of economic theory. In a review of John Hicks's *Value and Capital* (1939), Morgenstern dismissed the value of this well-received and widely read attempt to develop a more comprehensive economic theory based on Walrasian analysis by concluding that it was "outdated and lacking in rigor."[21]

The rigor that von Neumann and Morgenstern wished to introduce into economic theory was predicated on the belief, popular in intellectual circles at the time, that more sophisticated mathematical techniques could disclose the underlying dynamics of human consciousness and decision making. The notion that timeless, universal truths govern the dynamics of human thought and behavior and that the essence of these truths consists of immaterial ideas, or preexisting logics, that can be uncovered by advances in mathematical theory is everywhere present in their work. Both figures may have been very much aware that the mathematical clothes worn by the emperor of neoclassical economics in the 1930s were largely imaginary, but they firmly believed that a real or actual garment could be woven from the thread of higher mathematics.

One irony here is that their attempts to create this garment served to perpetuate the fiction that the invisible hand actually exists by disguising the metaphysical assumptions on which its existence is predicated under increasingly elaborate layers of mathematical formalism. Another is that von Neumann and Morgenstern attempted to do so during a period in which their conception of the relationship between mathematical theory and physical reality was completely undermined by developments in quantum physics. This conception was also undermined in a somewhat different way by Gödel's demonstration in his incompleteness theorem that no finite system of mathematics can be used to derive all true mathematical statements and, therefore, no algorithm, or calculation procedure, can prove its own validity.

Most of the research in neoclassical economics since the 1940s, particularly in general equilibrium theory, has been based on extensions and refinements of the work of von Neumann and Morgenstern. Paul Samuelson in *Foundations of Economic Analysis* (1947) attempted to systematize general equilibrium theory with the use of organic methodologies and mathematical techniques that were less rigorous than those used by von Neumann and Morgenstern. This is, however, the first treatise in economic theory in which the formal mathematical apparatus is embedded in the main argument and not placed in appendices. Samuelson clearly implies that the transcendent truths that lie at the core of economic behavior can be described and decoded by pure mathematics.

In *Foundations*, Samuelson assumes that any problem in economic theory can be reduced to a system of equations and that general equilibrium is the solution of all the equations that represent the lawful dynamics of a free-market system. He defines a meaningful mathematical theorem as "simply a hypothesis about empirical data which could conceivably be refuted, if only under ideal conditions."[22] Samuelson then goes on to specify that a theorem "may be indeterminate and practically difficult, or impossible to determine. . . . But it is meaningful because under ideal circumstances an experiment could be devised whereby one could hope to refute the hypothesis."[23]

The curious presumption that a system of idealized representations of economic activity in mathematical theorems could somehow be proven if an ideal experiment could somehow be conducted would soon become the primary justification for the real existence of the invisible hand in neoclassical economic theory. However, the mathematical formalism in this theory is such that it is not possible to define the specific roles or behavior of economic actors based on the functional form of the equations. Hence hypotheses normally refer to some qualitative properties of the functions that allegedly emerge from the formalism, such as convexity or monotony.

Aware of this problem, Samuelson rationalizes away the fact that experimental verification of general equilibrium is impossible by claiming that this is an indispensable aspect of theoretical economics: "It is precisely because theoretical economics does not confine itself to specific narrow types of functions that it is able to achieve wide generality in its initial formulation."[24] If a scientist claimed that a scientific theory is useful because it is sufficiently general to disallow any prospect that its predictions can be subjected to experimental proof, he or she would be the laughingstock of the profession. Mainstream economists, however, have rather consistently used this argument to justify the claim that neoclassical economics is a science comparable to the physical sciences and has much the same status as a theory in the physical sciences.

In the equations of physical theories, variables have a counterpart in physical reality that is observable or potentially observable, and new physical theories are deemed valid only if they make predictions that can be confirmed in repeatable experiments under controlled conditions. The primary reason why the predictions of general equilibrium theory cannot be confirmed in this manner is that the natural laws of economics do not exist. Another is that the variables in the mathematical formalism of this theory are self-referential functions that have no real or actual counterpart in physical reality. Given that these predictions are the product of a system of equations that refers only to itself, there is no basis in principle for confirming or denying them. This leads to the obvious conclusion that there is simply no way in which to prove that the theory is valid or invalid in scientific terms.

Gerald Debreu, who sought to complete the work begun by von Neumann and Morgenstern, published a complete axiomatization of general equilibrium theory in *Theory of Value* (1959) in which the emphasis is shifted from the mathematical techniques of infinitesimal calculus to those of algebra and typology.[25] He extends this mathematical apparatus to include a broad new range of quantitative and qualitative analysis with the aim of creating a formal structure that clearly reveals "all the assumptions and the logical structure of analysis."[26] This approach represents a major shift in neoclassical economic thought because it attempts to account for the formation of exchange values in pure mathematical language and without reference to the interpretive value of the concepts. As Debreu puts it, "Allegiance to rigor dictates the axiomatic form of the analysis where the theory, in the strict sense, is logically disconnected from its interpretations."[27]

The presumption behind this analysis is that a purely mathematical economic theory can uncover previously hidden lawful dynamics in economic reality just as purely mathematical theories in physics have uncovered hidden dynamics of physical reality. Given that the mathematical constructs in physics can be understood mathematically without any reference to their meaning in ordinary language, Debreu claims that this should also be the case for constructs in an axiomatized mathematical treatment of general equilibrium theory. The problem with these assumptions is not merely that there is no one-to-one correspondence between the variables in this theory and the actual behavior of economic systems. It is also that the metaphysical constructs on which the theory is based are the same as those in Walrasian general equilibrium theory and this fact is only thinly disguised by a mathematical formalism that differs in form and content from that used by Walras.

Debreu may have been successful in representing these constructs in a framework of hypotheses that are perfectly delineated and rigorously expressed in mathematical language. But this does not, in any sense, prove the validity of the assumptions and only serves to disguise their metaphysical foundations under another complex set of mathematical idealizations that say nothing in ordinary language about the actual character of the assumptions. And yet Debreu assumes that a self-referential mathematical system that has no real or actual counterpart in economic reality can disclose hidden lawful dynamics in this reality. For example, he claims that "uncertainties" about the future of market economies are "due to the unknown choice that nature will make from the set of possible states in the world" and that these uncertainties can be eliminated based on future extensions of axiomatization in neoclassical economic theory.[28]

Another neoclassical economist with a talent for higher mathematics, Kenneth Arrow, collaborated with Debreu to develop the Arrow-Debreu model for general equilibrium theory (1954).[29] This mathematical model describes a hypothetical perpetually expanding market system in which idealized economic actors possess an unlimited understanding of the consequences of their economic choices and engage in perfect competition without any transmission and information costs. In this model, general equilibrium theory is rigorously expressed in mathematical terms as a set of ideal conditions in an idealized economic system characterized by equilibrium of perfect competition. The mechanism in the model that allegedly confirms that these actors have made the mutually compatible decisions that result in this equilibrium is a set of signals, or market prices, which operates automatically even though the actors are totally unaware of its existence.

The history of general equilibrium theory is much more complex and detailed than this brief account suggests, and a complete history would require several volumes. But what is most important about this history for our purposes is that the theory is now and always has been predicated on assumptions about the relationship between parts (economic actors and firms) and wholes (market systems) articulated by the creators of neoclassical economics. It should now be clear that these assumptions were metaphysical in origin and assumed the guise of scientific truths after the creators of neoclassical economics incorporated them into a mathematical formalism borrowed from mid-nineteenth-century physics. This myth was perpetuated in theories that disguised the metaphysical foundations of the assumptions under an increasingly complex maze of mathematical formalism.

GAME THEORY

A fair number of economists over the past two decades, including luminaries such as Arrow and Hand, have expressed doubt about the efficacy of general equilibrium theory, but it is still the central legitimating construct in mainstream economics. Within the community of mainstream economists, the most serious objections have been raised by proponents of game theory. Game theory in economics originated in 1944 with the publication of *The Theory of Games and Economic Behavior* by John von Neumann and Oskar Morgenstern. A game, explained the authors, is a set of rules and objectives and a ranking of objectives by a set of players. Assuming that the sets are discrete and well defined, von Neumann and Morgenstern argued that they can be expressed in mathematical equations and manipulated by mathematical symbols to predict outcomes.

Martin Shubik, perhaps the best known and most influential of the game theorists, has been consistently critical of Walrasian general equilibrium theory because it assumes that economic actors have no freedom to make mistakes or even to make choices about the economic process. He claims that an alternate and more realistic description of the behavior of economic actors can be disclosed in noncooperative game theory. "Noncooperative game theory," writes Shubik, "appears to be particularly useful for the study of mass phenomena in which the communication between individuals must be relatively low and individuals interact with a more or less faceless economy, polity or society."[30]

These impersonal forces can be represented, says Shubik, "through the construction of mathematical models in which the 'rules of the game' derive not only from the economics and technology of the situation, but from the sociological and legal structure as well."[31] In Shubik's mathematical models, the basic features of an economy (tastes, technologies, and endowments) are essentially the same as those in conventional Walrasian models, and sociological, political, and legal forces are represented mathematically as the rules that act arbitrarily on the closed economy from the outside. These rules do not, claims Shubik, lie within the sphere of the closed economy, because they are not "natural" or do not operate in accordance the natural laws of economics. Although Shubik does not argue that the natural laws of economics are the single determinant of economic behavior, these laws function in his theory as the prime determinant of such behavior. The economic actor in his mathematical models may be buffeted by arbitrary variables that operate outside the closed market system, but this actor is still represented as a point particle subject to the influence of natural laws.

In a two-volume work titled *The Theory of Money and Financial Institutions,* Shubik attempts to reconcile micro- and macroeconomic theory by constructing a process-oriented theory of money and financial institutions based on a theory of games. He claims that it is possible to "construct process models of the economy that are as rigorous as general equilibrium theory but explain more phenomena."[32] Shubik then suggests that the essential problem with general equilibrium theory is that it is predicated on an absurdly reductive and restrictive view of economic actors: "The rational, economic, institution-free individual assumed in its models is an overly simplistic abstraction of a subtle and complex creature who must function with high constraints on perception and ability to calculate, who uses both internal and external memory, and whose goals can hardly be well defined outside the context of the society in which the individual functions."[33]

Shubik then notes that in the absence of "well-defined models of politico-economic and socio-economic behavior," he is obliged to make the "usual assumptions concerning the existence of well-defined preferences and utility functions, not because I believe in them, but because I want to show that even with these assumptions we can go beyond the results of general equilibrium theory."[34] This effort to transcend the limits of general equilibrium theory is predicated on an interesting view of the "institutions of society in general, and the financial institutions in particular." These institutions, writes Shubik, are the "neural network of the sensors of the body economic, guiding the flows of funds, credits, and other financial paper that guide the real goods and services of the economy." He then proceeds to demonstrate that the process of setting up playable games "forces us" to invent minimal financial and governmental institutions even if we do not invoke the maximization of utility or use equilibrium as a general solution.[35]

Based on the assumption that the "neural network" of financial institutions "emerges" as a logical necessity of decision making in market economies, Shubik claims that game theory can disclose the "emergent" logics that structure this network, and this becomes the basis for two large claims—"minimal financial institutions" emerge as a "logical, technological, and institutional necessity when economic activity is described as a playable game" and "both game theoretic and general-equilibrium models often predict the same apparently general, non-institutional outcome."[36]

In the conclusion of this densely mathematical treatise, Shubik cautions that his game-theoretic "process models that can be solved for general equilibrium solutions" are not meant to closely approximate reality. "They are meant to be well-defined playable games where details (money, credit, the rate of interest, and so forth) are clearly defined and causality can be considered."[37] Yet he also claims that the models can demystify the lawful dynamics of market economies, such as perfect insight, rational expectations and the laws of Walras and Say.[38]

Like most theoreticians in mainstream economics, Shubik is a very gifted mathematician, and his analysis is staggeringly complex in these terms.

However, the alleged symmetries between the outcomes of the playable games and those of general equilibrium theory are not emergent properties of a neural network of institutions that direct the future of a market economy in causal terms. They are simply artifacts of a mathematical analysis predicated on assumptions about the relationships between parts (economic actors and firms) and wholes (market systems) in general equilibrium theory. What is most important to realize here is that game theory, even in its most sophisticated forms, perpetuates belief in the real or actual existence of the invisible hand by disguising the natural laws of economics under a maze of different mathematical formalism. It does so by alleging that causal mechanisms in market economies are emergent properties of human decision making within the lawful constraints of market processes as opposed to the transcendent, godlike agencies that lurk behind the equations of general equilibrium theory.

Another fundamental problem faced by the game theorists is that since economic transactions in the real world are serial and multiple, any accurate depiction of the results of such transactions requires that games be repeated. However, repetition in noncooperative games leads to the addition of more ad hoc assumptions about how each player will interpret the moves of other players. And this, as many game theorists have discovered, undermines the prospect that the outcome will be either fixed or determinant.

The work of the game theorists has proved very unsettling for many mainstream economists. In Walrasian general equilibrium theory, the natural laws of economics allegedly determine the optimal outcome of an economic process, and economic actors are devoid of all distinctly human characteristics and obey fixed decision-making rules. In this theory, the realm of the economy is stable and unchanging, and economic actors are viewed as supremely rational entities who do not talk back. In opening the box of human subjectivity, game theorists have been obliged to posit an increasing number of ad hoc variables to account for the decision making of individual economic actors. This explains why the history of game theory is marked by a continual regression into the staggering complexities of language and culture.

Bargaining games led to cooperative games, to noncooperative games, and to games where players are free to interpret the meaning of economic variables and the intentions of other players. More than half of a typical textbook on game theory is devoted to describing a staggering array of variants on particular games based on quite different conceptions of uncertainty, and there is no sense of generality or unity. What the game theorists have unwittingly demonstrated is that the complexities of language and culture cannot be reduced to deterministic mathematical models and that attempts to do so undermine the validity of mechanistic rationality in general equilibrium theory. As R. Sugden puts it, "it is increasingly becoming clear that these foundations are less secure than we thought, and that they need to be examined and perhaps rebuilt. Economic theorists may have to become as much philosophers as mathematicians."[39]

Wassily Leontief, a Nobel laureate in economics, has expressed similar doubts about the efficacy of the orthodox neoclassical paradigm: "Page after page of professional journals are filled with mathematical formulas leading the reader from sets of more or less plausible but entirely arbitrary assumptions to precisely stated but irrelevant conclusions. . . . Year after year economic theorists continue to produce scores of mathematical models to explore in great detail their formal properties; and the econometrics fit algebraic functions of all possible shapes to essentially the same sets of data without being able to advance, in any perceptible way, a systematic understanding of the structure and the operations of a real economic system."[40]

The decision to award the 2001 Nobel Memorial Prize in Economic Science to economists who have done pioneering research on the imperfections of market systems is another indicator that mainstream economists have begun to question the validity of assumptions about the character of economic reality in the neoclassical economic paradigm. The winners, Joseph Stiglitz, George Akerlof, and Michael Spence, were chosen because they had demonstrated that "imperfect information" in actual economic processes challenges the assumption that atomized economic actors are fully aware of complex economic variables in every transaction. According to these economists, these imperfections lead to situations in which the alleged lawful dynamics of closed market systems cannot allocate resources in the most efficient way and government must, therefore, intervene and make the necessary adjustments. For example, Stiglitz has shown that if the Securities and Exchange Commission did not enforce full disclosure in financial markets, investors would not have sufficient information to determine a proper value for stocks and some sectors of the market would have more information than others.

These criticisms and revisions of assumptions about the character of economic reality in neoclassical economic theory do not mean, however, that mainstream economists are in the process of developing a new theory predicated on a different set of assumptions. Virtually all of the most advanced theoretical work in mainstream economics is premised on the assumptions that market systems are, by varying degrees, closed, self-correcting, and self-sustaining. The primary impulse in most of these theories is to disclose the hidden dynamics that move market systems toward optimal states of equilibria, with the use of increasingly more sophisticated mathematical techniques. For example, nonlinear analysis, particularly convex analysis, has been used to buttress the theoretical claims of the game theorists, and the resulting mathematical formalism, as the work of Jean-Pierre Aubin illustrates, is staggeringly complex. But as the title of Aubin's best-known book attests, *Optima and Equilibria: An Introduction to Nonlinear Analysis*,[41] his attempt to uncover the immaterial logics that sustain the orderly workings of market systems is predicated on the assumption that these logics result from mechanisms associated with the operations of natural laws of economics.

More important for our purposes, the vast majority of mainstream economists who work in business and government, including those at the International Monetary Fund and the World Bank, are not terribly concerned with the most advanced theoretical work in their discipline. Legions of these economists are engaged on a daily basis in developing analyses and making predictions that guide the decision making of global economic planners and that serve to legitimate assumptions about economic reality in the neoclassical economic paradigm. Many of these planners are aware of the negative impacts of their decisions on the global environment and seek to minimize these impacts as long as profit margins can be maintained. These good intentions are, however, typically defeated by our now familiar culprit—blatantly unscientific assumptions about economic reality that make it virtually impossible to resolve environmental problems in economic terms.

Because the predictions of neoclassical economic theory are not subject to empirical verification, the primary determinant of which theories are used to coordinate economic activities in particular market economies is the political process. Some theories may have more predictive value than others in dealing with specific sets of initial conditions. But the predictions themselves are merely useful approximations of tendencies that point toward directions in which an economy may move under relative stable conditions. When the predictions are grossly inaccurate, as they almost invariably are under unstable market conditions, neoclassical economists typically attempt to explain, or explain away, the discrepancies by attributing the causes to "market failures" that can potentially be corrected or to events that occur "outside" the closed market system and interfere with its operation.

It is also worth noting that the so-called Nobel "Memorial Prize in Economics" was not among the five prizes established by Alfred Nobel in his last will and testament in 1896. This prize, which is properly known the Bank of Sweden Prize in Economic Sciences in Memory of Alfred Nobel, was created and funded by the Central Bank of Sweden at the height of the Cold War in an effort to create the impression, at least, that one of the most politically charged issues in this war had been resolved. During the period in the late 1960s in which the managers of this bank managed to convince the members of Nobel Prize committee to award this prize, economists in both capitalist and communist countries claimed that their theories were scientific and that those used by economists on the other side of the ideological divide were not. At a time when the competition for global hegemony between these very disparate conceptions of political and economic reality could have easily escalated into a full-scale nuclear war, the question of which theories were actually scientific was no trivial matter.

From the perspective of the bank managers, this question had already been answered; they had been taught in graduate school that the creators of neoclassical economic theory had transformed the study of economics into a rigorously scientific discipline like the physical sciences. Because they firmly believed that this was the case, the bank managers insisted that the new economics prize should be awarded, like the prizes in physics and chemistry, by the Swedish Academy of Sciences. The members of this academy initially resisted this proposal. Their principal reason for doing so was that scientists should not be involved in selecting the recipients of this prize, because economics is a social science very different from the physical sciences. But after being persuaded that the proposed arrangement might serve to curb the spread of communism, the scientists reluctantly accepted the proposal. However, this did not prevent the scientists from expressing their dissatisfaction in other ways, and one of them was to insist that the names of the economics laureates be engraved on the edge of their gold medals rather than on the more visible front, where the names of the "real" Nobel laureates in physics and chemistry were engraved.

When mainstream economists are confronted with the charge that there is no basis in their mathematical theories for effectively dealing with environmental problems in economic terms, they typically deny that this is the case by arguing that environmental economists deal with these problems very effectively. This orthodox approach to positing economic solutions to environmental problems is taught in universities and practiced in government agencies and development banks, and the solutions are almost invariably embedded in the mathematical formalism of general equilibrium theory. One objective in the next chapter is to convincingly demonstrate that the claim that the economic solutions to environmental problems proposed by the environmental economists can effectively resolve environmental problems is false. The primary reason why this is the case is that there is no basis in the neoclassical economic paradigm for realistically assessing the environmental costs of economic activities and including these costs in pricing systems.

We will also briefly consider in the next chapter some efforts by a diverse group of interdisciplinary scholars known as ecological economists to enlarge the mathematical framework of neoclassical economic theory to include scientifically valid measures of the environmental costs of economic activities. These economists are not members of the community of mainstream economists, and their work has been rather consistently dismissed or ignored by mainstream economists. The intent in this portion of the discussion to demonstrate that there is one fundamental reason why mainstream economists have been quite unwilling to entertain the economic solutions to environmental problems proposed by the ecological economists—assumptions about the allegedly lawful or lawlike dynamics of closed market systems in the neoclassical economic paradigm are such that it is not possible to include scientifically valid measures of the environmental costs of economic activities.

7

A GREEN THUMB ON THE INVISIBLE HAND

Environmental Economics and Ecological Economics

In the end, our society will be defined not only by what we create, but by what we refuse to destroy.

— JOHN C. SAWHILL

The prospects of displacing neoclassical economics with an environmentally responsible economic theory would be greatly enhanced if mainstream economists were willing to recognize and come to terms with a scientifically valid truth—there is no basis in the neoclassical economic paradigm for realistically assessing the environmental costs of economic activities and internalizing these costs in pricing systems. The most expedient way to demonstrate that this is the case is to examine the manner in which neoclassical economists have attempted to graft a green thumb on the invisible hand in a subfield called environmental economics.

Virtually all the economic solutions to environmental problems proposed by environmental economists are based on the mathematical formalism of general equilibrium theory. These economists, like other mainstream economists, rarely talk openly about the natural laws of economics that are foundational to this formalism, but they often make references to assumptions about economic actors implicit in the formalism. Economic actors are typically described as completely rational decision makers who invariably make choices that maximize their utility, or their economic satisfaction or well-being. But when we examine the manner in which these actors are actually described in the mathematical formalism appropriated from mid-nineteenth-century physics, these assumptions become more than a little problematic. In this formalism, the actors are depicted as point particles that move about and interact in an immaterial field of utility, and economic decisions are allegedly predetermined, or massively conditioned by, mechanisms associated with the natural laws of economics.

This mathematical formalism obliges the environmental economists to assume that production and consumption do not alter the material substances out of which goods and commodities are made. Recall why the creators of neoclassical economists made this assumption—they did so to make the case that there is a symmetry between production and consumption in an immaterial field of utility in which lawful or lawlike mechanisms govern and control decisions made by economic actors and determine the value of goods and commodities. This explains why there is no basis in the mathematical formalism used by environmental economists for representing economic activities as physical processes embedded in and interactive with natural processes in the global environment. The environment in this formalism has value only as environmental goods, services, and amenities that can be bought, sold, traded, saved, or invested, like any other commodity, in a closed market system that must, if it is functioning properly, grow or expand.

When environmental economists calculate environmental costs, they assume that the relative price of each bundle of an environmental good, service, or amenity reveals the "real marginal values" of the consumer. In the mathematical theories used by these economists, a marginal value essentially represents how much more a consumer is willing to pay to acquire a little bit more of something. Note what the writers of a standard textbook on environmental economics have to say about the dynamics of this process: "The power of a perfectly functioning market rests in its decentralized process of decision making and exchange; no omnipotent planner is needed to allocate resources. Rather, prices ration resources to those that value them the most and, in doing so, individuals are swept along by Adam Smith's invisible hand to achieve what is best for society as a collective. Optimal private decisions based on mutually advantageous exchange lead to optimal social outcomes."[1]

In environmental economics, the presumption that optimal private decisions "based on mutually advantageous exchange" in an amorphous field of utility lead to optimal social outcomes for the state of the environment is a primary article of faith. But according to these economists, this will not occur unless the following conditions apply—the market system in which economic actors make optimal private decisions must operate more or less perfectly, and the prices, or values, of environmental goods and services must be represented as a function of those decisions. But if these conditions are met, environmental economists assume that the lawful or lawlike mechanisms of the market system will resolve environmental problems when the "prices are right."

Since the "right price" in neoclassical economic theory is a function of the dynamics allegedly revealed in the mathematical formalism, environmental economists assume that the results of computations based on this formalism will determine if a putative price is actually right. This explains why much of the work of the these economists attempts to represent environmental costs of economic activities in terms of prices that economic actors have paid, or are willing to pay, in order to realize some marginal benefits of environmental goods and services. This view of right prices also explains why the term "environmental externalities" has a rather peculiar meaning in the literature of mainstream economists.

Externalities are situations in which the production or consumption of something by one economic actor affects another who did not pay for the good produced or consumed, and externalities are viewed as either negative or positive. For example, environmental economists often cite pollution as an example of the former and preservation of biological diversity as an example of the latter. When these economists use the phrase "environmental externalities," they are referring to environmental goods and services that are "external" to market systems in the sense that they are presumed to exist outside the allegedly lawful or lawlike dynamics of these systems.

From the perspective of environmental economists, markets fail if prices do not accurately communicate the desires and constraints of a society, and an environmental problem is a negative externality that represents such a failure. A market system is alleged to operate properly when a set of competitive markets generates a sufficient allocation of resources at a level of efficiency known as "Pareto optimality." This term refers to a hypothetical idealized state or condition in which it is impossible to reallocate resources to enhance the utility of one economic actor without reducing that of another. The assumption here is that if the natural laws of economics are allowed to maximize the private net benefits of consumers and producers with minimal restraint, a set of markets will emerge in which each economic actor will have access to a socially optimal allocation of resources.

The most traditional approach to internalizing a negative environmental externality is to impose a tax, defined by Pigou in *The Economics of Welfare* (1932), that is presumably equal to the value of the marginal social damage associated with the externality. The aim of this tax, said Pigou, "is to ascertain how the free play of self-interest, acting under the existing legal system, tends to distribute the country's resources in the way most favorable to the production of a large national dividend, and how it is feasible for State action to improve upon 'natural' tendencies."[2] There are, said Pigou, "natural" tendencies at work in market systems associated with the operation of the natural laws of economics, and any tax imposed by the state should enhance these tendencies. He also claimed that the value of production will be maximized in the vast majority of economic situations if government refrains from interfering with these "natural" tendencies. Pigou also argued, however, that exogenous "human institutions" can interfere with the dynamics of closed market systems and, therefore, government must take some limited action "to control the play of economic forces in such ways as to promote the economic welfare, and through that, the total welfare, of their citizens as a whole."[3]

When environmental economists are asked to assess the potential impacts on market economies of environmental tax reforms, they typically factor a Pigouvian tax into the mathematical formalism of neoclassical economic theory. One problem with the optimal social outcomes that the calculations are intended to assess is that they are almost invariably premised on the assumption that the proposed environmental tax reforms must not impede the "natural" tendencies of market systems to grow and expand. Consequently, the calculated impacts of these reforms tend to emphasize economic losses associated with decreases in the consumption of environmental goods and services and to grandly minimize the environmental costs.

In dealing with pollution problems, environmental economists generally favor emissions charges or fees, and they often appeal to Pigou to make the case that this instrument is more efficient and effective than regulations imposed by the exogenous agency of government. They argue that these charges or fees will reduce the quantity or improve the quality of pollution by making polluters assume a portion of the costs for every unit of harmful pollution they release into the environment. The scheme is Pigouvian in the sense that the anticipated result is that the charges or fees will be equal to the marginal social damage associated with the externality. The expectation here is that firms will be induced to lower their emissions to the point where the incremental cost of pollution control equals the emissions charges they might otherwise pay. It is also presumed that if individual polluters use pollution control strategies that represent least-cost solutions, the invisible hand will cause the aggregate costs of pollution control to be minimized.

Another traditional approach in environmental economics to getting the prices right by internalizing negative environmental externalities was originally proposed by economist Ronald Coase in a paper published in 1960.[4] Coase objected to the use of any environmental tax or subsidy that would impose economic burdens not directly related to or a function of specific economic activities. He also argued that the value judgments implied in the use of taxes or subsidies were inconsistent with neoclassical assumptions about the character of economic reality and the lawful dynamics of market processes.

Coase claimed that the primary reason the mechanisms of market processes cannot resolve environmental problems is that many environmental resources are not owned and exist outside the domain in which these mechanisms allegedly operate. He concluded, therefore, that the most effective way to internalize negative environmental externalities was to revise the legal system to allow for the assignment of ownership rights to environmental resources. If these resources were owned, argued Coase, the invisible hand would eliminate undesirable uses, and adverse environmental impacts would disappear without the need for government intervention. In this situation, he said, there would be equivalence between paying someone for a good and charging someone for a bad in a state of general equilibrium where optimal social outcomes are necessarily realized.

Environmental economists often appeal to Coase to make the case that tradable pollution permits, like those mentioned earlier in the discussion of the Kyoto accords, are a more effective market-based solution for environmental problems than Pigouvian taxes. In these schemes, a predetermined level of emissions is established within a specific region, and permits equal to the permissible total emissions are distributed among producers in the region. Polluters who keep their levels of emissions below that allowed in their permits can sell or lease their surplus permits to other producers or use them to offset emissions in other parts of their production system. Because the permits are limited and have, therefore, scarcity value, the environmental economists claim that this should provide sufficient incentives to create a market in which they are actively traded.

Beginning in the 1970s, the U.S. Environmental Protection Agency allowed states to use tradable permits to implement the provisions of the Clean Air Act, and they were used in the 1980s in the petroleum industry to accomplish the phasedown of leaded gasoline.[5] This scheme was also employed to facilitate the worldwide reduction of emissions of ozone-depleting CFCs, to lower ambient ozone levels in the northeastern United States, and to implement stricter air pollution controls in the Los Angeles area.[6] Experience has shown, however, that tradable permits are costly to implement and difficult to administer, and that the infrastructure required for actively trading them rarely emerges. Also, some research suggests that tradable permits do not achieve more reductions in emissions than standard regulatory systems or stimulate more innovation in pollution control technology than emission restrictions imposed by governments.[7]

There is, however, a more fundamental reason why emissions charges and tradable permits cannot be viewed as viable economic solutions to the environmental crisis. The assumption in the neoclassical economic paradigm that the economic activities of production or distribution systems exist in closed market systems effectively undermines the prospect that these market-based solutions can effectively deal with pollution problems in economic terms. This assumption obliges the environmental economists to represent the costs of pollution as a function of the economic activities that have value only in the mental space of economic actors operating within closed and isolated regional economies or national economies. The fundamental problem here is obvious—economic activities are embedded in and interactive with the global environment, and there is no such thing in nature as discrete and isolated systems.

The fact that national economies are not closed or isolated systems should be obvious to anyone who has watched the Weather Channel. The precursors of acid rain produced in Great Britain (sulfur dioxide and nitrogen dioxide) travel on a prevailing western wind and are deposited in Scandinavia, and industrial facilities in northern Britain cause more pollution in Scandinavia than in southern England. Huge amounts of greenhouse gases and other pollutants produced in the United States cause environmental problems in Canada, and CFCs emitted from any region on the planet damage the global ozone layer. Because the thinning of the ozone layer is nonuniform, some countries, such as Australia and New Zealand, suffer more damage from thinning ozone and the consequent higher exposure to ultraviolet radiation than countries that are located farther from the poles.

It is, of course, theoretically possible to enlarge the zones, regions, or "bubbles" within which emissions schemes and tradable permits apply. Environmental economists did so in the failed U.S. proposal that would have allowed highly industrialized nations to meet the reductions in carbon dioxide emissions required in the Kyoto accords at less cost. This possibility does not, however, obviate the fact, as that agreement nicely demonstrated, that such schemes tend, almost invariably, to expand market economies at the great expense of a sustainable global environment. The market-based solutions of the environmental economists may appear to result in "win-win" outcomes in the equations of neoclassical economics. But this is only because blatantly unscientific assumptions about economic reality implicit in this formalism preclude the prospect that any realistic assessment of the damage done to the global environment by economic activities can be included in the calculations.

The fundamental disjunction between constructions of parts (closed economic systems) and whole (global market system) in the neoclassical economic paradigm and the actual dynamics of part-whole relationships in the global environment is also apparent in attempts by environmental economists to assess long-term economic impacts of changes in this environment. For example, a well-known environmental economist notes in a study on the potential impact of global warming on the global economy that "climate change is likely to have different impacts on different sectors in different countries." He then says the following about the U.S. economy: "In reality, most of the U.S. economy has little interaction with climate. For example, cardiovascular surgery and parallel computing are undertaken in carefully controlled environments and are unlikely to be directly affected by climate change. More generally, underground mining, most services, communications, and manufacturing are sectors likely to be largely unaffected by climate change—sectors that comprise about 85 percent of GNP."[8]

The assumption that various sectors of an economy can be isolated from the impacts of global warming because they have little or no "interaction" with climate makes no sense at all. In the climate models environmental scientists use to study global warming, it is quite clear that increases in the 3 to 6 degree Centigrade range would have disastrous impacts on all natural environments, including those within the borders of the United States. Imagine that 80 percent of the corn crop in this country failed, that the waters flowing down the Colorado River dropped in volume by 70 percent, that fisheries in most coastal waters collapsed, and one begins to get a sense of the scope of these potential impacts.

Other market-based instruments that environmental economists use to posit economic solutions to environmental problems, such as subsidies, incentive structures, performance bonds, and deposit refund schemes, are also premised on metaphysical assumptions about part-whole relationships in economic reality that are foundational to neoclassical economic theory. For those interested in a more detailed discussion of the entire range of market-based solutions developed by the environmental economists, a good place to begin is *Economics of the Environment,* edited by

Robert Stavins.[9] This book contains a number of useful overview articles and a wealth of bibliographical material.

ENVIRONMENTAL POLICY AND COST-BENEFIT ANALYSIS

Another way to illustrate why the neoclassical economic paradigm is incapable "in principle" of realistically assessing the costs of doing business in the global environment and internalizing these costs in pricing systems is to examine the methods used by environmental economists to value environmental externalities in cost-benefit analyses. Developing methods to conduct these analyses became a growth industry after Ronald Reagan issued Executive Order 12291 in 1981. The order required that cost-benefit analyses be performed for all environmental regulations in the United States with annual costs in excess of $100 million and stipulated that regulations could be implemented only if the benefits to society exceeded the costs.

In theory, this concept seems fairly straightforward and very appealing. Why should we spend money dealing with an environmental problem if the costs exceed the benefits? But when translated into the methods for evaluation used by environmental economists, "benefits to society" means the optimal social outcomes that result from the alleged operation of the natural laws of economics within closed market systems. And the "costs" against which those benefits are measured refer to other alleged manifestations of these nonexistent laws—the amounts that economic actors are willing to pay to protect or preserve environmental goods, services, and amenities, or the amounts they are willing to accept for the exploitation or consumption of those goods, services, or amenities.

One dilemma faced by environmental economists in doing cost-benefit analyses is that the only "real marginal values" they can confer on the environment are allegedly determined by the operation of the natural laws of economics within closed market systems. Given that the vast majority of the damage done to the global environment by economic activities cannot be valued in these terms, these economists have developed two methods for valuing "nonmarket" resources—indirect methods designed to estimate the "use value" of these resources (hedonic pricing and the travel cost method), and direct methods designed to estimate both "use value" and "nonuse value" of the resources (contingent valuation methods).[10]

In the hedonic pricing method, environmental economists try to estimate the market value of a commodity as a bundle of valuable characteristics, and one or more of these characteristics may be environmental.

For example, the value of a house may depend on the number of rooms, the size of the lawn, proximity to shopping, air quality levels, and distance from toxic waste sites. A hedonic price for this house would be arrived at by estimating a hedonic price function and calculating prices for the environmental variables by creating a demand curve that allegedly allows all the variables to be given an approximate monetary value. And the presumption is that the "real" marginal value of preserving air quality or eliminating toxic wastes can be reasonably inferred using this method.[11]

The travel cost method is predicated on the assumption that the value of a nonmarket resource, such as national parks and public forests, can be estimated based on the amount of money an economic actor would be willing to sacrifice to appreciate natural beauty. In this method, a statistical relationship between observed visits to nonmarket resources of natural beauty and the costs of visiting those resources is derived and used as a surrogate demand curve from which the consumer's surplus per visit-day can be measured. While the travel cost method of evaluation may seem rather esoteric and quite strange, it has been widely used in cost-benefit analyses of proposals in the United States and Britain to create or preserve publicly owned recreational areas.[12]

Contingent valuation methods have been used to assess the economic value of recreation, scenic beauty, air quality, water quality, species preservation, bequests to future generations, and other nonmarket environmental resources. The methods are intended to assess the willingness-to-pay function of economic actors who would prefer to preserve natural environments (preservation or existence values), maintain the option of using natural resources (option values), and bequeath natural resources to future generations (bequest values).[13] Most contingent valuation surveys seek to determine the maximal amount that individuals are willing to pay for an increase in the quality of an environmental resource and the minimal amount they are willing to accept as compensation to forgo this increase.

The word *contingent* is used to highlight the fact that the values disclosed by the respondents are contingent on conditions in the artificial or simulated market described in the survey. A description of this market might include an estimate of the costs of reducing annual mortality risk by improving air quality or the costs of providing more protection for an endangered species.[14] The questions take many forms, ranging from open-ended (What is the maximum you would be willing to pay for . . . ?) to specific yes-no responses (The government is considering a proposal X. Your per annum tax bill if this proposal passes would be Y. How would you vote?). The surveys also usually solicit information about the socio-

economic characteristics of the respondents, their environmental atti-
tudes and/or recreational behavior, and other variables that pertain to the
willingness-to-pay function.

However, there is no standard approach to the design of contingent
valuation surveys, and the level of environmental quality is typically predetermined by a third party, such as a government seeking to achieve a
particular level of air quality. The resulting methodological problems and
uncertainties have raised large questions about the efficacy of the results,
and there is a lively debate among mainstream economists about whether
the measures should be used at all. In spite of these problems, however,
contingent evaluations are still routinely used by government agencies
and the World Bank, and they have also been used in over forty countries
to determine values for a wide range of environmental goods and services.[15]

The primary reason why mainstream economists have questioned the
validity of contingent valuation studies has nothing to do, however, with
flaws in designs, problems with statistically based probability sampling,
or lack of controls.[16] According to most of these economists, the fundamental problem is that these studies are based on principles that are inconsistent with assumptions about the character of economic realty in
neoclassical economics.[17] Objections that appeal to these assumptions
are often presumed to be self-evident, but uncovering what these economists are really saying requires some explanation.

As we have seen, an economic actor in general equilibrium theory is
represented as an atomized entity moving like a point particle in a field
of utility in accordance with forces associated with the natural laws of
economics, and these forces allegedly govern or massively condition the decisions made by these actors. The hidden assumptions here are that the
subjective reality of the actors is atomized, the forces associated with the
natural laws act on this subjectivity from the outside, and the decisions
are largely unaffected by ideas, impulses, emotions, and desires that would
make the outcomes indeterminate. When, however, as the game theorists
have discovered, the black box of human subjectivity is opened and economic decisions are examined based on individual criteria of rational decision making, there is an infinite regress into the complexities of language and culture.

Given that this clearly suggests that the natural laws of economics do
not exist, what is the most effective way in which a mainstream economist
might seek to obviate this conclusion? Simply put, he or she can claim that
the laws manifest themselves only in actual decisions made in closed market systems and, therefore, the only data that can be used in the equations

of general equilibrium theory are those that reflect these decisions. Mainstream economists do not, of course, frame their objections to the use of contingent valuation methods in these terms. If, however, one carefully examines their arguments, this is essentially what they are saying.

Interestingly, a number of studies done by mainstream economists on the manner in which people make decisions in various economic contexts have shown that there are often no discernible regularities in the process. For example, one study suggested that "for many purchases a decision process never exists, not even for first purchase,"[18] and another on economic behavior in grocery stores found that shoppers construct a "choice heuristic on the spot about 25% of the time."[19] What these and other studies have revealed is something that most of us intuitively know—people often make complex consumer choices based on irrational impulses, which they rationalize after the fact by making up reasons why a purchase was needed or necessary.

For the sake of argument, however, let us assume that the natural laws of economics actually exist and that contingent valuation studies are capable of fully revealing maximal social outcomes of environmental policy decisions. Are we then to believe, as one such study showed, that reduction in chemical contaminants in drinking water was not important in economic terms because the value of a statistical life associated with a reduction in risk of death in thirty years was only $181,000?[20] Is $26 a measure of the real marginal costs of pollution because this is the average price that a household is willing to pay annually for a 10 percent improvement of visibility in eastern U.S. cities?[21] Is the value of whooping cranes the $22 per year average that one set of households was willing to pay to preserve this species[22] and that of bald eagles the $11 per year average that another set of households would spend to preserve this apparently less valuable species?[23] The point here is obvious, and I will not belabor it. These values are predicated on assumptions about economic reality that completely misrepresent and distort what should and must be the ultimate value of achieving the goal of a sustainable global environment.

It would be absurd to argue that the environmental economists are not committed to the resolution of the environmental crisis or that they fail to understand the enormity of this crisis. It would also be absurd to claim that there is anything wrong with attempts to assess economic impacts of environmental policies or to develop economic solutions to environmental problems that have minimal impacts on market economies. On the other hand, assumptions about the character of economic reality in the neoclassical economic paradigm are such that there is no basis in the mathematical theories used by neoclassical economists for realistically accounting for the costs of doing business in the global environment or internalizing these costs in pricing systems.

If environmental resources were unlimited, environmental sinks inexhaustible, and environmental impacts of global economic activities generally benign, the "usefulness" of neoclassical economic theory as a heuristic in managing market economies could be regarded as sufficient justification for its widespread application. But since none of these conditions apply, the theory can no longer be regarded as useful even in utterly pragmatic, utilitarian terms, because it fails to meet what must now be considered the fundamental criterion for the usefulness of any economic theory—the extent to which the theory allows us to coordinate experience with economic reality in ways that can achieve the goal of a sustainable global environment.

THE ECOLOGICAL ECONOMISTS

As noted earlier, the primary objective of the ecological economists has been to enlarge the framework of the neoclassical economic paradigm to include scientifically valid measures of the environmental costs of economic activities. Scholarship in this discipline is replete with carefully developed and well-documented reasons why the mathematical theories used by mainstream economists should include these costs and numerous demonstrations of how this can be accomplished. The mistake, if one can call it that, made by the ecological economists is the presumption that mainstream economists would be willing to revise assumptions that are foundational to their mathematical theories.

Given the enormous extent to which these assumptions contribute to the crisis in the global environment and frustrate its resolution, there is obviously nothing unreasonable about this presumption. But the fact that there has been virtually no dialogue between ecological economists and mainstream economists clearly indicates that the former are saying something that the latter simply do not wish to entertain or understand. Part of what mainstream economists clearly do not wish to confront is that there is absolutely no basis for assuming that the mathematical theories used in their profession are scientific. There is, however, a much more fundamental reason why neoclassical economists have been unwilling to engage in this dialogue.

Because ecological economists are normally familiar with research done in environmental science, they know that assumptions about economic reality in neoclassical economics are anything but sacrosanct. However, the presumption that mainstream economists would be willing to revise these assumptions is unrealistic because they are foundational to the mathematical theories used by these economists. The large problem here is that any proposed economic solutions to environmental problems that require even a slight modification of these assumptions would threaten to undermine the efficacy of the mathematical theories. This is the case because the presumed efficacy of these theories is entirely dependent on the belief that the assumptions are valid.

Even a slight change in these assumptions would force mainstream economists to redefine initial conditions in the equations of neoclassical economics in ways that would require the introduction of new sets of complex variables. This would not only play havoc with the neat symmetry in these equations between consumption and production and yield results that describe very different outcomes. It would also effectively undermine the presumption that the economic process exists in a separate and distinct domain of reality in which decisions of economic actors are a function of lawful or lawlike mechanisms that operate only within this domain. But as the following discussion of environmental economics illustrates, the refusal of mainstream economists to question, much less revise, the metaphysical assumptions that are foundational to their mathematical theories is an act of faith that has some very unfortunate consequences.

In an effort to incorporate scientifically valid measures of the environmental costs of economic activities into the neoclassical economic paradigm, many ecological economists have appealed to the first and second laws of thermodynamics. The first law states that energy is conserved and cannot be created or destroyed, and the second that low-entropy matter-energy in a closed system is always transformed into high-entropy matter-energy. As noted earlier, entropy in physics is essentially a measure of disorder in a system—the higher the entropy, the greater the disorder. From the perspective of thermodynamics, an economic system converts matter-energy from a state of low entropy to a state of high entropy, and matter-energy exists in two forms—available or free and unavailable or bound. For example, the chemical energy in a piece of coal, which is low in entropy, is viewed as free, and the heat energy in waters of the oceans, which is high in entropy, is viewed as bound. Since the amount of bound matter-energy in a closed system must continually increase, the only way to lower entropy in such a system is to introduce matter-energy from the outside. But after this matter-energy is introduced into the system, the price paid for consuming what might initially appear to be a free lunch is an overall increase in the level of entropy.

Virtually every object with economic value has a highly ordered structure, and the matter-energy required to manufacture these objects inevitably increases the overall level of entropy in the ecosystem. For example, an automobile is vastly more ordered that a lump of iron ore, and the matter-energy required to transform raw materials into an automobile is enormous. Manufacturing processes also produce waste, pollution, and greenhouse gases, and these by-products massively contribute to the overall level of disorder in the ecosystem. Even recycled products require energy inputs that increase entropy levels and convert free energy to bound energy. As Erwin Schrödinger put it, the life of all organisms, including our own, is necessarily an entropic process: "The device by which an organism maintains itself stationary at a fairly high level of orderliness (= a fairly low level of entropy) really exists in continually sucking orderliness from its environment."[24]

When the environmental movement in the United States emerged as a potent political force during the petroleum shortage in the 1970s, ecologist Howard Odum developed a systematic model based on energy flows to better understand the impact of human activity on the natural environment. He pointed out that wherever a flow of capital exists, there must be an energy flow in the opposite direction. Odum also noted that while a market system in neoclassical economics is represented as a closed loop with no inputs or outputs, low-entropy energy inputs always enter real or actual economic systems and become high-entropy energy outputs. He also convincingly argued that other essential energy flows, such as solar, water, and wind, are misused because they are not represented in the flow of capital.

The work of economists Nicholas Georgescu-Roegen and Herman Daly was also seminally important in the development of ecological economics. In *The Entropy Law and the Economic Process* (1971), Georgescu-Roegen demonstrates that the mathematical analysis of production in neoclassical economics is badly flawed because it fails to incorporate the laws of thermodynamics. In his view, an economy must be viewed in thermodynamic terms as a unidirectional flow in which inputs of low-entropy matter and energy are used to produce two kinds of outputs—goods and services, and high-entropy waste and degraded matter. Since neoclassical economic theory assigns value only to the first output and completely ignores the costs associated with the second, Georgescu-Roegen attempted to refashion the theory to include these costs.

"Man's natural dowry," writes Georgescu-Roegen, "consists of two essentially distinct elements: (1) the stock of low-entropy on or within the globe; and (2) the flow of solar energy." And we have not, in his view, used these resources well: "We need no elaborated argument to see that the maximum of life quantity requires the minimal rate of natural resource depletion. By using these resources too quickly, man throws away that part of the solar energy that will still be reaching the earth after he has departed. And everything he has done during the last two hundred years or so puts him in the position of a fantastic spendthrift. There can be no doubt about it: any use of the natural resources for the satisfaction of non-vital human needs means a smaller quantity of life in the future."[25]

The writings of Georgescu-Roegen are well known and appreciated by ecological economists, but there are, to my knowledge, no discussions of his work in standard textbooks on mainstream economics. The reason for this omission is that Georgescu-Roegen challenged three fundamental assumptions on which the mathematical formalism of neoclassical economic theory is predicated: (1) market systems are closed; (2) nonmarket environmental resources must be viewed as existing outside market systems and treated as externalities; and (3) there are no limits on the growth and expansion of market economies.

In *Steady State Economics* (1977), Herman Daly, who was a student of Georgescu-Roegen's at Vanderbilt, criticizes the failure of mainstream economics to account for the throughput of low-entropy natural resources. He also argues that the preoccupation with money flows, or with movement of quantities of money over periods of time, serves to perpetuate the fiction that perpetual economic growth is possible and morally desirable. One solution to this problem, says Daly, is to use constraints associated with the second law of thermodynamics to formulate policies for long-term sustainability, such as taxes on energy and virgin resources. He claims that such policies would increase social awareness of ecological limits and promote the realization that "physical flows of production and consumption must be minimized subject to some desirable population and standard of living."[26]

In Daly's view, the three basic goals of an economic system should be efficient allocation, equitable distribution, and sustainable scale. The first two goals are included in mainstream economics, and specific public policies have been formulated to realize them. But scale is not included, and consequently there are no policy instruments in mainstream economics that deal with scale. Daly defines scale as the total physical volume of low-entropy raw materials that move through the open subsystem of an economy and back into the finite and nongrowing global environment as high-entropy wastes.[27]

Since the scale of the global economy has grown dangerously large relative to the fixed size of the ecosystem, this economy is sustainable, says Daly, only if it does not erode the carrying capacity of the ecosystem. He is, therefore, critical of his fellow economists for assuming that environmental resources and sinks are infinite relative to the scale of the economy and that decisions about allocation merely move natural resources between alternative uses. The unfortunate result, says Daly, is that scale is not viewed as a constraint and economic policies encourage growth that cannot be sustained by the ecosystem.

The fundamental problem here is that there is no basis in neoclassical market price mechanisms, which are tied to the preferences of individual consumers, to account for scale. "Distribution and scale," writes Daly, "involve relationships with the poor, the future, and other species that are fundamentally social in nature rather than individual." Pretending that these social choices exist on the same plane as the choice between chewing gum and a candy bar seems, he continues, "to be dominant in economies today and is part of the retrograde reduction of all ethical choice to the level of personal tastes weighted by income."[28]

Given that Daly privileges market mechanisms, one might suppose that his views would have been welcomed by mainstream economics. But this has not been the case, because his scientifically valid claim that economic systems are open to and interactive with the global environment challenges the assumption that market systems are closed. If mainstream economists admit that these systems are open, they will be obliged to recognize that the allegedly lawful or lawlike dynamics of these systems do not exist, for a now obvious reason—the presumed existence of these dynamics in the mathematical theories used by mainstream economists is entirely dependent on the axiomatic assumption that the dynamics operate within closed market systems. In the absence of that assumption, there is no basis for believing in the existence of the dynamics, and it would become clear that the god with the invisible hand exists only in the minds of those who believe in his existence.

Many ecological economists have also been concerned with the "tragedy of the commons," a dilemma first described by American biologist Garrett Hardin in 1968.[29] A commons, said Hardin, is any area where property rights regimes do not apply and users have open access to its exploitation. He used the example of a common grazing land where each cattle owner continues to enlarge his or her herd as long as doing so increases his income. Since each owner derives all the economic benefits from the sale of his cattle, and since the loss of grazing resources consumed by his or her cattle is borne by all the other owners, the tragedy is that all owners will increase the numbers in their herds to the point at which the grazing capacity of the land is utterly depleted or destroyed.

Economist H. S. Gordon came to very similar conclusion in an earlier study of fisheries. As long as fishermen can earn a profit, they continue to catch fish to the point at which overfishing occurs. If a particular species of fish is valuable, which often correlates with scarcity, fishermen tend to develop more technologically efficient means of catching these fish, and this often threatens the species with extinction.[30] The problem here is that exploiters of common resources have little incentive to conserve them and a great deal of incentive to exploit them recklessly before others can do so, and this applies to the global commons of oceans, frozen poles, forests, and the entire genetic reserve.

Ecological economists have tried to deal with this problem by proposing some substantive changes in the system of national accounts that mainstream economists use to evaluate the relative performance of national economies. The two standard measures are Gross Domestic Product (GDP) and Gross National Product (GNP), and both paint an utterly distorted picture of the relationship between human systems and environmental systems. The principal reasons why this is the case are that these accounts do not reflect the costs of pollution and general environmental degradation and the costs associated with the deterioration of the environmental resource base.

The first comprehensive case for developing new accounting techniques was made in the World Bank report *Environmental Accounting for Sustainable Development* (1989). The authors of this report argued that a measure of sustainable income, which is not included in standard GDP measures, is badly needed. They noted that the GDP measures not only fail to distinguish between income derived from production and income derived from depleting natural assets, such as forests, soils, and mineral reserves. GDP measures also do not account for defensive expenditures, such as the costs of cleaning up oil spills or dealing with radioactive wastes.

Herman Daly and John Cobb have developed an alternative to GNP, the "Index of Sustainable Development," that essentially divides national income accounts into sectors and imposes standards of sustainability, as well as equity, on these sectors.[31] When Daly and Cobb used their index to adjust GNP in the United States during the period from 1945 to 1980, the surprising result was that net income has been virtually flat over this twenty-five year period. In another study of the U.S. economy from 1951 to 1990, a period during which per capita GNP more than doubled, the economy according to this index grew less than 20 percent and even declined slightly between 1980 and 1990. If these results are reasonably accurate, the conclusion is rather devastating—all apparent economic growth in the U.S. economy from 1951 to 1990 is a delusion that results from a failure to account for losses in natural capital.

Robert Repetto and his associates at the World Resources Institute have done a number of natural-resource accounting studies on developing nations such as Indonesia, the Philippines, and Costa Rica.[32] These studies show that growth trends in GNP massively distort the health of economies in these developing nations because they do not account for such factors as petroleum depletion, forest loss, and soil erosion. When net investment was adjusted to account for these factors, the results showed that it was negative during a period when gross investment by standard GDP measures was very high and rising. When ecological economist Kirk Hamilton factored in resource depletion and environmental damage to calculate net savings in national economies, he arrived at the disturbing conclusion that these savings in most of the developing world have been negative since the mid-1970s.[33]

Mark Sagoff makes a convincing case that neoclassical market valuation is not capable of realistically assessing the environmental costs of economic activities. He points out that market value in mainstream economics is based on a vague something that is not subject to direct observation or measurement—individual utility or individual happiness and well-being. He then argues that even if individuals could be enticed into placing a marginal money valuation on an environmental "amenity," they might be happier if they paid this amount in exchange for the opportunity to destroy the amenity. To lend weight to this argument, Sagoff cites the results of a study in Wyoming in which participants refused to recognize that the environment had any monetary value.[34]

Ecological economist Bruce Hannon has taken a different approach. Rather than revise standard GNP measures, he proposes that we develop a contrasting measure of the health of the ecosystem—the Gross Ecosystem Product or GEP.[35] He argues that the GEP would demonstrate that increased economic output has some very destructive environmental impacts. If the proposed GEP existed, and if economic planners were committed to making GEP and GNP more compatible, this could, says Hannon, result in more efficient production techniques and promote the recognition that there are limits to economic growth.

Not surprisingly, all these suggestions for revising the system of national accounts used by mainstream economists have been dismissed or ignored by these economists. The problem is not merely that there is no viable basis in the neoclassical economic paradigm to establish market prices for environmental resources that are commensurate with their real or actual value in ecological terms. It is also that any successful attempt to value the resources in these terms would require the introduction of a new set of variables that would falsify the assumption that markets are closed and tend toward a state of equilibrium.

Ecological economists have been successful in convincing some leaders in other nations that GNP is not necessarily the best indicator of human satisfaction and that accounting for the depreciation of natural capital is a necessary part of the economic process. Norway has developed a system for calculating balances of mineral and living resources, France is using a system of accounts that attempts to track the status of all resources influenced by human activity, and the Netherlands has a system that includes environmental damage and the costs of repairing this damage. The governments of these nations use this information to assess environmental impacts of economic activities and to make policy decisions. However, these studies are rarely taken seriously by the governments' own mainstream economists, and they are routinely ignored by the mainstream economists who assess the relative "health" of their national economics.

The work done by the ecological economists is quite extensive, and this brief overview does not even begin to represent the range and complexity of this scholarship. However, the discipline of ecological economics has become increasingly fragmented into a variety of different, often contradictory, approaches, and there is no single economic paradigm that encompasses these approaches.[36] On one side, there are those who take the more traditional approach and argue that ecological criteria for sustainability should serve as the basis for making policy recommendations. On the other, there are those who are attempting to redefine the discipline as a science of social change that is committed to developing institutional frameworks that feature sustainable production and consumption patterns.[37] This inability to evolve a set of assumptions that can serve as the basis for a commonly shared economic paradigm also explains why many ecological ecologists have migrated toward solutions derived from more humanistic disciplines in the social sciences, such as public policy, psychology, and sociology.

It should now be clear that the primary reason why mainstream economists have not been willing to engage the ecological economists in a meaningful dialogue about how to resolve the environmental crisis is that there is no basis for this dialogue. And the now obvious reason why this is the case is that blatantly unscientific assumptions about economic reality in the neoclassical economic paradigm disallow the prospect of enlarging mathematical theories used by mainstream economists to include scientifically valid assessments of the environmental costs of economic activities. Ecological economists are, of course, very much aware that mainstream economists are quite unwilling to abandon these assumptions. But since the ecological economists are committed to positing solutions to environmental problems by extending the mathematical framework of the neoclassical economic paradigm, they have been understandably reluctant to openly question the validity of the assumptions.

This is, in my view, very unfortunate because the ecological economists have the background and experience required to develop an environmentally responsible economic theory. In this theory, the environmental costs of economic activities would be based on scientifically valid measures of the relationship between parts (large-scale human activities) and whole (a sustainable global environment), and these costs would included in pricing systems. And most ecological economists seem to realize that this is the only viable basis for developing an environmentally responsible economic theory.

However, it seems very unlikely that these economists will be able to make substantive contributions to developing this theory unless they are willing to openly declare and rigorously defend two truths that are implicit in virtually all of their proposed solutions to environmental problems. The first truth is that the natural laws of economics which are foundational to the mathematical theories used by mainstream economics do not exist. And the second related truth is that those who believe in their existence are unwittingly undermining the prospect of positing viable economic solutions to the crisis in the global environment during the relatively short time frame in which this crisis can be resolved.

UNSEEN GODS AND MARKET MYTHS

A fair number of mainstream economists have argued that assumptions about the character of economic reality in the neoclassical economic paradigm are fundamentally flawed. It is also significant that those who have made the most convincing case that the mathematical theories used by neoclassical economists cannot be viewed as scientific have been trained as economists. For example, Alfred Eichner in *Why Economics Is Not Yet a Science* first provides a devastating critique of the many ways in which mainstream economists fail to adhere to the methods and procedures of science and then offers the following commentary on the discipline of economics as a social system:

The refusal to abandon the myth of the market as a self-regulating system is not the result of a conspiracy on the part of the "establishment" in economics. It is not even a choice that any individual economist is necessarily aware of making. Rather it is the way economics operates as a social system—including the way new members of the establishment are selected—retaining its place within the larger society by perpetuating a set of ideas which have been found useful by that society, however dysfunctional the same set of ideas may be from a scientific understanding of how the economic system works. In other words, economics is unwilling to adhere to the epistemological principles which distinguish scientific from other types of intellectual activity because this might jeopardize the position of economists within the larger society as the defender of the dominant faith. This situation in which economists find themselves is therefore not unlike that of many natural scientists who, when faced with mounting evidence in support of first, the Copernican theory of the universe and then, later, the Darwinian theory of evolution, had to decide whether undermining the revelatory basis of Judeo-Christian ethics was not too great a price to pay for being able to reveal the truth.[38]

Disclosing the "revelatory basis" of neoclassical economic theory is not, as we have seen, terribly difficult. The French moral philosophers who first posited the existence of the natural laws of economics presumed that these laws, like the laws of Newtonian physics, were created by the Judeo-Christian God. The creators of classical economics appealed to this conception of natural law to legitimate the real or actual existence of the invisible hand, and they did so within the context of a mechanistic Newtonian worldview that did not need or require the presence of the willful and mindful agency of God. They concluded, therefore, that both the laws of Newtonian physics and the natural laws of economics originated in the mind of a Deistic God who withdrew from the universe following the first moment of creation.

The presence of these metaphysically based assumptions about the natural laws of economics was disguised by the creators of neoclassical economics under a maze of mathematical formalism borrowed from a mid-nineteenth-century physical theory. This disguise become more convincing after these economists managed to promulgate the fiction that they had transformed economics into a rigorously scientific discipline with the use of higher mathematics. The totally unwarranted assumption that mainstream economics is a scientific discipline was massively reinforced by subsequent generations of economists who refined and extended general equilibrium theory with the use of increasingly more sophisticated mathematical devices and techniques.

In the next chapter, we will examine how belief in the actual existence of the natural laws that allegedly manifest themselves as lawful or lawlike dynamics in free-market economies became foundational over the last few decades to the market consensus (also called the Washington consensus). One objective in this portion of the discussion is to demonstrate that the market or Washington consensus has been used to legitimate a program for economic globalization that can fairly be described as a recipe for ecological disaster. The other is to make the case that systematic attempts by the United States and other prosperous countries to impose this vision of a new global order on all peoples and governments has occasioned deep divisions and conflicts in the international community. The large problem here is that if the divisions and conflicts are not eliminated very soon, they can easily undermine the prospect that the members of the international community will be able to achieve the level of cooperation required to resolve the environmental crisis.

8

AN UNNATURAL RELIGION
The Telos of the Market Consensus

Free trade is the religion of our age. With its heaven in the global economy, free trade comes complete with comprehensive analytical and philosophical underpinnings. But in the final analysis, free trade is less an economic strategy than a moral degree. Although it pretends to be value-free, it is fundamentally value-driven.

– DAVID MORRIS

The eighteenth-century authors of new narratives about democratic systems of government and free-market economies posited the existence of two sets of natural laws that they viewed as ontologically equivalent to the laws of Newtonian physics. They assumed that one set of natural laws governed the movement and interaction of people in political reality and that another governed the movement and interaction of people in economic reality. Virtually all of these figures firmly believed that both sets of laws originated in the perfect mind of the Creator of the mechanistic universe. But they did not assume that the two sets of laws operate in concert, or that the existence of democratic governments was dependent on the preexistence or simultaneous development of what the French more accurately call laissez-faire market systems.

My intent in this chapter is to demonstrate that the market or Washington consensus is predicated on this assumption and functions as a quasi-religious belief system. In this belief system, the primary article of faith is that the lawful or lawlike mechanism associated with the natural laws of economics will necessarily result in a new global order in which all economies will be free-market systems and all governments will operate in accordance with the principles of democratic capitalism. Later in this chapter, we will examine the origins of the market or Washington consensus in mainstream economic theory and the large role played by this teleological view of the human future in Great Britain and the United States. For the moment, however, the case will be made that this alleged consensus is predicated on metaphysical assumptions that derive from and are deeply embedded in the Judeo-Christian tradition. If this discussion were enlarged to include all the relevant evidence from sources such as news reports in print and electronic media, political speeches and commentaries, advertising campaigns, public policy debates, and so on, this would require several hefty volumes. For our purposes, however, a brief examination of some statements made in books and articles published in the United States over the last two decades should suffice.

During this period, *New York Times* columnist Thomas Friedman argued in numerous articles and a best-selling book that the mechanisms of free-market systems are inextricably connected with and inseparable from the dynamics of democratic systems of government. In one of these articles, Friedman concludes that although people once thought that human affairs could be ordered in the absence of free markets, this is no longer the case in the new era of globalization: "I don't think there will be any alternative ideology this time around. There are none."[1] The central theme in his best-selling book, *The Lexus and the Olive Tree*, is that the forces of free-market capitalism will necessarily transform the governments of all sovereign nation-states into functional democracies.

These forces are responsible, claims Friedman, for the "democratization of technology," the "democratization of finance," and the "democratization of information." Countries that resist this inexorable movement toward the new global order will be severely punished for their lack of faith because the "Electronic Herd," or the traders in the global financial system in which securities and currencies are exchanged at the speed of light, will "stampede away." If this occurs, says Friedman, the investment capital required to grow economies in the resisting countries will no longer be available, currencies will be greatly devalued, stock markets could easily crash, and the prospects of improving economic conditions and enhancing individual freedoms will be greatly diminished.[2]

What is important here for our purposes is not whether the withdrawal of foreign investment in developing countries is likely to have these outcomes. It is why Friedman assumes that the process of economic globalization will necessarily result in a new global order in which all national economies will be free-market systems and all governments will be based on the principles of democratic capitalism. The answer to this question is implicit on virtually every page of *The Lexus and the Olive Tree*.

In this hugely popular book, Friedman suggests that this outcome is preordained by the dynamics of the free-market system, and he occasionally alludes to the prospect that these dynamics are associated with the willful purpose and design of a benevolent Creator. For example, Friedman wonders in the last chapter of this book how a "visionary geo-architect," or God, would design an ideal nation-state, and concludes that this state would undoubtedly be the "most flexible market in the world."[3]

Francis Fukuyama in another best seller, *The End of History*, does not openly declare that the process of economic globalization is proceeding in accordance with a sacredly ordained plan. But he does argue that this process is inexorably moving the global community toward the "end point of mankind's ideological development and the final form of human government."[4] Fukuyama claims that human history is "coherent and directional" because the mechanisms of the "free market" and the dynamics of democratic systems of government operate in concert. According to Fukuyama, this explains why the forces of democratic capitalism have "conquered rival ideologies like hereditary monarchy, fascism, and most recently communism." He also claims that when this process is complete, history will end in the sense that a "single coherent, evolution process" will have resulted in a new global order in which all governments are "liberal democracies" and all economies are linked to the global market system.[5]

In other best-selling books, the metaphysically based assumptions that are foundational to the telos of the market or Washington consensus are virtually impossible to ignore. George Gilder, the author of numerous popular books on business, states in *The Sprit of Enterprise* that "it is the entrepreneur who knows the rules of the world and the laws of God."[6] In *Wealth and Poverty*, Gilder declares that virtually all societal problems in the United States can be resolved by the unfettered operation of the natural laws of economics. He attempts to reinforce this conclusion by arguing that the greatest source of poverty in this country is lack of family values, the primary cause of economic problems is the liberals and socialists in government and the academy, and the greatest threat to the security and peace of the United States is the hedonism associated with the surviving remnants of the counterculture revolution of the 1960s.[7] The clear suggestion here is that the natural laws of economics and the moral laws of the Judeo-Christian tradition are dictated by God and the willful violation of these laws is the principal cause of virtually all economic and social problems in the United States and, by implication, in all other countries.

Similarly, Kevin Kelly in another best seller, *Out of Control: The New Biology of Machines, Social Systems and the Economic World*, consistently conflates God's providential design for the universe with technological in-novation and refers to his own list of allegedly lawful dynamics in the global market system as "The Nine Laws of God."[8] Robert Samuelson, an economist who writes a column for *Newsweek,* suggests that the ex-istence of this providential design is particularly obvious in the United States. In an article on the stock market titled "The Markets 'R' Us," Samuelson says that the dynamics of the free-market system always act in the best national interests of the United States, whether we know it or not, and against the interests of countries that do not embrace this sys-tem.[9] Robert Bartley, the editor of the *Wall Street Journal,* has embraced a similar view. According to Bartley, the "world is not ruled by politicians but by markets," and national governments "will evolve toward some-thing like state governments today. Each will have its own industrial de-velopment program to show why it has the best business and investment climate."[10]

Walter Wriston, when president of Citibank, argued in *The Twilight of Sovereignty* that the market "will flee from manipulation or onerous regu-lation of its value or use, and no government can restrain it for long."[11] In this book, the presumption that the mechanisms of free markets are virtually indistinguishable from the dynamics of democratic governance is particularly obvious. "Markets," writes Wriston, are "voting machines" and "general plebiscites" that "conduct a running tally on what the world thinks of a government's diplomatic, fiscal, and monetary polices."[12] He claims that markets are giving "power to the people" and anticipates a time when the entire global population will "fight to reduce government power over the corporations for which they work, organizations far more democratic, collegial, and tolerant than distant state bureaucracies."[13]

Also consider how the word "market" is used in virtually all commen-taries on the telos of the market or Washington consensus—the market moves, responds, determines, directs, resolves, points, and creates. This language clearly suggests that the dynamics of free-market systems are both mindful and purposeful, and the assumption that presumably justi-fies this belief is that these dynamics are associated with the operations of transcendent, universal, and teleological natural laws. The resulting view of the human future is hugely problematic for three reasons.

First, it is predicated on a belief in the actual existence of nonexistent gods—the natural laws of economics that allegedly result in functional democracies only in countries with free-market economies. Second, the presumption that the new global order is preordained by the dynamics as-sociated with the operations of these laws massively informs the decision-making process in a program for economic globalization that is a recipe for ecological disaster. And third, this telos functions as a quasi-religious belief system, and the true believers are convinced that they know the truth and all others must know it as well. This true believing has not only occasioned deep divisions and conflicts between developed countries in the Northern Hemisphere and underdeveloped or developing countries in the Southern Hemisphere. It has also generated enormous hostility toward the United States and other economically prosperous countries in regions of the world where a large percentage of the population is resisting the process of globalization for religious or ideological reasons.

What the true believers in the market or Washington consensus fail to recognize is a self-evident scientific truth that is obscured by the mathematical theories of neoclassical economics—the agency that creates incredible complex economic systems and manages them in ways that allow for a fairly high level of coherence and stability is entirely human. Such coherence and stability result from stochastic processes in human cognition that inform economic decisions, and the system exists because large numbers of economic actors have assimilated narratives that describe roles, habits, and ritualized behavior within institutional frameworks and processes that deal in units of money. The fact that the institutional rules that govern monetary transactions are fairly stable and resistant to change also contributes to the relative stability of markets.

Any unbiased examination of the dynamics of an actual economic process reveals that the only regularities involved are emergent from the cognitive processes of individuals who base their economic decisions on widely known and shared economic narratives. The monetary value of a property, stock, bond, contract, commodity, or service as it is represented in these narratives becomes real by mutual consent, and the withdrawal of consent as a result of what mainstream economists call a lack of "belief" or "confidence" in the "market" has major economic impacts. The narratives that inform economic decisions may feature numerically based analyses that can be quite staggering in their complexity and very daunting in their abundance of details. But any order that emerges from an economic process has nothing to do with a transcendent godlike agency with a hand to spare. It results from cognitive processes in the minds of individuals that manifest themselves as decisions to use available capital resources in ways that are consistent with their perceptions of potential monetary gains or losses.

One can, of course, employ sophisticated mathematical techniques to describe emergent regularities in economic behavior within a range of probabilities, and these descriptions can be useful in coordinating experience with market economies. But this does not mean that the mathematical description discloses lawful dynamics in this behavior that point to the existence of natural laws that govern this behavior. It simply means that mathematical language is an effective tool for modeling tendencies to occur in stochastic processes in which patterns of behavior are a function of widely shared and mutually reinforced economic narratives. This becomes quite obvious when the conduct of normal or everyday life is disrupted by disturbing events and people express their fear, uncertainty, and confusion by deviating from scripts in the economic narratives.

MAINSTREAM ECONOMIC THEORY AND THE POLITICAL PROCESS

When two physical theories in science describe the same range of phenomena and make disparate predictions about the outcomes of observations or experiments, the theory that accurately predicts these outcomes is accepted as scientifically valid while the other is not. But since the predictions of disparate theories in neoclassical economics cannot be confirmed by observation or experiment, the primary determinant of which theory is used to coordinate economic activities in particular market economies is the political process. In countries with functional democracies, large-scale changes in the organization of market systems typically occur after a political party that closely identifies with a particular understanding of the character of economic reality wins a general election during a period of economic crisis and manages to implement an alternate economic program.

In the vast majority of cases, the economic crisis can be directly attributed to, or has been massively aggravated by, what mainstream economists call nonmarket variables, or events that are presumably not subject to the lawful mechanisms of the closed market system. The alternate economic program is normally based on the views of economists that are most consistent with the ideological commitments of the victorious candidate for president or prime minister, with the ideological agenda that distinguishes the party of this candidate from that of other parties, and with the ideologically driven solutions to economic problems that appeal to large numbers of dissatisfied voters.

Perhaps the best way to illustrate that this is the case is to briefly examine the large role played by the competition between Keynesian and anti-Keynesian economic theory in the electoral process in Great Britain and the United States. In the aftermath of World War II, there was no private sector capable of mobilizing the investment, capital goods, and skills required to rebuild economies devastated by this conflict, and international trade was massively disrupted. Only governments seemed capable of marshaling the resources needed to deal with these large problems, and the economic model used in most industrial nations in the West and in large parts of the developing world was based on Keynes's vision of a reformed and managed national economy. In these so-called "mixed economies," state ownership, industrial policy, and fiscal management were used in various combinations in an effort to protect capitalism from its own excesses and to save capitalism from the lure of socialism.

Until the late 1970s, Keynesian "new economics," with its emphasis on managing the overall economy with the fiscal tools of taxation and spending, appeared, for the most part, to have fulfilled its promise of sustained economic growth and full employment. Many economists during this period challenged Keynes's vision, but the most fervent anti-Keynesians, whose names would become household words during the Thatcher-Reagan era, were Martin Hayek and Milton Friedman. What is most interesting about the work of Hayek and Friedman for our purposes is that their theories are narrowly predicated on the assumptions about the lawful or lawlike dynamics of free-market systems that the creators of neoclassical economic theory embedded in the mathematical formalism borrowed from mid-nineteenth-century physics. Both of these economists extended and refined this formalism with their own original contributions, and each received the Bank of Sweden Prize in Economic Sciences in recognition of these contributions. But their understanding of the lawful dynamics of the economic process closely resembles that of Jevons, Walras, Edgeworth, and Pareto, and it is premised on the same metaphysical assumptions.

The legacy of Hayek, the most influential proponent of the Austrian free-market school of economics, is encapsulated in the response of Larry Summers, former secretary of the treasury in the second Clinton administration and currently president of Harvard University, to the question, "What's the single most important thing to learn from an economics course today?" Summers replied, "What I leave my students with is the view that the invisible hand is more powerful than the hidden hand. Things will happen in well-organized efforts without direction, control, plans. That's the consensus among economists."[14] This view is everywhere present in a book that became the "bible of economics" for Margaret Thatcher and the blueprint and rationale for the changes in the structure of the British economy that occurred during her tenure as prime minister— Hayek's *Road to Serfdom*.[15]

Originally published in 1944, this extremely conservative rendering of the truths of neoclassical economics denounces the welfare state, the mixed economy, and all forms of collectivism. The book was published in the United States by the University of Chicago Press and achieved much wider fame in this country after a condensed version appeared in *Reader's Digest*. Keith Joseph, who had been elected to Parliament as a member of the Conservative Party in 1956 and who served as minister in charge of social services after Edward Heath become prime minister in 1970, read *The Road to Serfdom* and experienced what he later described as a "conversion to conservatism."[16] This conversion took place during a period in which the British economy was severely disrupted by the Yom Kippur War, the 1973 oil crisis, and a prolonged coal miners' strike.

Following this conversion experience, Joseph joined a right-of-center think tank called the Institute of Economic Affairs that would, under his leadership, promote Hayek's views and popularize the economic agenda that eventually became the basis for the "Thatcherite revolution." Always impatient with the pace of change, Joseph established the Centre for Policy Studies with the professed aim of converting the members of the Conservative Party to belief in the "more pristine" understanding of the lawful workings of the market system championed by Hayek. He recruited Margaret Thatcher, a member of Parliament who had previously served as minister of education in the Heath government, to serve as his vice chairman, and the Centre for Policy Studies began to promote its understanding of the lawful or lawlike dynamics of the free-market system by sponsoring a flood of books, pamphlets, seminars, dinners, and luncheons.

At the top of the reading list Joseph distributed to his vice chairman and to other Tory politicians was Hayek's *Road to Serfdom,* which Thatcher had first read as an undergraduate student at Oxford. After rereading the book, she had her own conversion experience and became a true believer in the notion that the unimpeded operations of the invisible hand could resolve virtually all economic and social problems.[17] During the two years before Thatcher became prime minister, the British economy had performed badly, and alternate economic solutions were high on the political agenda. The British government was forced to borrow money from the International Monetary Fund to prevent a further devaluation of its currency, and the conditions of the loans required sizable cuts in public expenditures.

These cuts sparked a rebellion within the ranks of the Labour Party, and Labour prime minister Callaghan added more fuel to this flame by supporting plant closures and a reduction in the labor force at state-owned companies. The economic situation reached crisis proportions after a strike by public-sector employees resulted in the rationing of medical care in hospitals and mounds of uncollected garbage in city streets. To make matters even worse, another strike by truck drivers brought the entire British economy to the point of virtual collapse. On a day when even the catering staff at the House of Commons was on strike, the Labour government lost a vote of confidence, and Callaghan was obliged to call the general election that made Thatcher prime minister in 1979.

Thatcher made it quite clear that she wished to chart a future for the British economy based on a distinctly un-Keynesian view of the market system in which the "Nanny State" would be replaced by the risks and rewards of "enterprise culture."[18] But during her first three years in office, Thatcher was not successful in translating this vision into reality, and the planned Thatcherite revolution was a failure or, more accurately, a nonevent. Interest rates rose to 16 percent, inflation was anticipated to reach 20 percent, and government deficits continued to climb.

Keith Joseph, who remained Thatcher's unofficial minister of thought and who served officially as secretary of state for industry in her government, was eager to privatize state-owned industries and to confront the politically powerful trade unions. To prepare for this struggle, he presented senior civil servants in his ministry with a reading list containing Hayek's *Road to Serfdom,* Adam Smith's *Wealth of Nations* and *Theory of Moral Sentiments,* and eight pamphlets that he had written himself.[19] Meanwhile, the Tory government was embroiled in an effort to displace Keynesian monetary policy with monetarism by attempting to ensure that increases in the money supply would be commensurate with economic growth. When economic conditions failed to improve and political unrest increased, Thatcher's support in the polls dropped to 23 percent, making her the most unpopular prime minister since the advent of modern polling in Britain.

What saved the Thatcher government from almost certain defeat in the 1983 general election was the decision to respond to what economists term an exogenous or nonmarket event. The event was the invasion by Argentine troops of islands eight thousand miles from the isle of Great Britain, and the decision was to counter this action with an impressive display of military force. After several naval battles, a full-scale landing, and three weeks of fierce fighting, Britain emerged victorious in the Falklands War, and the nationalistic fervor that accompanied this victory changed Thatcher's political fortunes dramatically. She won the general election with a 144-seat majority, and her government suddenly had the political clout to implement a legislative agenda designed to create a market system in Britain consistent with that envisioned by Hayek.

The other confrontation that enhanced Thatcher's standing in the polls took the form of a standoff with the National Union of Coal Miners, led by Marxist Arthur Scargill, which began in 1984. When Scargill and other union leaders refused to allow some mine pits to be closed, the Thatcher government anticipated a strike and asked the Central Electricity Generating Board to stockpile enough coal inventories to prevent the blackouts and power cuts that had crippled the British economy during the 1974 strike. After a year the strike was broken, and the terms of the relationship between labor, management, and government in Great Britain changed dramatically. This new relationship allowed the Thatcher government to privatize state-owned industries, such as British Gas, British Airways, British Steel, British Coal, and British Rail, and to sell off government shares in North Sea Oil and British Petroleum. By 1992, two-thirds of the state-owned industries, forty-six businesses employing roughly 900,000 employees, were privately owned.[20]

These changes did not occur without a great deal of social unrest and political opposition, and this accounted in large part for the overwhelming 179-seat majority won by Tony Blair's "New Labour Party" in the 1997 general election. Although Blair rejected the emphasis in the "Old Labour Party" on government intervention and state ownership, his vision of the free market, which was premised on compassion, social democracy, and inclusiveness, was more Keynesian and quite different from that of Thatcher and her mentor Hayek. A devout Christian since his undergraduate years at Oxford, Blair was committed to what he termed an "ethical socialism," meaning a socialism more rooted in the ideals of Christian community and personal responsibility and that placed less emphasis on the class struggle and dependence on the state.[21] Nevertheless, Blair was a firm believer in the telos of the market or Washington consensus, and this partly explains why he was willing several years later to support the decision of President Bush to topple the regime of Saddam Hussein by invading Iraq.

MAINSTREAM ECONOMIC THEORY AND AMERICAN POLITICS

The intimate connection between the competition between Keynesian and anti-Keynesian economics and the political process is also apparent in the more market oriented United States during the post–World War II era. The United States, in contrast with most other highly industrialized countries, has consistently favored a regulatory approach to solving economic problems with the use of a web of regulatory agencies and antitrust legislation enforced by a powerful judiciary. Because the United States emerged from World War II with an intact and greatly strengthened economic system, it was not necessary, as it was in Europe, for government to play a large and central role in the management of the postwar economy.

Economic planners in Washington first began to apply Keynesian fiscal policies in 1938, and subsequent planners were heavily influenced by the work of Keynesian "new economists" at Harvard through the Johnson and Kennedy administrations. Richard Nixon, who attributed his 1960 defeat by John Kennedy to the recession of that year, declared, "Now, I am a Keynesian" shortly after winning the presidency in 1968.[22] He then proceeded to implement a Keynesian full-employment budget in which deficit spending was used to reduce unemployment and the trade-offs between inflation and unemployment were addressed with an income policy in which government intervention was used to control wages.

Against the advice of Federal Reserve chairman Arthur Burns, a conservative anti-Keynesian economist, Nixon took the nation off the gold standard, which weakened the dollar against other currencies and added to inflation by driving up the prices of imported goods. This action created a situation in which mainstream economists at central banks were obliged to take on the role of seeking to protect the stability of international commerce in the currency markets by buying or selling national currencies in response to sudden swings in their relative values. The Nixon administration also extended government regulation into new areas with the creation of the Environmental Protection Agency, the Occupational Safety and Health Administration, and the Equal Opportunity Commission. What is remarkable here is that the influence of Keynesian economics explains, in large part, why the administration of one of America's most conservative politicians instituted more liberal economic reforms than any other administration with the exception of that of Franklin Roosevelt.

During the 1970s, the U.S. economy did not perform well, owing to the large-scale impacts of the 1973 oil boycott. In 1974, inflation was at its highest level since World War I and unemployment reached 9.2 percent, two points greater than at any time in the years since that war. This situation became much worse after the shah of Iran was toppled from power in 1979 and a second major drop in the supply of oil raised the price from $13 to $34 a barrel. As lines at gas stations grew progressively longer and inflation hit 13.2 percent, President Carter was desperate for ways in which to slay the inflationary dragon and remain in office. Several of his advisers told him that economist Paul Volcker, who was exposed in graduate school at Princeton to professors from the Austrian school where Hayek did his doctoral work, might be able to deal with the problem of inflation as chairman of the Federal Reserve. After Carter appointed Volcker to this office, the chairman chose to fight inflation with a blunt instrument that produced dramatic results. Rather than merely set the prime rates, which affect the cost of borrowing money, Volcker also elected to control the actual supply, or quantity, of money by managing bank reserves. As the Fed restricted the money supply, interest rates climbed to 20 percent, unemployment hit 10 percent, and the American economy entered the worst recession since the Great Depression.[23] The sad state of the economy and the Iran hostage crisis were the major factors contributing to the defeat of Carter by Ronald Reagan in the 1980 election.

Martin Hayek's more direct influence on the American political process and on an economist who would serve as the minister of economic thought for Ronald Reagan, Milton Friedman, began in 1950. In that year, Hayek left the London School of Economics and accepted an appointment at the University of Chicago. By the end of the 1950s, economists in the "Chicago School" had distinguished themselves as the most vocal opponents of Keynesian new economics and its influential proponents at Harvard. Their central argument was that government intervention disturbs the lawful mechanisms of closed market systems and that these mechanisms, if left alone, can resolve both social and economic problems more effectively and efficiently. The Chicago economists also believed that a small number of mathematical theorems can predict the manner in which decision makers will allocate resources and how these allocations will result in prices.

Milton Friedman, who did his graduate work at the University of Chicago and became a professor there in 1946, launched a direct assault on virtually every aspect of Keynesian economics in the late 1950s. In response to charges that the Chicago School was dogmatic, rigid, and given to a simpleminded reductionism, Friedman set out to demonstrate that there is a direct and explicit connection between free-market capitalism and democracy. In *Capitalism and Freedom,* published in 1962, he argued that the mechanisms of the market system cannot function properly in the absence of economic freedom and that this freedom cannot exist in the absence of political liberty.[24]

This marked the beginning of Friedman's celebrity status among conservatives, and that status was considerably enhanced when he served as the principal economic adviser to Republican presidential candidate Barry Goldwater in 1964. After receiving the Bank of Sweden Prize in Economic

Sciences in 1976, Friedman further popularized his views in a mass-market best seller, *Free to Choose,* which became the basis for a series of programs on public television.[25] He soon retired from teaching, joined the Hoover Institution at Stanford, and established direct contact with Ronald Reagan and his advisers.

By the time Reagan defeated Carter in the 1980 presidential election, economic problems during the 1970s had caused many to question the efficacy of Keynesian new economics, and this greatly enhanced the influence of the Chicago economists, who claimed that government intervention was the primary source of these problems. In this climate, a group of economists known as "supply-siders" became very influential. These economists firmly believed that the best way to fight inflation was to control the money supply and that the value of international currency should be based on fixed rates, preferably that of gold. However, the concept of the supply-siders that had the largest impact on the Reagan administration was the notion that government revenues lost as a result of tax cuts would be more than made up by the additional tax revenues resulting from higher economic growth rates.

Based on the claim of the Chicago economists that the market system would perform better with less interference by government and the argument of the supply-siders that economic growth would be enhanced by cutting taxes, the Reagan administration cut the top marginal rates for federal income taxes from 70 percent to 28 percent. After the increases in tax revenues predicted by the supply-siders failed to materialize and the large tax cut was accompanied by massive increases in defense expenditures, the gross national debt during the Reagan presidency rose from $995 billion to $2.9 trillion, and the annual federal budget deficit tripled.[26] It is also worth noting that between 1979 and 1989, the portion of the national wealth held by Americans in the top 1 percent increased from 22 percent to 39 percent, and some experts have estimated that by the mid-1990s the top 1 percent had captured 70 percent of all earnings since the mid-1970s.[27]

When the senior George Bush took office in 1989, his "read my lips, no new taxes" campaign slogan made tax increases politically undesirable, and his administration elected to confront the problem of the ballooning deficits by containing government spending. Fortunately for this administration, two "exogenous" events, the fall of the Berlin Wall and the collapse of the Soviet Union, made it politically feasible to reduce defense spending. But after the Reagan tax cuts for affluent Americans failed to generate the anticipated additional tax revenues and overall revenues fell during the recession of the early 1990s, the annual deficit by the end of Bush's term in 1992 had climbed to $290 billion.

The successful campaign against big government and excessive government spending during the late 1990s coincided with a heady period of economic growth fueled by lower interest rates, cheap oil, expanding global markets, high-tech innovations, and dot-com mania. These developments largely explain why fiscal conservatives gained ground in both parties and why the anti-Keynesian, promarket "New Democrats" became power brokers after Bill Clinton was elected president in 1993. These developments also made it possible for Newt Gingrich and his "Contract with America" to take center stage in American domestic politics after the Republicans captured both houses of Congress in 1994.

The goal of the Gingrich Republicans was to enact a budget that would eliminate federal deficits in seven years by curbing the growth of Medicare, Medicaid, and welfare programs, and by turning over the administration of most of these programs to the states. This group also called for very large tax cuts for high-income Americans based on the assumption that this would encourage investment and stimulate the economy. When Clinton vetoed this budget, the Gingrich Republicans refused to pass the continuing resolution that would provide the temporary funds to keep the federal government going, and this resulted in shutdowns of selected government agencies and services in November and December of 1995. As it turned out, the American public was more frightened than pleased by this action, Gingrich and his followers fell out of favor, and the primary source of this conflict, the federal deficit, ceased to be a burning issue in 1997.

The remarkable decrease in the annual federal deficit, from 5 percent of GDP in 1992 to less than 1 percent in 1997, was not anticipated by any economists, and those who attempted to explain it did so after the fact. In 1993, economists working for the Clinton administration and at the Congressional Budget Office predicted that the 1997 deficit would be over $200 billion, and there were absolutely no indications that the actual deficit in that year could be about a tenth of that figure, $22.6 billion.[28] The economists who proffered after-the-fact explanations said that the turnaround resulted from reductions in government spending, particularly on defense, slightly higher taxes, and a dramatic increase in the flow of additional tax revenues generated by a strong economy.

The tensions between the vestiges of Keynesian new economics, which allows for prudent government spending to sustain a safety net of social services and programs, and the anti-Keynesian economics of the sort promulgated by the Chicago School, which calls for displacing or augmenting government activities with the mechanisms of the closed market system, were quite apparent in the 2000 presidential campaign. While Democrat Al Gore argued for increased federal spending to sustain the Social Security Retirement System and the Medicare and Medicaid programs, Republican George W. Bush claimed that market mechanisms could reduce government spending and provide more beneficial outcomes for already overburdened taxpayers. And while Gore made the case that increased regulations and more government spending were required to deal with problems in the global environment, Bush took the position that these measures would hurt the U.S. economy and that market mechanisms would resolve environmental problems.

In the American two-party system, presidential elections in which the Democratic and Republican candidates endorse disparate solutions to economic and social problems have often been decided by very narrow margins. The margin was so close in the 2000 election that most analysts concluded that the result would have been different if a third-party candidate, Ralph Nader, had withdrawn and thrown his support to Gore. The outcome was finally determined by a Supreme Court ruling that gave Bush a majority of votes in the Electoral College even though Gore had won the popular vote by a margin of roughly 500,000.

Polls taken during and after this election indicated that the American public was deeply divided on virtually every issue, including that of the environment. Because Gore had systematically studied the linkage between global economic activities and the crisis in the global environment and had even published a best-selling book on the subject, *Earth in the Balance,* in 1993, he was clearly more informed on this issue than Bush.[29] In one of the televised debates, Bush even suggested that there was no valid scientific evidence indicating that global warming is a problem.

From our perspective, the fact that Bush did not feel that there was any great need for government to play a substantive role in resolving environmental problems makes sense. Virtually everything he said about this matter during the campaign was based on the presumption that the mechanisms of market systems will resolve environmental problems even if individual economic actors are not aware that they are doing so. This rather pristine belief that the invisible hand will, if left alone, produce such a remarkable result and still promote maximal economic growth is profoundly religious in character. But since this metaphysical construct is embedded in assumptions about the dynamics of part-whole relationships in neoclassical economic theory and arrayed in the garment of scientific knowledge, it has some real-world consequences. Some of these consequences during the first Bush administration were economic initiatives that massively contributed to the crisis in the global environment, a refusal to cooperate with other industrialized countries in dealing with this crisis, and an environmental policy, if one can call it that, which was little more than a thinly veiled attempt to serve the economic interests of corporate America.

In July of 2003, a report was issued by the U.S. Environmental Protection Agency that was originally intended to provide a comprehensive review of what was known about environmental problems and areas in which additional research was needed. But after some heavy-handed censorship by the White House Council on Environmental Quality and the Office of Management and Budget, a long section on the risks of global warming was replaced by a noncommittal note on the problem. The censors also deleted statements indicating that the decade of the 1990s was the warmest in the Northern Hemisphere in the last thousand years, that human activities are contributing to global warming, and that global climate change has environmental and health impacts.[30]

The systematic attempts by the Bush administration to suppress scientific knowledge about the environmental crisis have been so flagrant that members of the scientific community have recently been willing to overcome their usual reluctance to engage in partisan politics. For example, the Union of Concerned Scientists issued a report in February of 2004 that made a very convincing case that the Bush administration has displayed "a well-established pattern of suppression and distortion of scientific findings by high-ranking political appointees across numerous federal agencies."[31] This document, signed by sixty prominent scientists, including twenty Nobel laureates and former science advisers to both Republican and Democratic administrations, also accused the administration of consistently abusing scientific knowledge in the service of an ideological agenda.

During the months prior to the presidential election of 2004, the Bush administration continued to pursue its ideological agenda by preventing a 144-page study called the Arctic Climate Impact Assessment from becoming public. This study was sponsored by a council of eight nations with territories in the Arctic—the United States, Canada, Russia, and several Nordic countries—and the research was done over a four-year period by a group of over three hundred internationally known scientists. The scientists determined that global warming is melting the Arctic ice sheet at an alarming rate and that this phenomenon can be directly attributed to increased global emissions of greenhouse gases. If nothing is done to dramatically decrease these emissions, the scientists warned that abrupt, large-scale changes in the global climate system similar to those described in chapter 2 ("Godgames at the Pentagon") could occur.[32]

All members of the council, with the exception of those from the United States, concluded that there was only one way to prevent massive changes in the global climate system from endangering the lives of billions of people—the international community must establish mandatory limits on the global emissions of carbon dioxide and other greenhouse gases with all deliberate speed. But the U.S. delegation, operating under direct orders from the Bush White House, argued that the study was not sufficiently detailed to justify the formulation of any concrete proposals and refused to endorse any recommendations that called for mandatory curbs on greenhouse gas emissions.

THE GOSPEL ACCORDING TO GEORGE W. BUSH

Numerous public policy analysts and political commentators have struggled to understand why the Bush administration has systematically attempted to undermine environmental regulations that are not commensurate with the financial interests of American businesses and corporations. Many of these individuals have argued that Bush and his economic advisers are "neocons" who embrace the narrow view of the dynamics of free-market systems articulated by Hayek and Friedman and that this largely accounts for the abysmal environmental record of the Bush administration. Some of these critics have also claimed that Bush and his most influential advisers are scientifically illiterate and that this explains their well-documented tendency to allow environmental policies to be scripted by friends and associates they previously worked with or for in the energy business.

But virtually nothing has been said about the principal reason why the environmental record of the Bush administration resembles a tale told by an idiot signifying nothing more than a blissful lack of awareness that the crisis in the global environment is real and must be resolved with all deliberate speed. President George W. Bush is one of the prime examples in American politics of a true believer in the market or Washington consensus who conflates the natural laws of economics and with the laws of God. When we examine the record of the Bush administration from this perspective, there are no inconsistencies between religious truths as they are conceived by this president and the domestic and foreign policies and legislative agenda in his administration. This explains why President Bush assumes that privatization and market-based initiatives can resolve virtually all human problems, why he has consistently supported faith-based government-sponsored programs that violate the constitutionally sanctioned division between church and state, and why he has favored tax policies for the rich that may eventually undermine the capacity of the federal government to fund Social Security and other entitlement programs. But what is most invidious about the gospel according to George W. Bush is that it apparently serves in the mind of this president to sacredly legitimate the totally specious assumption that the allegedly lawful or lawlike mechanisms of free-market systems can resolve environmental problems if the prices are right.

During the week following the 2004 presidential election, the Bush White House and the Republican leadership in Congress appealed to this assumption to justify their efforts to revamp regulations on air pollution and endangered species and to revive a moribund bill that would open the Arctic National Wildlife Refuge to energy exploration. The proposed "Clear Skies" initiative, which gives new meaning to the term "Orwellian newspeak," would dramatically lower emissions standards for pollutants such as nitrogen oxide, sulfur dioxide, and mercury. And the proposed revisions of the thirty-two year old Endangered Species Act would allow lumber companies and the mining industry to exploit environmental resources in previously protected habitats for endangered species by making it virtually impossible for scientists to demonstrate that a species is endangered. The Republican leadership during the week after the election was also moving legislation through Congress that would open up protected areas in the West, such as the Roan Plateau in Colorado and the Otero Mesa in New Mexico, to the exploitation of environmental resources by business interests. Even more invidious, President Bush made it clear a few days after the election that his administration would fight any regulations that would reduce emissions of carbon dioxide and other greenhouse gases and any efforts by Congress to approve the Kyoto Accords.[33]

In the next chapter, the case will be made that any successful effort to resolve the environmental crisis will be entirely dependent on the willingness of the international community to accomplish two very daunting tasks in the most responsible ways in the least amount of time. The first is to displace the present system of international government with a supranational federal system, and the second is to simultaneously develop and implement an environmentally responsible economic theory. Obviously, these are formidable enterprises. There are, however, indications that we are in the process of witnessing some massive changes in the geopolitical climate that could allow these remarkable developments to occur over a relatively short period of time.

THE ENDGAME

Resolving the Crisis in
the Global Environment

Humanity's dominance of Earth means that we cannot escape responsibility for managing the planet. Our activities are causing rapid, novel, and substantial changes in the Earth's ecosystems. Maintaining populations, species, and ecosystems in the face of these changes, and maintaining the flow of goods and services they provide humanity, will require active management for the foreseeable future.

— PETER VITOUSEK

The business-as-usual approach to resolving the environmental crisis is predicated on the following list of now familiar assumptions: (1) the lawful or lawlike dynamics of free-market systems can resolve virtually all environmental problems; (2) these dynamics will necessarily result in technological solutions; (3) governments should deal only with those environmental problems that cannot be resolved in these terms; (4) any actions taken by government must be commensurate with the understanding of the dynamics of free-market systems in the neoclassical economic paradigm; (5) the sole source of political power in dealing with environmental problems is the sovereign nation-state; (6) the sovereign nation-state exists, like all forms of government, in a domain of reality separate and distinct from the domain of economic reality; (7) the international system of government does not in itself have any political power; and (8) any attempts by this government to resolve environmental problems that might interfere with the growth and expansion of national economies and the global market system must be resisted by the governments of sovereign nation-states.

If the natural laws of economics and the sovereign nation-state were sacredly ordained aspects of a cosmic scheme or plan, business as usual could be very good business indeed. But since these constructs exist only in the minds of those who believe in their existence, and since belief in their actual existence is effectively undermining efforts to revolve the crisis in the global environment, the time has clearly come to recognize that living in the service of false gods is not in the interests of human survival. If this does not happen and the international community refuses to abandon the business-as-usual approach to resolving the environmental crisis, we may soon find ourselves living in a world that resembles the one described in the Pentagon report. In this world abrupt, large-scale changes in the global climate system would have disastrous impacts on people living in every region or territory on the planet; the competition for scarce resources between nation-states would result in endless cross-border conflicts and armed invasions; and such conflicts could easily escalate to the point where one or more countries may elect to use nuclear bombs and other weapons of mass destruction.

But if political leaders and economic planners realize that the gods they now serve are false and proceed to do what is required to resolve the environmental crisis, we can soon be living in a very different world. In this world, human populations cease over time to suffer from the ravages of hunger, starvation, and disease; extreme and hopeless poverty is no longer tolerated or ignored; the rights and freedoms now enjoyed by the citizens of fully functional democracies will be extended to the rest of humanity; and cross-border conflicts and wars of aggression will be viewed as remnants of a benighted human past that have no place or function in the vastly more enlightened human future.

Realists and pragmatists have routinely dismissed such dreams as products of the overheated imaginations of muddleheaded idealists who fail to recognize or properly understand what the critics regard as self-evident truths—the more invidious aspects of human nature, the harsh realities of geopolitical politics, the intimate connection between economic prosperity and competitive advantage, and the vital role and function of a strong military in protecting and enhancing the interests of sovereign nation-states. The problem with this conventional wisdom is that the usual distinctions between idealism and realism, between moral considerations and pragmatic solutions, and between idealistic conceptions of the better world that can be versus realistic assessments of the world as it is are no longer commensurate with the terms of human survival.

What these terms dictate is that the international community must begin very soon to coordinate large-scale human activities on a global or planetary scale in ways that will allow for the emergence of sustainable conditions in the global environment. And the only pragmatic and realistic way of accomplishing this feat is to create a fully functional system of international government and to simultaneously develop and implement an environmentally responsible economic theory. But why should the successful implementation of these realistic and practical solutions result in a more peaceful, humane, and equitable world for all of the 6.4 billion members of the extended human family? The answer is that if there is not a very active commitment to creating this world at every stage in this process, it will not be possible to achieve the totally unprecedented level of cooperation between peoples and governments required to prevent a human tragedy on a truly apocalyptic scale.

Granted, the prospects that these solutions can be implemented in the present geopolitical climate may seem rather bleak. The prediction here, however, is that this climate will change dramatically over the next few years in ways that will greatly enhance the likelihood that these remarkable developments can and will occur. This, in my view, will be the case because the numbers of scientific studies that clearly indicate that the crisis in the global environment is rapidly becoming a zero-sum endgame in which the winners or losers could be all of humanity are increasing exponentially. This research has demonstrated that large-scale human activities are massively disrupting environmental systems everywhere on the planet and that we are rapidly approaching the point where far-from-equilibrium conditions can trigger abrupt, large-scale changes in the global climate system. Because the bad news about the state of the global environment will be very alarming and quite impossible to ignore, concerns about the crisis in the global environment should soon rise to the top of the political agenda in virtually all nation-states.

Some recent research on how massive changes occur in geopolitical reality lends weight to this argument. This research, based on dynamical systems theory, suggests that during periods of gradual change, negative feedbacks predominate; these feedbacks tend to maintain political systems in something like the same state; and radical proposals and public policy initiatives are rare. But during periods of rapid change, a real or imagined crisis occasions the emergence of positive feedbacks; each action generates proportionately larger positive feedbacks; and these feedbacks increase in almost direct proportion to the numbers of people who are aware of and concerned about the crisis. When this occurs in democratic societies, large numbers of previously apathetic citizens become involved in the political process, many new programs and public policies are implemented, and fundamental changes in political and economic reality tend to occur over a relatively short period of time.[1]

One of the early indicators that the geopolitical climate may be changing in ways that can enhance the prospects of resolving the environmental crisis involves some actions recently taken by the United Nations. When the United Nations approved the Universal Declaration of Human Rights and the International Covenant on Genocide and created a set of ethical norms designed to regulate the manner in which a government deals with its own population, this not only challenged the assumption that no external agency or power should interfere with the internal affairs of a sovereign nation-state. It also legitimated the principle that if a government of a nation-state violates these norms, the international community can declare that this government is no longer legitimate. Based on this principle, the international community challenged, under the auspices of the United Nations, the legitimacy of the apartheid regime in South Africa in the 1980s by authorizing the use of sanctions and embargoes. In the 1990s, the U.N. Security Council applied this same principle in response to the internal despotism in Cambodia and Somalia and created de facto U.N. trusteeship governments in both countries.

Equally significant, the Security Council responded in 1999 to the massive abuses of human rights and freedoms in the Federal Republic of Yugoslavia by approving Resolution 1244. This resolution authorized the use of force to curtail these abuses, and NATO, acting on the authority of the resolution, declared that the government in Kosovo was illegitimate and intervened militarily. After obtaining another resolution from the United Nations, NATO replaced the Belgrade government with a U.N. trusteeship that governed Kosovo with the assistance of a NATO military force. These actions are significant because they were motivated by the growing conviction that international government has an obligation to protect the universal rights and freedoms of all the 6.4 billion people on this planet even if this results in a violation of the old rule that no external government should intervene in the internal affairs of a sovereign nation-state.

The willingness of France, Germany, and other European countries to advocate over the last few years the creation of a World Environment Organization may be another indicator that we may soon witness a phase change in geopolitical climate that can facilitate a timely resolution of the environmental crisis. This proposed international agency, which would operate under the auspices of the United Nations, would have as much power as the World Trade Organization. In one proposal, the new agency would manage all existing environmental treaties, determine international standards that can contribute to the emergence of a sustainable global environment, and be invested with the legal authority to enforce these standards.[2]

TOWARD A NEW SYSTEM OF INTERNATIONAL GOVERNMENT

Obviously, it is not possible to predict with absolute certainty a series of events that could lead to the emergence of a system of international government capable of coordinating large-scale human activities in environmentally responsible ways on a global or planetary scale. However, it is reasonable to assume that any such process will be driven by efforts in the international community to resolve the environmental crisis and that any effective solutions must be commensurate with our best scientific understanding of the actual dynamics of the interactions between human systems and environmental systems. In the first phase of this process, governments of nation-states should become increasingly more committed to resolving the environmental crisis. And this should stimulate the international community, under the auspices of the present system of international government, to create and adequately fund a massive research project similar to that described in the first chapter of this book.

In the first phase of this project, an international group of environmental scientists could determine baseline measures of sustainability and the overall reductions in the environmentally destructive activities of current production and distribution systems required to achieve a sustainable global environment. In the second phase, the environmental scientists could work closely with social scientists to develop specific proposals to coordinate large-scale human activities in ways that could achieve the baseline measures of sustainability during the time frame in which this will remain a possibility. This international research project, which would be far more extensive than similar projects that now exist, could also take into account the social, political, and economic variables involved in implementing the solutions.

The results of this research would make it quite clear that the actual dynamics of the interactions between human and environmental systems are categorically different from and completely incompatible with arbitrary assumptions about the relationship between parts (sovereign nation-states and national economies) and wholes (international government and the global market system) in our present conception of geopolitical reality. One major reason why this would be the case is that any viable solutions must be capable of coordinating human activities in environmentally responsible ways on a global or planetary scale. Another is that the successful implementation of these solutions would require the creation of institutional frameworks and processes that are not restricted in their operations by the artificial boundaries between nation-states.

In the initial stages of this process, governments will probably attempt to forge new agreements within the present system of international government.

But this effort, like all previous efforts of this kind, will fail for a now obvious reason—there is no basis in a system of international government predicated on the metaphysically based construct of the sovereign nation-state for positing, much less implementing, viable solutions. The players of this godgame would soon realize that any viable solutions must be based on the assumption that all large-scale human activities exist in embedded and interactive relationships with environmental systems and processes on a planetary scale. And they would also be obliged to recognize that the usual tendency in the international community to discount or dismiss, for political or ideological reasons, our best scientific understanding of the causes of the global environmental crisis and the manner in which it can be resolved would undermine any prospect that the crisis can be resolved.

During the next phase of the negotiations, it should become quite apparent that viable solutions cannot be implemented in the absence of a fully functional system of international government. Assuming that the usual sources of resistance to creating such as government are overcome, the process of developing and implementing viable solutions should eventually result in the emergence of an international government capable of resolving this crisis—a supranational federal system. The only legitimate grounds for creating this government will be to protect the individual rights and freedoms and to improve the conditions of life for all members of the extended human family. It is, therefore, reasonable to assume that the founding documents will state that the government of any nation-state can be displaced by a transitional government that operates under the aegis of the new international government if any of the following conditions apply: (1) a government of a nation-state has violated the human rights and freedoms of significant numbers of people living within its regions or territories; (2) a government of a nation-state has failed to adequately respond to natural or human-caused disasters that threaten the lives of large numbers of people; and (3) the destructive environmental impacts of large-scale human activities in regions or territories governed by a nation-state have reached levels where the goal of achieving sustainable conditions in the global environment are being undermined.

However, the greatest challenge faced by the emerging international government will not be the enormous difficulties involved in developing viable solutions to the environmental crisis. It will be the process of implementing these solutions, which will require a very active commitment to improving the conditions of life for all 6.4 billion people on this planet. Obviously, translating this commitment into effective policies and programs will not be easy. At present, the richest 20 percent of the global human population own 85 percent of the wealth and the poorest 20 percent own 1.4 percent.[3] In spite of the claim by the true believers in the Washington or market consensus that the rising tide of the global market system will necessarily lift all boats, the income differential between the fifth of the global population in the wealthiest countries and the fifth in the poorest is growing at alarming rates—30 to 1 in 1960, 60 to 1 in 1990, and 74 to 1 in 1995.[4] There are also 1.1 billion people on this planet who do not have access to sufficient potable water, 2.4 billion who lack adequate sanitation facilities, and 2.8 billion who live on less than $2 a day.[5] In sub-Saharan Africa, half of the population survives on less than 65 cents a day, and average per capita income is lower than in the 1960s. The World Food Program has recently indicated that 40 million Africans are on the verge of starvation and that almost three-quarters of those in this population are suffering from either HIV or AIDS.[6]

Also consider that global population increased 35 percent over the past twenty years, that this population is projected to increase another 25 percent over the next twenty years, and that virtually all these increases have been and will be in underdeveloped or developing countries. The developed countries experienced their population explosions earlier and have gone through what is called the "demographic transition." This transition begins when improvements in health and nutrition reduce infant mortality rates and increase average life spans. In the initial phase, fertility rates do not decline and population growth is even more rapid. Later, however, fertility rates decline and population size tends to become stable. In other words, the transition is from high birth and death rates and to low birth and death rates. If this process continues, birthrates tend to fall below replacement levels, as they have done in some industrialized countries, and native populations become smaller.[7]

Because there is a positive correlation between increases in global population, the percentage of this population that lives in extreme poverty, and the damage done to the global environment by large-scale human activities, this leads to an obvious conclusion—the effort of the new international government to resolve the environmental crisis will fail in the absence of dramatic improvements in living conditions in poorer countries. Such improvements are needed in order to bring about a worldwide demographic transition. This, in turn, can enable a peaceful stabilization, then decline, in the global human population—as opposed to the nightmarish free for all of collapsing ecosystems and escalating wars envisioned in the Pentagon report. Granted, inequities in standards of living will probably be a feature of human life for a very long time. On the other hand, any realistic and pragmatic assessment of what will be required to resolve the crisis in the global environment clearly indicates that the gross inequities between the lives of the haves and have-nots on this planet are not commensurate with the terms of human survival.

TOWARD AN ENVIRONMENTALLY RESPONSIBLE ECONOMIC THEORY

The godgame, which is rapidly becoming a zero-sum endgame, will also be lost if we fail to develop and implement with all deliberate speed an environmentally responsible economic theory. The developers of this theory must first contend with a scientifically valid truth that is ignored or obscured in the mathematical theories used by neoclassical economists—there is no basis for accurately predicting the choices that economic actors will make in response to any economic situation in which there are large numbers of variables. Human cognition is an emergent phenomenon in the nonlinear system of the human brain; a large number of variables are involved in making any complex decision, and there is no way to precisely predict how acts of human cognition will inform any such decision.

Granted, a hungry person will in all probability choose to eat, and a thirsty person will choose to drink. But if we exclude choices driven by basic biological needs, there is nothing more indeterminate in nature than the mental processes that inform human decisions in any domain of experience, including economic reality. The fact that we cannot "in principle" accurately predict the choices that an individual economic actor will make in response to a situation in which there are even a limited number of economic variables obliges us to draw the following conclusion: there is no basis for positing general laws or lawful or lawlike regularities that would allow us to accurately predict the choices that will be made by economic actors.

This means that an environmentally responsible economic theory cannot be a science like the physical sciences in dealing with choices made by economic actors, and yet this theory must be predicated on our best scientific understanding of the interactive relationships between parts (large-scale economic activities) and whole (the state of the global environment). This new theory will feature means and methods for understanding the bases on which economic actors make choices in terms of real or imagined needs and preferences and ability to pay. It will do so, however, based on a much more robust understanding of the multiple factors that inform these choices, and this should result in more accurate assessments of consumer needs and preferences and more reliable stochastic predictions of both short-term and long-term economic trends. However, this theory will not be predicated on the absurd assumption that the only dynamics at work in economic reality are the decisions made by economic actors in reified market systems in which the god of the invisible hand resolves all human problems without any conscious design or intent by those who make these decisions.

There must be a basis in this new theory for realistically assessing the costs of environmental impacts of economic activities and internalizing these costs in pricing systems, and this will require a concerted and well-funded effort in the international community to accomplish the following tasks:

- Develop scientifically valid means and methods for measuring the relationship between the economic activities of parts (major production and distribution systems) and the state of the whole (ecosystem or biosphere).
- Develop means and methods for translating these measures into price mechanisms that realistically reflect the costs of doing business in the global environment.
- Devise a plan that can lead to the creation of international organizations or agencies that will attempt to ensure that these price mechanisms are applied in a fair and consistent manner throughout the global economic system.

Any environmentally responsible economic theory must also be predicated on empirically valid quantifiable measures of the environmental impacts of production and distribution systems. The following measures, which we can already estimate with a reasonable degree of accuracy, can be used for this purpose:

- amounts of low-entropy materials consumed in production and distribution systems;
- amount of high entropy generated in the production of materials and goods and in the distribution of products;
- total amount of throughput in production and distribution measured in units of energy;
- amounts of greenhouse gases, pollutants, and toxic substances generated;

- amounts of nonrenewable resources consumed;
- amounts of biologically important nutrients removed from the nutrient-cycling process in the biosphere;
- environmental impacts over the lifetime of products;
- environmental impacts of product wastes;
- recycling of products;
- efficient use of energy resources.[8]

Equally obvious, any environmentally responsible economic theory must also be predicated on measures of sustainable conditions in the global environment, which we can also now determine with a reasonable degree of accuracy. The list of these measures can include the following:

- levels of greenhouse gases in the atmosphere;
- ozone levels in the atmosphere;
- percentage increases or decreases in global warming;
- conditions of rain forests, fisheries, arable lands, rangelands, and coral reefs;
- amounts of arable land, potable water, open water, and groundwater;
- extinction rates;
- loss of species diversity.

One of the most challenging problems faced by the developers of this theory will be to determine how to translate the relationships between parts (production and distribution systems) and whole (state of the global environment) into units of money. Some have argued that this is not possible, because we do not know how to define baseline measures for a sustainable global environment in scientific or empirical terms.[9] But this is not, in fact, the case, because we have recently developed vastly more sophisticated computer models that can simulate the dynamics of nonlinear systems and climate-modeling computers that can handle the orders-of-magnitude increases in computation required by the models.

For example, Japan has spent over $400 million on the development of a linked array of supercomputers that will be able to calculate orders of magnitude faster than the best existing climate-modeling systems. A typical array used for climate modeling in the United States can process about 20 gigaflops, or 20 billion floating operations per second, and the best European systems can process about 100 gigaflops. The performance of the new Japanese system, appropriately called the Earth Simulator, is measured in teraflops, or thousands of gigaflops.[10] With the use of these new research tools, along with the vast amounts of improved data from satellites and ground-based observation systems, scientists are confident that they can reasonably determine baseline measures for sustainability in the global environment over the next few years if the resources to accomplish this task are available. But since life on Earth is an enormously complex nonlinear system in which indeterminacy is a macrolevel phenomenon, the only way in which the baseline measures can ever be defined is within a range of probabilities. This means that those who develop the new economic theory must realize that measures for sustainability can be determined only in proximate terms and that the baseline measures included in the economic theory must be based on the precautionary principle.

Those involved in this formidable development project must also decide how to deal with another major dilemma that we have, thus far, been unable to resolve. How can we value a sustainable global environment in monetary terms? This dilemma has resulted in another catch-22 situation for those who have attempted to confer a monetary value on environmental resources by enlarging the framework of neoclassical economics in ways that can allow these resources to be viewed as "natural capital." For example, ecological economist Robert Costanza has developed a model in which global ecosystem services have a central value of $33 trillion per year with a range of $16 to $54 trillion per year.[11] Although this scheme confers a value on global environmental resources that is roughly one to three times global GNP, it cannot and will not work, because there is no basis in the value theory of neoclassical economics for realistically assessing the costs, or value, of environmental resources.

This theory obliges Costanza to represent the costs of environmental resources as market values, and his estimates of these costs may not be taken seriously by those who believe that "real" costs can be determined only by decisions made by economic actors within closed market systems. The neoclassical conception of value also forces Costanza to link the value of the natural capital of environmental resources to a volatile and unpredictable variable—global consumption of scarce resources based on market prices. Consequently, the resulting market value of the natural capital is related to the value of a sustainable environment only in the sense that the opportunity costs associated with the use of this capital are higher. If we assume that the total value of environmental resources is at its maximum three times that of global GNP, it might be possible to argue that there is plenty of room to grow the global economy. But the most fundamental problem with any such scheme is that the alleged monetary values of environmental resources as they are assessed in main-stream economics can never be equal to or the same as the value of a sustainable environment.

The most reasonable way to resolve this dilemma in an environmentally responsible economic theory is to begin with the following assumptions:

- The absolute value is a sustainable global environment.
- The prime values are the costs of achieving this environment.
- All other values are a function of these values.

In this value theory, the absolute value will be represented in monetary terms by some large and robust measure of the whole of the global economy, and the prime values will be a function of this value. One can, for example, represent the absolute value as an amount equivalent to the total flows of global capital for the previous ten years. There are probably more suitable ways to determine how to represent this value in monetary terms. However, the amount must be large enough to clearly indicate that the absolute value of achieving a sustainable global environment is vastly greater than that associated with the exchange value of goods, commodities, and services.

The next major task of the developers of the new economic theory will be to define the absolute value of a sustainable global environment in terms of monetary values of the designated measures for sustainable conditions. The percentage differences between the sustainable measures and the actual measures can be computed by an algorithm that runs on a desktop computer, and this algorithm can be updated and refined on an annual basis to reflect advances in knowledge and improved observational data. The value assigned to each of the measures of sustainability can then be translated into dollar amounts that represent in the aggregate the total value of a sustainable environment.

In other words, the dollar amount assigned to each measure will represent its value as a percentage of the absolute value of a sustainable global environment, and this amount can serve as the basis for calculating prime values, or the costs associated with achieving sustainable conditions in this environment. These costs can be calculated by first determining in percentage terms the extent to which specific measures of the economic activities of a part (production or distribution system) in the previous year contributed to the movement toward or away from specific optimal values for sustainability in the whole (global environment). These percentages can then be translated into dollar equivalents that represent the prime values, or the environmental costs of the economic activities of each part.

One major concern here is that the prime values, or the costs of doing business in the global environment, in the initial phase of implementation of an environmentally responsible economic theory may be so high that they could easily cause a breakdown in the global market system. For example, recent scientific studies have indicated that achieving the goal of a sustainable global environment will require that material flows in industrialized economies be reduced by 90 percent, or by a factor of ten. This means that any attempt to immediately translate all the environmental costs associated with these flows into prime values in pricing systems would have disastrous consequences.[12]

The developers of the new theory must, therefore, devise a strategy for phasing in these costs in a series of escalating prime values that will not cause massive disruptions in the global economy. At the same time, however, they must be certain that these costs are consistent with the goal of achieving a sustainable global environment based on the best scientific estimates of the time frame in which this will remain a possibility. The translation of these costs into prime values in very different economies, such as those in the first and third worlds, will be a large problem. However, this problem can be resolved in equitable ways based on measures such as the Index for Sustainable Economic Welfare and the Human Development Index.[13]

The index of optimal measures for sustainability in the whole (the global ecosystem or biosphere) and the index of measures of the activities of parts (production and distribution systems) can be perpetually reviewed, extended, and refined based on improved observational techniques and more advanced computer models. As this knowledge base expands, the new economic theory can be continually refined to include more physical variables and advances in scientific knowledge, such as an improved understanding of the dynamics of nonlinear systems.

Another major challenge is to develop a value theory that is not premised, like that of neoclassical economics, on a categorical distinction between market values and ecological values. Value theory in neoclassical economics reifies choices made by economic actors by alleging that these choices are governed or directed by the god of the invisible hand. If an actor is willing to pay, the god has spoken, and there is nothing else that can be said about the matter. In the new economic theory, markets will not be viewed as separate in any sense from the global environment or the subsystems of this environment. They will be viewed as collections of human activities embedded in and interactive with the "real economy" of the global environment. Hence the price paid for a sustainable environment in the new pricing mechanisms will be viewed as a cost of doing business in this environment and not as a tax on business activities.

This distinction between a cost and a tax is not a trivial matter. A tax is a compulsory levy by government on private individuals and organizations to raise revenue to finance public goods and services. A cost is a measure of what must be given up in order to obtain or acquire something in a purchase or exchange. In an environmentally responsible economic theory, government will continue to levy taxes for all the usual reasons. But since economic activities in this theory will be represented as parts that exist in embedded and interactive relationships with the real economy of the global environment, the costs of goods and commodities will necessarily include the costs that reflect this relationship. These costs will be understood as the costs of doing business in the global environment and no different in kind from any other costs, and they will be represented as such in pricing mechanisms and in systems of accounting. The column labeled taxes will not include these costs, and there will be no tax advantage associated with paying this cost.

It is important to realize that the greatest barrier to the implementation of an environmentally responsible economic theory is not lack of scientific knowledge or technological expertise. We have the means to measure the inputs and outputs of major economic systems, to measure the variables on the state of the global environment, and to establish baseline measures of sustainability. The greatest barrier to implementation is the need to obtain widespread acceptance of the assumption that a sustainable environment is an absolute value, that the prime value is the goal of achieving this environment, and that all other values in economic terms must be a function of these values. In the absence of these assumptions, it will not be possible to develop and implement an environmentally sound economic theory. Keep in mind, however, that as the environmental crisis intensifies, the value of a sustainable global environment may well be perceived as an ultimate value for a simple reason—the activities of human beings will eventually have no value, economic or otherwise, in the absence of a sustainable global environment.

After we begin to coordinate large-scale economic activities based on an environmentally responsible economic theory, the environmental impacts of these activities will be reflected in units of money, and monetary values will be linked to ecological values. Price mechanisms will constantly remind consumers of the intimate connection between economic activities and the state of the global environment. And since these mechanisms will reflect a continually improving scientific understanding of the evolving relationship between parts (production and distribution systems) and whole (sustainable conditions in the global environment), ecological values will be closely wed to monetary values.

This should make the overall scale of consumption more commensurate with basic needs than with unlimited desires, and distributions of income and wealth should become far more equitable than they are today. An international system of labeling laws, similar to the food labeling law in the United States, might require that a label be attached to all goods and commodities. Such a label could represent in easily understood graphic format the relationship between the environmental impacts associated with the production and distribution of a particular product or service and the state of the global environment measured in terms of the baseline measures of sustainability.[14]

This description of an environmentally responsible economic theory, like the earlier description of how a supranational system of international government could emerge, is not very sophisticated and does even begin to deal with the "devils in the details." On the other hand, any environmentally responsible economic theory must be capable of realistically assessing the environmental costs of economic activities and internalizing these costs in pricing systems. Equally obvious, these costs must be based on scientifically valid measures of the embedded and interactive relationships between the parts (large-scale economic activities) and sustainable conditions in the whole (the global environment or ecosystem).

It is also important to note that the environmentally responsible economic theory described here can preserve virtually all the substantive benefits of the free-market economies. In fact, there is only one major difference between a free-market system predicated on metaphysically based assumptions about part-whole relationships in the neoclassical economic paradigm and a free-market system predicated on a valid scientific understanding of these relationships. In the environmentally responsible economic theory, it will no longer be possible to ignore the environmental costs of economic activities.

ENVIRONMENTAL TAX REFORM AND GREEN TECHNOLOGIES

Given the relatively short time frame in which there will be an opportunity to create sustainable conditions in the global environment, it is imperative that we implement existing economic solutions to environmental problems during the period in which an environmentally responsible theory

is being developed. One of these solutions is to make much more extensive use of a device that the vast majority of neoclassical economists view
as external to closed market systems and an impediment to economic
growth—environmental tax reforms. The basic principle in these reforms,
which have been enacted in Germany, the Netherlands, and the Scandinavian countries, is very simple—raise taxes on activities that should be
discouraged and lower taxes on those that should be encouraged.

A large-scale imposition of environmental taxes will obviously retard
growth in industries where production and distribution systems are large
contributors to the crisis in the global environment. But it will also create
new markets for products that have less adverse environmental impacts.
Based on a detailed account of existing green technologies and others that
will soon be available, Paul Hawken, Amory Lovins, and Hunter Lovins
have made a convincing case in *Natural Capitalism: Creating the Next
Industrial Revolution* that companies that exploit these technologies can
reap enormous financial gains.[15] Because a widespread implementation
of these technologies will be labor-intensive, these authors also argue that
this will create large numbers of jobs and dramatically increase levels of
employment internationally.

Some recent developments also suggest that existing technological systems can be replaced by green technologies relatively quickly if there is a
political will to do so and appropriate economic incentives are in place.
From 1990 to 1998, wind energy technologies grew at an annual rate of
10 percent and photovoltaic technologies at 16 percent. Denmark has
banned the use of coal in all its industries and now generates 18 percent
of its electricity from wind turbines. Germany uses this technology to generate 3.5 percent of its total electricity needs today and plans to reach 25
percent by 2025. Globally, wind turbines are already generating about 10
percent of the energy generated by nuclear power plants. The percentage
of electricity generated by photovoltaic cells also increased more than 30
percent globally between 1998 and 2001, and several European countries
along with Japan have instituted subsidy programs to promote the development and implementation of photovoltaic systems.[16]

When, however, we view these hopeful signs within the larger economic context, they become considerably less hopeful. For example, governments now provide powerful vested interests in agriculture, energy,
transportation, fisheries, and forestry with enormous amounts of capital
in the form of subsidies. Norman Meyers and Jennifer Kent have labeled
these subsidies "perverse" because they have enormously destructive impacts in environmental terms and they are not cost-effective in economic

terms. The total amount of these subsidies worldwide each year is a staggering $869 billion, or about 2.3 percent of the $35 trillion global economy.

This means that governments are now providing huge economic incentives to industries engaged in environmentally destructive economic activities. They do so by giving away enormous amounts of money, most of which comes from taxes paid by ordinary citizens, to powerful economic interests that manipulate the political process to further enrich themselves without public consent and with little or no regard for the public good. The obvious solution to this problem is for ordinary citizens to engage the political process in ways that will promote legislation that serves the public good. This legislation should eliminate the perverse subsidies and stipulate that public money that was previously used for this purpose will now be devoted to developing and implementing environmentally friendly technologies.[17]

TOWARD A GLOBAL ENVIRONMENTAL ETHIC OR ETHOS

It may be comforting to know that science has provided us with the knowledge required to resolve the crisis in the global environment. On the other hand, there is nothing in this knowledge that obliges us to do so or that dictates how we must respond in moral terms. Arguing "ought" from "is" by appealing to scientific knowledge is a dangerous exercise, and real moral thinking cannot be achieved through mindless application of formulas. There is no system of ethics that is computationally reducible, and an environmental ethic or ethos will not emerge based on more rationality, more rules, and more justifications.[18] Those who have sought to articulate a system of universal ethics, from Plato to the present, have often found themselves in a situation aptly described by philosopher Colin McGinn: "The head spins in theoretical disarray; no explanatory model suggests itself; bizarre ontologies loom. There is a feeling of intense confusion, but no clear idea about where the confusion lies."[19]

There are, however, three recently discovered scientific truths that have large implications in philosophical and religious terms, and these implications can serve as the basis for articulating an environmental ethic or ethos that can be critically important in the effort to resolve the environmental crisis. The first truth is that all 6.4 billion people on this planet are members of one extended family and profoundly similar to one another in genetic, cognitive, and behavioral terms. The second is that human life and consciousness are emergent from and grounded in the evolution of the cosmos and the self-organizing and self-perpetuating system of life.

And the third truth is that the evolutionary pathway that allowed our ancestors to acquire and use fully complex language systems and to become aware of their own awareness was highly improbable and utterly unique.

There is, however, another scientific truth that can serve as the basis for articulating an environmental ethic or ethos that is even more profound in philosophical and religious terms. The most fundamental law of environmental science is that everything is connected to everything else, or that all activities in biological reality, including human activities, are embedded in and interactive with the whole of the global environment or ecosystem. But the whole as we are now obliged to conceive it in both the new biology and the new physics is not a collection of externally related parts. It is an emergent phenomenon in which the whole exists within the parts and cannot be explained in terms of the sum of the parts or the sum of the properties that exist within the parts.

At the most basic level of organization in physical reality, quanta interact with other quanta in and between fields, and fundamental particles interact with other fundamental particles to produce the roughly one hundred naturally occurring elements that display emergent properties that do not exist in the particles themselves. The parts represented by the elements combine to form new wholes in compounds and minerals that display emergent properties not present in the elements themselves. For example, the properties in salt, or sodium chloride, are novel and emergent, and do not exist in sodium or chloride per se. Long ago, in the ancestor of DNA, some of the parts associated with compounds and minerals combined to form a new whole that displayed emergent properties associated with life. During the first 2 billion years of evolution, the exchange of parts of DNA between prokaryotes as well as mutations within parts resulted in new wholes that displayed new emergent properties. Combination through synergism of these parts resulted in new wholes in eukaryotes that displayed emergent properties not present in prokaryotes.

Meiotic sex, or the typical sex of cells with nuclei, allowed for an exchange of parts of DNA that eventually resulted in new wholes with emergent properties in speciation. Mutation and recombination of the parts resident in DNA resulted in emergent properties in whole organisms that do not exist within the parts or in the series of nucleotides in DNA. Through a complex network of feedback loops the interaction of all organisms as parts resulted in a whole, biological life, that exists in some sense within the parts and displays emergent regulatory properties not present in the parts.

The "essential reality" in quantum field theory, says physicist Steven

Weinberg, "is a set of fields subject to the rules of special relativity and quantum mechanics; all else is derived as a consequence of the quantum dynamics of those fields."[20] Because events at the quantum level cannot be directly perceived by the human sensorium, we are not normally aware that every aspect of physical reality "emerges" through the interaction of fields and quanta. But from the perspective of our most advanced scientific knowledge, this is the actual ground for our existence, and the part that is our "self" emerges from and is embedded in a seamless web of activity that is the entire cosmos.

In superstring theory, the fundamental entity is a tiny vibrating filament of energy that physicists call a string, and quanta and elementary particles correspond to distinct patterns of vibrating strings. The strings can be visualized as incredibly small loops or strands that emerge from quantum interactions with particular vibrational patterns and a minuscule but finite circumference. According to this theory, specific patterns of vibrating strings result in the emergence of both matter particles and messenger particles and account for the properties of these particles, such as charge and spin. The mathematics of superstring theory requires a universe that has nine spatial dimensions and the most recent version of the theory, known as M-theory, features ten spatial dimensions. In this view, material reality emerges from a seamless web of quantum interactions in ten dimensions in space and one in time, and nothing in this reality can be viewed as isolated, separate, and discrete.

As the philosopher of science Errol Harris notes in thinking about the special character of wholeness in modern physics and biology, a unity without internal content is a blank or empty set and is not recognizable as a whole.[21] In a genuine whole, writes Harris, the relationships between the constituent parts must be "internal or immanent" in the parts, as opposed to a more spurious whole in which parts appear to disclose wholeness because of relationships that are "external" to the parts.[22] The collection of parts that allegedly constitute the whole in classical physics is an example of a spurious whole. Harris argues that parts constitute a genuine whole when the principle of order is "inside" the parts, and thereby adjusts each to all so that they interlock and become mutually complementary.[23] This not only describes the character of the whole revealed in both relativity theory and quantum mechanics. It is also consistent with the understanding of part-whole relationships in the new biology.

From the perspective of modern science, the cosmos is a single significant whole that evinces progressive order during successive stages of development. If one chooses to believe that the universe is a self-reflective and self-organizing whole, this lends no support whatsoever to conceptions of design, meaning, purpose, intent, or plan associated with any religious tradition. On the other hand, there is nothing in the scientific description of nature that can be used to refute this belief. Put differently, it is no longer possible to assume that a profound sense of unity with the whole, which has long been understood as the foundation of religious experience, can be undermined or invalidated with appeals to scientific knowledge.

It now seems clear that the scientific study of physical reality will take us perpetually closer to a horizon of knowledge where the whole that is the cosmos can never be completely explained or defined by a scientific "theory of everything." One reason why this is the case is that the progress of science has revealed that a purely reductionist approach to understanding the whole of physical reality cannot disclose any ultimate or final truths about this reality. This should have been obvious when Kurt Gödel published his Incompleteness Theorem in 1930. This extremely important but often ignored theorem shows that mathematics, the language of physical theory, cannot reach closure, because no algorithm, or calculation procedure, that uses mathematical proofs can prove its own validity. In other words, any mathematical description of physical reality that claims to have reached closure, or to have exhaustively described any aspect of this reality, cannot prove itself. As physicist Freeman Dyson puts it, "Gödel proved that in mathematics the whole is always greater than the sum of the parts."[24]

According to mathematician Rudy Rucker, "Mathematics is open-ended. There can never be a final best system of mathematics. Every axiom-system for mathematics will eventually run into certain simple problems that it cannot solve at all."[25] If a mathematical system cannot reach closure, it follows that no physical theory built on mathematical systems can reach closure. Even if we could manage to construct a "theory of everything" that allegedly disclosed all dynamics at every level of complexity in both physical and biological reality, this theory could not in principle be the final or complete description. From my point of view, this is rather fortunate. As William Blake put it in the age of Newton, the "bounded is loathed by its possessor," and what loathing we would surely feel if the meaning of all being and becoming could be completely understood and defined in scientific or religious terms.

The most seminally important religions thinkers in the five major religious traditions concluded some time ago that the whole, God or Being, can never be reduced to human understanding or explained in human terms. The fundamental religious truth in all these traditions is that the source and ground of human life and consciousness is an indivisible God or Being and any sense of separateness is an illusion that is not in accord with the actual character of spiritual reality. Equally significant, this truth is foundational to the moral dictum that spiritually active and aware individuals must treat others as they would wish to be treated. Both of these profound ideas were articulated in slightly different ways by Zoroaster, Confucius, the Buddha, Jesus, Mahavira, Mohammed, Hillel, and the authors of the Hindu epic Mahabharata and the Judeo-Christian book Leviticus.[26]

The realization by religious thinkers that all human beings are profoundly the same was remarkably prescient—science did not even begin to convincingly demonstrate that is the case until the last few decades of the twentieth century. But what is most significant here for our purposes is that the single most profound religious truth in all these religious traditions is in accord with or analogous to our most advanced scientific understanding of part-whole relationships in both physics and biology. Obviously, distinctions must be made here between scientific knowledge and philosophical or religious speculations based on this knowledge, and the most important of these distinctions is that there is no empirically valid linkage between the former and the latter. Those who wish to dismiss the speculations made on this basis are obviously free to do so. But there is another conclusion that can be drawn here that is firmly grounded in scientific theory and experiment—there is no basis in the scientific description of nature for believing in the radical Cartesian division between mind and world sanctioned by classical physics. It now seems clear that this radical separation between mind and world was a macrolevel illusion fostered by limited awareness of the actual character of physical reality.

This may be the stuff out of which revolutions in human thought and sensibility are made, but this new paradigm will not be apparent to those who refuse to recognize the epistemological authority of scientific knowledge or insist that scientific truths must be in accord with anthropocentric versions of religious truths. The assumption that one must make to enter the new dialogue between science and religion, which may be impossible for many, is that God or Being assumes the anthropomorphic guise of particular conceptions of beings in diverse linguistic and cultural contexts. In this dialogue, religious truths must be viewed in much the same way that we now view scientific truths, as metaphors for aspects of a seamlessly integrated whole that cannot be fully disclosed or described in ordinary language or mathematical language.

Those who are capable of profound spiritual awareness are already very much aware that the single significant whole is vastly more than the sum of its parts. If people who have this awareness are willing to become familiar with what science has to say about the character of part-whole relationships in physical reality, they should have no difficulty understanding the causes of the crisis in the global environment and the manner in which it must be resolved. The challenge is to wed this understanding to an active commitment to resolving this crisis and to create in the process a global religious movement in which the primary aim and purpose is to enlarge the circle of human compassion in ways that can contribute to a timely resolution.

This prospect is not as unreasonable as some might imagine, because there are already concrete indications that we are witnessing the emergence of such a movement. The religious leaders and thinkers who are members of the National Religious Partnership for the Environment and the Earth Charter Commission are attempting to wed ecological values to fundamental religious truths as they are defined in all the great religions of the world.[27] The Tellus Institute is also engaged in this effort, and the Harvard Divinity School has sponsored a ten-volume set of books on "religions of the world and ecology" that is being published by Harvard University Press.[28]

We are, however, free to deny that there is a basis for a new dialogue between the truths of science and religion for the same reason that we are free to recognize it exists—there is nothing in the knowledge we call science that can prove the existence of God or Being and nothing that legitimates any anthropocentric conceptions of God or Being. The question of belief in ontology remains what it has always been, a question, and the physical universe remains what it has always been, a riddle. And the ultimate answer to the question and the ultimate meaning of the riddle are now, and probably always will be, a matter of personal choice and conviction.

There is, however, a large difference between a profoundly religious belief in God or Being as the source and ground of human existence and a belief in the actual existence of the false gods that are foundational to the neoclassical economic paradigm and to the present system of international government. People who worship at the altar of these false gods will not appreciate being told that their gods do not exist and that belief in their existence undermines the prospect of resolving the crisis in the global environment and preventing a human tragedy of staggering dimensions. But if we can extend the circle of our compassion and enlarge the bases for mutual recognition and understanding, most should realize that the death of false gods is a small price to pay in exchange for a once-in-all-human-lifetimes opportunity. The opportunity is to protect the lives of existing members of the extended human family and the future existence of subsequent generations of this family by resolving the crisis in the global environment. And if this enterprise is successful, we may soon find ourselves living in a more just and peaceful world in which extreme poverty does not exist and universal rights and freedoms are extended to all humanity. This is not merely the work of an age, but a work that can preserve the memory of all ages, and it is hard to imagine that anyone can serve a greater good or answer a higher calling.

NOTES

INTRODUCTION
1. E. O. Wilson, *The Future of Life* (New York: Knopf, 2002), p. 28.
2. Thomas Berry, *The Dream of the Earth* (San Francisco: Sierra Club, 1988), p. 123.

1. THE MAKING OF THE GODGAME
1. Peter Behr, "A Car for the Distant Future," *Washington Post,* March 9, 2003.
2. Union of Concerned Scientists, "World Scientists' Warning to Humanity," November 18, 1992, http://deoxy.org/sciwarn.htm.
3. *United Nations World Development Report,* March 2003; Rick Weiss, "Threats Posed by Water Scarcity Detailed: U.N. Report Warns of Looming Crisis," *Washington Post,* March 5, 2003; "Nor Any Drop to Drink," *Economist,* March 6, 2003; Rick Weiss, "Water Scarcity Prompts Scientists to Look Down," *Washington Post,* March 10, 2003.
4. Paul H. Ehrlich and John P. Holdren, "Impact of Population Growth," *Science* 171 (1971): 1212–1217.
5. E. O. Wilson, *Consilience: The Unity of Knowledge* (New York: Knopf, 1998), p. 262.
6. The most comprehensive summary of data on the global environment is provided by the Worldwatch Institute. A good summary can be found in *State of the World and Vital Signs: Trends That Are Shaping Our Future* (New York: Norton, 1997).
7. Philip P. Pan, "Scientists Issue Dire Prediction on Warming," *Washington Post,* January 22, 2001; Craig S. Smith, "150 Nations Start Groundwork for Global Warming Projects," *New York Times,* January 18, 2001.
8. Reed F. Noss and Robert L. Peters, *Endangered Species: A Status Report of America's Vanishing Habitat and Wildlife* (Washington, D.C.: Defenders of Wildlife, 1995); Reed F. Noss, T. LaRoe III, and Michael Scott, *Endangered Species of the United States: A Preliminary Assessment of Loss and Degradation* (Washington, D.C.: U.S. Department of the Interior, National Biological Service, 1995).
9. E. O. Wilson, *The Future of Life* (New York: Knopf, 2002), pp. 98–99.
10. "The Least Developed Countries Report 2002," *Escaping the Poverty Trap* (New York: United Nations, 2002).
11. Robert Levine, "The Sims Online," *Wired Magazine,* November 11, 2002.
12. NSF Advisory Committee for Environmental Research and Education, *Complex Environmental Systems: Synthesis for Earth, Life, and Society in the 21st Century* (Washington, D.C.: U.S. Government Printing Office, 2003).
13. NSF Advisory Committee, *Complex Environmental Systems,* pp. 1–20.

2. GODGAMES AT THE PENTAGON
1. David Stipp, "Pentagon Says Global Warming Is a Critical Security Issue," *Fortune Magazine,* January 26, 2004.
2. Peter Swartz and Doug Randall, "An Abrupt Climate Change Scenario and Its

Implications for United States National Security," www.ems.org/climate/pentagon-climate-change.pdf

3. Swartz and Randall, "Abrupt Climate Change Scenario," pp. 4–5.

4. Swartz and Randall, "Abrupt Climate Change Scenario," p. 19.

5. Swartz and Randall, "Abrupt Climate Change Scenario," p. 7.

6. Swartz and Randall, "Abrupt Climate Change Scenario," p. 2.

7. Swartz and Randall, "Abrupt Climate Change Scenario," p. 18.

8. Oleg Anisimov, quoted in Usha Lee McFarling, "Fear Growing over a Sharp Climate Shift, *Los Angeles Times,* July 13, 2001.

9. Terry Root, Jeff Price, Kimberly Hall, Stephen Schneider, Cynthia Rosenzweig, and Alan Pounds, "Fingerprints of Global Warming on Wild Animals and Plants," *Nature* 421 (2003): 57–60.

10. Andrew C. Revkin, "Warming Is Found to Disrupt Species," *New York Times,* July 2, 2003.

11. Alex Kirby, "Climate Risk to Millions of Species," *BBC News World Edition,* January 7, 2004.

12. Mark Townsend, *Ecologist,* August 26, 2002.

13. William Speed Weed, "Climate Jumping," *New York Times Magazine,* December 15, 2002.

14. Ed Johnson. "Global Warming at Critical Point," Associated Press, January 25, 2005.

15. Anthony D. Smith, *Myths and Memories of the Nation* (Oxford: Oxford University Press, 1999), p. 102.

16. Anthony W. Mark, *Exclusionary Origins of Nationalism* (Oxford: Oxford University Press, 2003); Hagen Schulze, *States, Nations and Nationalism* (Oxford: Blackwell, 1998); Ronald S. Bremer, *Theorizing Nationalism* (Albany: State University of New York Press, 1999); Walker Connor, *Ethno-nationalism: The Quest for Understanding* (Princeton, N.J.: Princeton University Press, 1994); Ernest Geller, *Nations and Nationalism* (Oxford: Blackwell, 1983); Paul Gilbert, *The Philosophy of Nationalism* (Oxford: Westview Press, 1998); Eric J. Hobsbawm, *Nations and Nationalism Since 1780,* 2nd edition (Cambridge: Cambridge University Press, 1992); John Hutchinson, *The Dynamics of Cultural Nationalism* (London: Allen and Unwin, 1987); Avishai Margalit, *The Morality of Nationalism* (New York: Oxford University Press, 1997); Margaret Moore, *The Ethics of Nationalism* (New York: Oxford University Press, 2001); Anthony D. Smith, *Nations and Nationalism in a Global Era* (Cambridge: Polity Press, 1995); Anthony D. Smith, *Nationalism and Modernism: A Critical Survey of Recent Theories of Nations and Nationalism* (London: Routledge, 1998); Benedict Anderson, *Imagined Communities: Reflections on the Origins and Spread of Nationalism* (London: Verso, 1991); John Armstrong, *Nations before Nationalism* (Chapel Hill: University of North Carolina Press, 1982); J. Cohen, ed., *For Love of Country: Debating the Limits of Patriotism* (Boston: Beacon Press, 1996); Adrian Hastings, *The Construction of Nationhood* (Cambridge: Cambridge University Press, 1997); K. McKim and J. McMahon, eds., *The Morality of Nationalism* (New York: Oxford University Press, 1997); Conor C. O'Brien, *God-Land: Reflections on Religion and Nationalism* (Cambridge, Mass: Harvard University Press, 1988); Charles Tilly, ed., *The Formation of National States in Western Europe* (Princeton, N.J.: Princeton University Press, 1975); Leon Tipton, ed., *Nationalism in the Middle Ages* (New York: Holt, Rinehart and Winston, 1972).

17. Robert Heilbroner, *The Worldly Philosophers,* 6th edition (New York: Simon & Schuster, 1992).

18. K. J. Arrow and F. H. Hahn, *General Competitive Analysis* (San Francisco: Holden Day, 1971), p. 1.

19. Adam Smith, *An Inquiry into the Nature and Causes of the Wealth of Nations,* ed. R. H. Campbell, A. S. Skinner, and W. B. Todd (Oxford: Oxford University Press, 1976) book 4, chap. 2.

20. Philip Mirowski, *Against Mechanism: Protecting Economics from Science* (Lan-

ham, Md.: Rowman & Littlefield, 1988); Bruno Ingrao and Giorgio Israel, *The Invisible Hand: Economic Equilibrium in the History of Science*, tr. Ian MacGilvray (Cambridge, Mass.: MIT Press, 1990).

21. Robert L. Nadeau, *The Wealth of Nature: How Mainstream Economics Failed the Environment* (New York: Columbia University Press, 2003).

22. Michael M'Gonigle and Mark W. Zacher, *Pollution, Politics and International Law* (Berkeley: University of California Press, 1979).

23. James Gustave Speth, *Red Sky at Morning: America and the Crisis in the Global Environment* (New Haven, Conn.: Yale University Press, 2004), pp. 77–98.

24. Mostafa Tolba, quoted in Carolyn Thomas, *The Environment in International Relations* (London: Royal Institute of International Affairs, 1992), p. 228.

25. The following is an interesting case study on the manner in which scientific evidence was explicitly rejected as the basis for decision making on ocean dumping of radioactive wastes: Judith Spiller and Cynthia Haden, "Radwaste at Sea: A New Era of Polarization or a New Basis for Consensus?" *Ocean Development and International Law* 19 (1988): 345–366.

26. Quoted in William Ruckelshouse, "Toward a Sustainable World," *Scientific American,* September 1989.

27. Christine Todd Whitman, quoted in Erin Pianin, "U.S. Rebuffs Europeans Urging Change of Mind on Kyoto Treaty," *Washington Post,* April 4, 2001.

28. George W. Bush, quoted in Edmund L. Andrews, "Bush Angers Europe by Eroding Pact on Warming," *New York Times,* April 1, 2001.

29. Romano Prodi, quoted in Andrews, "Bush Angers Europe."

30. Peter Baker, "Russia Backs Kyoto to Get on Path to Join WTO," *Washington Post,* May 22, 2004.

31. Paul R. Ehrlich, *Human Nature: Genes, Cultures, and the Human Prospect* (New York: Penguin, 2000), p. 331.

3. A NEW VIEW OF NATURE

1. Charles Darwin, "The Linnaean Society Papers," in Philip Appleman, ed., *Darwin: A Norton Critical Edition* (New York: Norton, 1970), p. 83.

2. Charles Darwin, *The Origin of Species* (New York: Mentor, 1958), p. 75

3. Ernst Mayr, *The Growth of Biological Thought: Diversity, Evolution and Inheritance* (Cambridge, Mass.: Harvard University Press, 1982), p. 63.

4. P. B. Medawar and J. S. Medawar, *The Life Sciences: Current Ideas in Biology* (New York: Harper and Row, 1977), p. 165.

5. Ilya Prigogine and Isabelle Stengers, *Order out of Chaos* (New York: Bantam, 1984), p. 292.

6. Stuart Kauffman, *The Origins of Order: Self-Organization and Selection in Evolution* (New York: Oxford University Press, 1993); Kauffman, *At Home in the Universe: The Search for the Laws of Self-Organization and Complexity* (New York: Oxford University Press, 1995).

7. John Holland, *Adaptation in Natural and Artificial Systems: An Introductory Analysis with Applications to Biology, Control & AI* (Cambridge, Mass.: MIT Press, 1992); Holland, *Hidden Order: How Adaptation Builds Complexity* (New York: Addison Wesley, 1995); Holland, *Emergence: From Chaos to Order* (New York: Helix Books, 1998).

8. Christopher G. Langton, *Artificial Life* (Redwood City, Calif.: Addison Wesley, 1989).

9. Per Bak, *How Nature Works: The Science of Self-Organized Criticality* (New York: Springer-Verlag, 1996).

10. Robert Nadeau, *The Wealth of Nature: How Mainstream Economics Has Failed the Environment* (New York: Columbia University Press, 2003).

11. Harold Morowitz, *Beginnings of Cellular Life* (New Haven, Conn.: Yale University Press, 1992); Morowitz, *The Emergence of Everything* (New York: Oxford University Press, 2002).

12. Lynn Margulis and Dorian Sagan, *Microcosmos: Four Billion Years from Our Microbial Ancestors* (New York: Simon & Schuster, 1986), p. 18.

13. Margulis and Sagan, *Microcosmos,* p. 18.

14. Margulis and Sagan, *Microcosmos,* p. 19.

15. Marjori Matzke and Antonius J. M. Matzke, "RNAi Extends Its Reach," *Science* 391 (2003): 1060–1061.

16. J. Shaxel, *Gruduz der Theorienbuldung in der Biologie* (Jena: Fisher, 1922), p. 308.

17. Natalie Angier, "Constantly in Motion, Like DNA Itself," *New York Times,* March 2, 2004.

18. James L. Gould, *Ethology: Mechanisms and Evolution of Behavior* (New York: Norton, 1982), p. 467.

19. Paul Colinvaux, *Why Big Fierce Animals Are Rare: An Ecologist's Perspective* (Princeton, N.J.: Princeton University Press, 1978), p. 145.

20. Colinvaux, *Why Big Fierce Animals Are Rare,* p. 146.

21. Peter Farb, *The Forest* (New York: Time Life, 1969), p. 116.

22. P. Klopfer, *Habitats and Territories* (New York: Basic, 1969), p. 9.

23. Charles Perrins, "Reserved Rationality and the Precautionary Principle: Technological Change, Time, and Uncertainty in Environmental Decision Making," in Robert Costanza, ed., *Ecological Economics: The Science of Management and Sustainability* (New York: Columbia University Press, 1991) p. 157.

4. THE AMAZING GIFT OF LANGUAGE

1. Ernst Mayr, *Toward a New Philosophy of Biology* (Cambridge, Mass.: Harvard University Press, 1988), pp. 66–74.

2. Lynn Jorde, Michael Bamshad, and Alan Rogers, "Using Mitochondrial Nuclear DNA to Reconstruct Human Evolution," *BioEssays* 20 (1998): 126–136; A. Gibbons, "The Mystery of Humanity's Missing Mutations," *Science* 267 (1995): 35–36; L. L. Cavalli-Sforza, P. Menozza, and A. Piazzi, "Demic Expansions and Human Evolution," *Science* 259 (1993): 639–646.

3. Richard G. Klein, *The Human Career: Human Biology and Cultural Origins,* 2nd edition (Chicago: University of Chicago Press, 1999).

4. J. D. Bergtson and M. Ruhlen, "Global Etymologies," in M. Ruhlen, ed., *On the Origins of Languages: Studies in Linguistic Taxonomy* (Stanford, Calif.: Stanford University Press, 1994), pp. 278–337.

5. Joseph Chang, "Recent Common Ancestors of All Present-Day Individuals," *Advances in Applied Probability* 31 (1999): 1002–1026.

6. Steven Molnar, *Human Races, Types, and Ethnic Groups,* 4th edition (Upper Saddle River, N.Y: Prentice Hall, 1988); Nina Jablonski and George Chaplin, "The Evolution of Human Skin Coloration," *Journal of Human Evolution* 39 (2000): 57–106.

7. Lyle Campbell, *Historical Linguistics* (Cambridge, Mass.: MIT Press, 1999).

8. Rafael E. Nimez, "Eating Soup with Chopsticks: Dogmas, Difficulties and Alternatives in the Study of Conscious Experience, " *Journal of Consciousness Studies* 4, no. 2 (1997): 143–166.

9. Jared Diamond, *Guns, Germs, and Steel: The Fates of Human Societies* (New York: Norton, 1999), pp. 134–143.

10. Diamond, *Guns, Germs, and Steel,* pp. 132–133.

11. Steven Budiansky, *The Nature of Horses: Exploring Equine Evolution, Intelligence and Behavior* (New York: Free Press, 1997).

12. E. O. Wilson, *The Future of Life* (New York: Knopf, 2002), p. 115.

13. Alfred Crosby, *The Columbian Exchange: Biological and Cultural Consequences of 1492* (Westport, Conn.: Greenwood, 1972).

14. Richard P. Clark, *Global Life Systems* (New York: Rowan & Littlefield, 2000), pp. 165–186.

15. William Cronon, *Changes in the Land: Indians, Colonists, and the Ecology of New*

England (New York: Hill and Wang, 1983); Timothy Silver, *A New Face on the Country-side: Indians, Colonists and Slaves in South Atlantic Forests, 1500–1800* (Cambridge: Cambridge University Press, 1990).

16. Alfred Crosby, *Germs, Seeds and Animals: Studies in Ecological History* (Armonk, N.Y.: Sharpe, 1994), pp. 148–156.

17. Clive Pointing, *A Green History of the World: The Environment and the Collapse of Great Civilizations* (New York: St. Martin's Press, 1991).

18. William McNeil, *Plagues and Peoples* (New York: Doubleday, 1977).

19. Joseph Konvitz, *The Urban Millennium: The City Building Process from the Early Middle Ages to the Present* (Carbondale: Southern Illinois University, 1985), chap. 4.

20. Michael Kremer, "Population Growth and Technological Change: One Billion B.C. to 1900," *Quarterly Journal of Economics* 108, no. 3 (1993): 681–716; Edward Deevey, "The Human Population," *Scientific American,* September 1960.

21. Robert Ross and Kent Trachte, *Global Capitalism: The New Leviathan* (Albany: State University of New York Press, 1990); William Grieder, *One World, Ready or Not: The Manic Growth of Global Capitalism* (New York: Simon & Schuster, 1997).

22. *Economist,* April 25, 1992, p. 48.

23. Herman Prager, "Commentary on U.N. Environment Programme," in *Global Marine Environment* (Lanham, Md.: University Press of America), pp. 61–62.

24. Peter Freund and George Martin, *The Ecology of the Automobile* (Montreal: Black Rose, 1993).

25. James J. MacKenzie and Michael P. Walsh, *Driving Forces: Motor Vehicle Trends and Their Implications for Global Warming* (Washington, D.C.: World Resources Institute, 1990); "One Billion Cars," *Worldwatch,* January–February 1996.

26. J. R. McNeill, *Something New under the Sun: An Environmental History of the Twentieth Century* (New York: Norton, 2000), p. 311.

27. Michel Meybeck, Deborah Chaplin, and Richard Helmer, eds., *Global Freshwater Quality: A First Assessment* (Oxford: Blackwell Scientific, 1989).

28. Peter Singer, *The Expanding Circle: Ethics and Sociobiology* (New York: Farrar, Strauss & Giroux, 1991).

29. D. L. Horowitz, *The Deadly Ethnic Riot* (Berkeley: University of California Press, 2001); J. Keegan, *The Face of Battle* (New York: Penguin, 1976).

5. THE GODS OF THE SOULLESS MACHINE

1. John Locke, *An Essay Concerning Human Understanding,* ed. Peter H. Nidditch (Oxford: Oxford University Press, 1979) book 1, chap. 1.

2. Locke, *Essay Concerning Human Understanding,* book 2, chap. 1.

3. Jean le Rond d'Alembert, *Sketch for a Historical Picture of the Progress of the Human Mind,* trans. Richard N. Schwab (Indianapolis: Bobbs-Merrill, 1963), pp. 83–84.

4. Locke, *Essay Concerning Human Understanding,"* book 2, chap. 18.

5. Thomas Hobbes, *Leviathan* (Oxford: Oxford University Press, 1957), pp. 185–186.

6. R. Aron, *Les étapes de la pensée sociologique* (Paris: Gillimard, 1967), p. 40.

7. F. Quesnay, "Analyse de la formule arithmétique du Tableau économique de al distribution des dépenses annuelles d'une nation agricole," *Journal de l'Agriculture du Commerce et des Finances* 5, no. 3 (1766): 921.

8. Quesnay, "Analyse de la formule arithmétique," pp. 921–922.

9. Bruno Ingrao and Giorgio Israel, *The Invisible Hand: Economic Equilibrium in the History of Science,* tr. Ian MacGilvray (Cambridge, Mass.: MIT Press, 1990), p. 44.

10. A.R.J. Turgot, "Reflections on the Formation and Distribution of Riches," in R. L. Meek, ed., *Turgot on Progress, Sociology and Economics* (Cambridge: Cambridge University Press, 1973), pp. 83–84.

11. Marquis de Condorcet, "Discours prononcé dans l'Académie francaise le jeudi 21 fevier 1792 a la reception de M. Le marquis de Condorcet," in A. Condorcet-O'Connor and F. Arago, eds., *Oeuvres de Condorcet* (Paris, 1847) vol. 1, pp. 390ff.

12. Ingrao and Israel, *Invisible Hand,* pp. 50–51.

13. Kerry S. Walters, *The American Deists* (Lawrence: University of Kansas Press, 1992); Walters, *Rational Infidels* (Durango, Colo.: Longwood Academic Press, 1992).

14. James Madison, *The Federalist Papers,* ed. C. Rossiter (New York: New American Library, 1961), p. 78.

15. John Adams, quoted in J. O. McGinnis, "The Human Constitution and Constitutive Law: A Prolegomenon," *Journal of Contemporary Legal Issues* 8 (1997): 236.

16. Alexander Hamilton, *Federalist Papers,* p. 437 (see n. 14 above).

17. James Madison, *Federalists Papers,* p. 322.

18. Robert Heilbroner, *The Worldly Philosophers: The Lives, Times and Ideas of the Great Economic Thinkers* (New York: Simon & Schuster, 1992), pp. 42–43.

19. Heilbroner, *Worldly Philosophers,* pp. 33–50.

20. Adam Smith, *An Inquiry into the Nature and Causes of the Wealth of Nations,* ed. R. H. Campbell, A. S. Skinner, and W. B. Todd (Oxford: Oxford University Press, 1976), Astronomy Intro. 1, 7, II, 2.

21. Smith, *Wealth of Nations,* III, 2.

22. Smith, *Wealth of Nations,* III, 2.

23. Smith, *Wealth of Nations,* Astronomy, II, 12, III, 3.

24. Smith, *Wealth of Nations,* Astronomy, II, 12, III, 3.

25. Smith, *Wealth of Nations,* IV, ix, 51.

26. Smith, *Wealth of Nations,* V, i, f. 28.

27. Smith, *Wealth of Nations,* Physics, 9.

28. Smith, *Wealth of Nations,* Physics, 9.

29. Adam Smith, *The Theory of Moral Sentiments,* ed. D. D. Raphael and A. L. Macfie (Oxford: Oxford University Press, 1976), IV, 1, 10.

30. Smith, *Theory of Moral Sentiments,* IV, 1, 10.

31. Smith, *Theory of Moral Sentiments,* VII, ii, 1, 20.

32. Smith, *Theory of Moral Sentiments,* I, i, 4, 2.

33. Smith, *Wealth of Nations,* VI, i, 11–12.

34. Smith, *Wealth of Nations,* VI, i, 13.

35. Smith, *Theory of Moral Sentiments,* IV, I, 10.

36. William Godwin, quoted in James Bonar, *Malthus and His Work* (New York: Augustus M. Kelly, 1967), p. 15.

37. Thomas Robert Malthus, *An Essay on the Principle of Population,* ed. Philip Appleman (New York: Norton, 1976), pp. 15ff.

38. Malthus, *Essay on Population,* pp. 15ff.

39. Heilbroner, *Worldly Philosophers,* p. 95.

40. David Ricardo, *On the Principles of Political Economy and Taxation* (New York: Cambridge University Press, 1951).

41. Robert L. Nadeau, *The Wealth of Nature: How Mainstream Economics Has Failed the Environment* (New York: Columbia University Press, 2003), pp. 20–36.

6. THE GOD WITH THE INVISIBLE HAND

1. Robert L. Nadeau, *The Wealth of Nature: How Mainstream Economics Has Failed the Environment* (New York: Columbia University Press, 2003).

2. Philip Mirowski, Against Mechanism (Lanham, Md.: Roman and Littlefield, 1988); Mirowski, *More Heat Than Light* (New York: Cambridge University Press, 1989).

3. Bruno Ingrao and Georgio Israel, *The Invisible Hand: Economic Equilibrium in the History of Science* (Cambridge, Mass.: MIT Press, 1990).

4. Mirowski, *Against Mechanism,* pp. 19–20.

For readers interested in a detailed discussion of the manner in which the creators of neoclassical economics abused mid-nineteenth-century physics, the best available source is Mirowski's *Against Mechanism.* The following is a less robust treatment that illustrates how these economists appropriated the mathematics of this physics and redefined energy as the equivalent of utility.

Assume that a mass point is displaced from point A to point B in a three-dimensional plane by force vector F and that the force vector is decomposed into its perpendicular components, $F = iF_x + jF_y + kF_z$, where the notations i, j, and k represent unit vectors along the three spatial axes. In the same manner, assume that the vector of displacement dq can also be decomposed into its perpendicular components, $dq = id_x + jd_y + kd_z$. Hence the work accomplished, or the product of the force and the infinitesimal displacements, is defined as the integral of the force times the displacement:

$$T = \int_A^B (F_x d_x + F_y d_y + F_z d_z) = \tfrac{1}{2}mv^2 |B - \tfrac{1}{2}mv^2 |A.$$

The mid-nineteenth-century physicists redefined the change in mv as the change in the kinetic energy of the particle and represented this as a single value vector function with T representing the change in kinetic energy. Assume that $(F_x d_x + F_y d_y + F_z d_z)$ is an exact differential and that there exists a uniquely identified scalar function $U(x, y, z)$ such that

$$F_x = -\partial U/\partial_x;\ F_y = -\partial U/\partial_y;\ F_z = -\partial U/\partial_z.$$

The scalar function U was viewed as the unobserved potential energy of the particle, and the total energy of the particle, which is presumably conserved through any motion, was represented as $T + U$. William Hamilton had earlier defined the action integral over time of the path of the particle as

$$\int_{t_1, A}^{t_2, B}(T - U)dt.$$

The Hamiltonian principle of least action asserts that the actual path of the particle from A to B will be the one that makes the action interval stationary, and this path can be calculated by finding the constrained extrema using either Langrangian constrained maximization/minimization techniques or the calculus of variations. In a conservative system where $T + U =$ a constant, action is a function only of position.

Walras borrowed these equations and made F the vector of the prices of a set of traded goods and q the vector of the quantities of those goods purchased. He then defined the integral $\int F\,dq = T$ as the total expenditure on these goods, integrated the expression as an exact differential, and defined the scalar function of the goods x and y as $U = U$ (x, y, z). Amazingly enough, he concluded that the resulting scalar function represents or describes the "utilities" of those goods.

Walras assumed that these utilities, like the concept of potential energy in the physics, are unobservable and that their existence can only be "inferred" through linkage with observable variables. He then argued that relative prices are equal to the ratios of the marginal utilities of goods by defining the "potential field" of utility as the locus of the set of constrained extrema. Although the other creators of neoclassical economic theory treated utility as a derived phenomenon by viewing the utility field as the exogenous data to which market transactions adjusted, they used the same mathematics. The assumption that this "market system" is reversible and without history did not seem totally unreasonable, because the second law of thermodynamics, the entropy law, had not been formulated.

5. William Stanley Jevons, *The Principles of Science*, 2nd edition (London: Macmillan, 1905), pp. 735–736.

6. William Stanley Jevons, *The Theory of Political Economy* (New York: Penguin, 1970), p. 736.

7. Ingrao and Israel, *Invisible Hand*, p. 97.

8. Léon Walras, "Letter to Louis Ruchonnet," in W. Jaffe, ed., *Correspondence of Léon Walras and Related Papers* (Amsterdam: North-Holland, 1965), I, p. 201.

9. Léon Walras, *Elements of Pure Economics* (New York: Kelly Watson, 1960), p. 61.

10. Walras, *Elements of Pure Economics*, p. 63.

11. Walras, *Elements of Pure Economics*, p. 69.

12. Walras, *Elements of Pure Economics*, p. 40.

13. Léon Walras, quoted in Philip C. Newman, Arthur D. Gayer, and Milton H. Spencer, eds., *Source Readings in Economic Thought* (New York: Norton, 1954), pp. 466–467.

14. Miroswki, *More Heat Than Light*, pp. 193–195.

15. Francis Ysidro Edgeworth, *Mathematical Physics* (London: Routledge, 1881), pp. 9, 12.

16. Vilfredo Pareto, *Manual of Political Economy* (New York: Augustus M. Kelly, 1971), pp. 36, 113.

17. Alfred Marshall, *Principles of Economics,* 8th edition (London: Macmillan, 1920), p. xiv.

18. John Maynard Keynes, letter to Bernard Shaw, quoted in Roy Harrod, *The Life of John Maynard Keynes* (New York: Augustus M. Kelly, 1969), p. 462.

19. John Maynard Keynes, quoted in Robert Glower, "Reflections on the Keynesian Perplex," *Zeitschrift fur National Okonomie* 35 (1975): 5.

20. John von Neumann in conversation with Oskar Morgenstern, in Oskar Morgenstern, "The Collaboration between O. Morgenstern and J. von Neumann on the Theory of Games," *Journal of Economic Literature* 12 (1976): 805–816.

21. Oskar Morgenstern, "Professor Hicks on Value and Capital," *Journal of Political Economy* 29, no. 3 (1949): 361–393.

22. Paul A. Samuelson, *Foundations of Economic Analysis* (Cambridge, Mass.: Harvard University Press, 1947), p. 3.

23. Samuelson, *Foundations of Economic Analysis,* p. 4.

24. Samuelson, *Foundations of Economic Analysis,* p. 258.

25. Gerald Debreu, *Theory of Value: An Axiomatic Analysis of Economic Equilibrium* (New Haven, Conn.: Yale University Press, 1959).

26. Debreu, *Theory of Value,* p. x.

27. Debreu, *Theory of Value,* p. x.

28. Gerald Debreu, *Mathematical Economics: Twenty Papers of Gerald Debreu* (Cambridge: Cambridge University Press, 1983), p. 5.

29. Kenneth J. Arrow and Gerald Debreu, "Existence of an Equilibrium for a Competitive Economy," *Econometrica* 22 (1954): 265–290.

30. Martin Shubik, *Game Theory in the Social Sciences* (Cambridge, Mass.: MIT Press, 1982), p. 300.

31. Shubik, *Game Theory in the Social Sciences,* p. 10.

32. Martin Shubik, *The Theory of Money and Financial Institutions* (Cambridge, Mass.: MIT Press, 1999), I, p. 3.

33. Shubik, *Theory of Money and Financial Institutions,* I. p. 4.

34. Shubik, *Theory of Money and Financial Institutions,* I, p. 4.

35. Shubik, *Theory of Money and Financial Institutions,* I, pp. 4–5.

36. Shubik, *Theory of Money and Financial Institutions,* I, pp. 4–5.

37. Shubik, *Theory of Money and Financial Institutions,* II, p. 333.

38. Shubik, *Theory of Money and Financial Institutions,* II, pp. 334–337.

39. R. Sugden, "Rational Choice: A Survey of Contributions from Economics and Philosophy," *Economic Journal* 101 (1991): 783.

40. Wassily Leontief, letter in *Science* 217 (1981): 104–107.

41. Jean-Pierre Aubin, *Optima and Equilibria: An Introduction to Nonlinear Analysis* (New York: Springer-Verlag, 1998).

7. A GREEN THUMB ON THE INVISIBLE HAND

1. Nick Hanley, Jason E. Shogren, and Ben White, *Environmental Economics in Theory and Practice* (New York: Oxford University Press, 1997), p. 358.

2. A. C. Pigou, *The Economics of Welfare,* 4th edition (London: Macmillan, 1932), p. 183.

3. Pigou, *Economics of Welfare,* p. xii.

4. R. H. Coase, "The Problem of Law and Economics," *Journal of Law and Economics* (October 1960): 1–44.

5. Nathaniel O. Keohane, Richard L. Revesz, and Robert N. Stavins, "The Choice of Regulatory Instruments in Environmental Policy," in Robert N. Stavins, ed., *Economics of the Environment,* 4th edition (New York: Norton, 2000), p. 563.

6. Keohane, Revesz, and Stavins, "Choice of Regulatory Instruments," p. 563.

7. Office of Technology Assessment, Technical Assessment Board of the 103rd Congress, *Environmental Policy Tools: A User's Guide* (Washington, D.C.: U.S. Government Printing Office, 1995).

8. William D. Norhaus, "Reflections on the Economics of Climate Change," *Journal of Economic Perspectives* 7 (Fall 1993): 14.

9. Robert N. Stavins, ed., *Economics of the Environment,* 4th edition (New York: Norton, 2000).

10. W. Michael Hanneman, "Valuing the Environment through Contingent Value," *Journal of Economic Perspectives* 8 (Fall 1994): 19.

11. A. M. Freeman III, "The Measurement of Environmental Resource and Values: Theory and Methods," in *Resources for the Future* (Washington, D.C.: U. S. Government Printing Office, 1993).

12. J. W. Fletcher, W. Adamowicz, and T. Graham-Tomasi, "The Travel Cost Model of Recreation Demand," *Leisure Studies* 12 (1990): 119–147.

13. Mark Sagoff, "Some Problems with Environmental Economics," *Environmental Ethics* 10 (Spring 1988): 55.

14. Paul J. Portney, "The Contingency Valuation Debate: Why Economists Should Care," *Journal of Economic Perspectives* 8 (Fall 1994): 3.

15. Richard T. Carson et al., *A Bibliography of Contingent Valuation Studies and Papers* (La Jolla, Calif.: Natural Resource Damage Assessment, 1994).

16. Hanneman, "Valuing the Environment," pp. 19–43.

17. J. A. Hausman, ed., *Contingent Valuation: A Critical Assessment* (New York: North-Holland, 1993).

18. Richard W. Olschavsky and Donald H. Granbois, "Consumer Decision Making— Fact or Fiction?" *Journal of Consumer Research* 6 (1977): 93–100.

19. J. R. Bettman and M. A. Zins, "Constructive Processes in Consumer Choice," *Journal of Consumer Research* 4 (1977): 75–78.

20. Robert C. Mitchell and Richard T. Carson, "Valuing Drinking Water Risk Reduction Using the Contingent Valuation Methods: A Methodological Study of Risks from THM and Giardia," paper prepared for *Resources for the Future* (Washington, D.C.: U.S. Government Printing Office, 1986).

21. George Tolley et al., "Establishing and Valuing the Effects of Improved Visibility in Eastern United States," paper prepared for the U.S. Environmental Protection Agency, Washington, D.C., 1986.

22. James Bowker and John R. Stoll, "Use of Dichotomous Choice Nonmarket Methods to Value the Whooping Crane Resource," *American Journal of Agricultural Economy* 23, no. 5 (1987): 372–381.

23. Kevin J. Boyle and Richard C. Bishop, "Valuing Wildlife in Benefit-Cost Analyses: A Case Study Involving Endangered Species," *Water Resources Research* 23, no. 5 (1987): 943–950.

24. Erwin Schrödinger, *What Is Life?* (London: Cambridge University Press, 1967), p. 79.

25. Nicolas Georgescu-Roegen, *The Entropy Law and the Economic Process* (Cambridge, Mass.: Harvard University Press, 1971), pp. 20–21.

26. Herman E. Daly and Kenneth N. Townsend, eds., *Valuing the Earth: Economics, Ecology, Ethics* (Cambridge, Mass.: MIT Press, 1993), p. 21.

27. Herman E. Daly, "Allocation, Distribution, and Scale: Toward an Economics That Is Efficient, Just, and Sustainable," *Ecological Economics* 6 (1992): 186.

28. Daly, "Allocation, Distribution, and Scale," pp. 190–191.

29. Garrett Hardin, "The Tragedy of the Commons," *Science* 162 (1968): 1243–1248.

30. H. S. Gordon, "The Economic Theory of a Common-Property Resource: The Fishery," *Journal of Political Economy* 62 (1954): 124–142.

31. Herman E. Daly and John B. Cobb, Jr., "Appendix: The Index of Sustainable Development," in *For the Common Good: Redirecting the Economy toward Community, the Environment and a Sustainable Future* (Boston: Beacon Press, 1989), pp. 443–507.

32. Robert Repetto et al., *Wasting Assets: Natural Resources in the National Income*

Accounts (Washington, D.C.: World Resources Institute, 1989); Wilfrido Cruz and Robert Repetto, *The Environmental Effects of Stabilization and Structural Adjustment Programs: The Philippines Case* (Washington, D.C.: World Resources Institute, 1992); Maria Concepcion Cruz et al., *Population Growth, Poverty and Environmental Stress: Frontier Migration in the Philippines and Costa Rica* (Washington, D.C.: World Resources Institute, 1992).

33. Kirk Hamilton, "Monitoring Environmental Progress" and "Green Adjustments to GDP," World Bank Environment Discussion Papers, 1994.

34. Mark Sagoff, "Some Problems with Environmental Economics," *Environmental Ethics* 3 (Spring 1988): 55–74.

35. Bruce Hannon, "Measures of Economic and Ecological Health," in Robert Costanza, Brian Norton, and Benjamin Haskell, eds., *Ecosystem Health: New Goals for Environmental Management* (Washington, D.C.: Island Press, 1992).

36. F. Hinterberger, "Another Plea for Pluralism in Ecological Economics," *ESEE Newsletter* (November 1997): 3–7.

37. Andreas Renner, "Some Methodological Reflections: A Plea for a Constitutional Ecological Economics," in Jorg Kohn et al., eds., *Sustainability in Question: The Search for a Conceptual Framework* (Northampton, Mass.: Edward Elgar, 1999), p. 320.

38. Alfred S. Eichner, ed., *Why Economics Is Not Yet a Science* (Armonk, N.Y.: Sharpe, 1983), p. 238.

8. AN UNNATURAL RELIGION

1. Thomas Friedman, *New York Times,* August 15, 1998.

2. Thomas Friedman, *The Lexus and the Olive Tree* (New York: Random House, 2000), pp. 87–88.

3. Friedman, *The Lexus and the Olive Tree,* pp. 298, 302.

4. Francis Fukuyama, *The End of History and the Last Man* (New York: Penguin, 1992), p. 1.

5. Fukuyama, *End of History,* pp. 2–3.

6. George Gilder, *The Spirit of Enterprise* (New York: Simon & Schuster, 1984).

7. George Gilder, *Wealth and Poverty* (New York: Basic, 1981), p. 80.

8. Keven Kelly, *Out of Control: The New Biology of Machines, Social Systems and the Economic World* (Reading, Mass: Perseus, 1994).

9. Robert Samuelson, "Markets 'R' Us," *Newsweek,* December 20, 1998.

10. Robert Bartley, in David Brooks, ed., *Backward and Upward: The New Conservative Writing* (New York: Vintage Press, 1996), pp. 197–198.

11. Walter B. Wriston, *The Twilight of Sovereignty: How the Information Revolution Is Transforming Our World* (New York: Scribner's, 1992), pp. 61–62.

12. Wriston, *Twilight of Sovereignty,* pp. 9, 45, 170.

13. Wriston, *Twilight of Sovereignty,* pp. 46, 121.

14. Larry Summers, interviews with Jeffrey Sachs and Lawrence Summers, *The World Bank Development Report* (New York: Oxford University Press, 1991), p. 20.

15. F. A. Hayek, *The Road to Serfdom* (Chicago: University of Chicago Press, 1994).

16. Morrison Halcrow and Keith Joseph, *A Single Mind* (London: Macmillan, 1989), p. 152.

17. Richard Cockett, *Thinking the Unthinkable: Think-tanks and the Economic Counter Revolution, 1931–1983* (London: HarperCollins, 1994), p. 174.

18. Margaret Thatcher, *The Path to Power* (New York: HarperCollins, 1995), p. 26.

19. Halcrow and Joseph: *Single Mind,* pp. 136–138.

20. John Vickers and George Yarrow, *Privatization: An Economic Analysis* (Cambridge, Mass.: MIT Press, 1993), p. 127.

21. Jon Sopel, *Tony Blair: The Modernizer* (London: Bantam, 1995), p. 35.

22. Herbert Stein, *Presidential Politics: The Making of Economic Policy, from Roosevelt to Reagan and Beyond* (New York: Touchstone, 1985), pp. 135–136.

23. William R. Neikirk, *Volker: Portrait of the Money Man* (New York: Congdon & Weed, 1987), pp. 137–138.

24. Milton Friedman, *Capitalism and Freedom* (Chicago: University of Chicago Press, 1962).

25. Milton Friedman, *Free to Choose* (New York: Harcourt Brace Jovanovich, 1980).

26. William A, Niskanen, *Reaganomics: An Insider's Account of the Politics and the People* (New York: Oxford University Press, 1988).

27. Paul Ruscavage, *Income Inequality in America* (Armonk, N.Y.: Sharpe, 1999).

28. *The Economic and Budget Outlook: Fiscal Years 1998–2005* (Washington, D.C.: U.S. Government Printing Office, 1997).

29. Al Gore, *Earth in the Balance: Ecology and the Human Spirit* (New York: Penguin, 1993).

30. "Censorship on Global Warming," *New York Times,* July 20, 2003.

31. "Scientific Integrity in Policymaking: An Investigation into the Bush Administrations' Misuse of Science," Union of Concerned Scientists, February 18, 2004, http://web exhibits.org/bush/1.html.

32. Juliet Eilperin, "U.S. Wants No Warming Proposal: U.S. Aims to Prevent Arctic Council Suggestions," *Washington Post,* November 3, 2004.

33. Felicty Berringer and Michael Janofsky, "G.O.P. Plans to Give Environmental Rules a Free Market Tilt," *New York Times,* November 8, 2004.

9. THE ENDGAME

1. Frank R. Baumgartner and Bryan D. Jones, *Agenda and Instability in American Politics* (Chicago: University of Chicago Press, 1993).

2. Frank Biermann, "The Case for a World Environmental Organization," *Environment* 42, no. 9 (2000); Daniele C. Esty and Maria H. Ivanova, "Revitalizing Global Environmental Governance: A Function Driven Approach," in Esty and Ivanova, eds., *Global Environmental Governance: Options and Opportunities* (New Haven, Conn.: Yale School of Forestry and Environmental Studies, 2002); Steve Charnovitz, "A World Environmental Organization," *Columbia Journal of Environmental Law* 27, no. 2(2002): 324.

3. United Nations Development Program, *Human Development Report* (New York: Oxford University Press, 1996).

4. United Nations, *Human Development Report;* Thomas F. Homer-Dixon, *Environment, Scarcity and Violence* (Princeton, N.J.: Princeton University Press, 2000).

5. *Global Economic Prospects and the Developing Countries 2000* (Washington, D.C.: World Bank, 2000), p. 29.

6. Barry Bearak, "Why People Starve," *New York Times Magazine,* July 13, 2003.

7. United Nations Fund for Population Activities, *Population and Environmental Change* (New York: United Nations Population Fund, 2001); Richard E. Benedict, "Human Population and Environmental Stresses in the Twenty-First Century," *Environmental Change and Security Project Report* 6 (2000): 5; Robert Engelman et al., *People in the Balance* (Washington, D.C.: Population Action International, 2000); Anne H. Ehrlich and James Salzman, "The Importance of Population Growth to Sustainability," *Environmental Law Reporter News and Analysis* 32 (2002): 10559–10570.

8. Other indexes that could be useful for this purpose are The Environmental Sustainability Index, The Living Planet Index, The Ecological Footprint, and The Compass of Sustainability.

9. D. A. Underwood and P. G. King, "On the Ideological Foundations of Environmental Policy," *Ecological Economics* 1 (1989): 315–334; J. M. Gowdy and C. N. Mc-Daniel, "One World, One Experiment: Addressing the Biodiversity-Economics Conflict," *Ecological Economics* 15 (1996): 181–192.

10. Andrew C. Revkin, "U.S. Losing Status as a World Leader in Climate," *New York Times,* June 6, 2001.

11. Robert Costanza et al., "The Value of the World's Ecosystem Services and Natural Capital," *Nature* 387 (1997): 253–260.

12. J. Spangenberg, ed., *Toward a Sustainable Europe* (Brussels: Friends of the Earth, 1995); R. A. Waterings and J. B. Spschoor, "The Ecocapacity as a Challenge to Technological

Development," Publication RNMO 74a, Advisory Council for Research on Nature and Environment, Rijswijk, 1992.

13. Herman E. Daly and John B. Cobb, Jr., *For the Common Good: Redirecting the Economy toward Community, the Environment and a Sustainable Future* (Boston: Beacon Press, 1989), pp. 443–507.

14. Gareth Porter et al., *Global Environmental Politics* (Boulder, Colo.: Westview Press, 2000), pp. 212–218; Lawrence E. Suskind, *Environmental Diplomacy: Negotiating More Effective Global Agreements* (Oxford: Oxford University Press, 1994).

15. Paul Hawken, Amory Lovins, and L. Hunter Lovins, *Natural Capitalism: Creating the Next Industrial Revolution* (New York: Little, Brown, 1999).

16. Worldwatch Institute, *Vital Signs, 2002* (New York: Norton, 2002), pp. 42–45.

17. Arthur P. J. Mol, *Globalization and Environmental Reform* (Cambridge, Mass.: MIT Press, 2001), pp. 199–200.

18. Daniel C. Dennett, *Darwin's Dangerous Ideas: Evolution and the Meanings of Life* (New York: Simon & Schuster, 1996), pp. 494–500.

19. Colin McGinn, *Problems in Philosophy: The Limits of Inquiry* (Cambridge: Blackwell, 1993), p. 241.

20. Steven Weinberg, quoted in Heinz Pagels, *The Cosmic Code* (New York: Bantam, 1983), p. 239.

21. Errol E. Harris, "Contemporary Physics and Dialectical Holism," in Richard E. Kitchener, ed., *The World View of Contemporary Physics* (Albany: State University of New York Press, 1988), p. 161.

22. Harris, "Contemporary Physics and Dialectical Holism."

23. Harris, "Contemporary Physics and Dialectical Holism," p. 162.

24. Freeman Dyson, quoted in J. Cornwall, ed., *Nature's Imagination* (Oxford: Oxford University Press, 1995), p. 8.

25. Rudy Rucker, *Infinity and Mind* (Boston: Birkhauser, 1982), p, 157.

26. Leonard Swindler, ed., *For All Life: Toward a Universal Declaration of a Global Ethic* (Ashland, Ore.: White Cloud Press, 1999).

27. www.npre.org; www.earthharter.org.

28. www.tellus.org; www.hup.org.

INDEX

ABOUT THE AUTHOR

Robert Nadeau is an interdisciplinary scholar who has attempted throughout his career to bridge the gap between the two cultures of humanists-social scientists and scientists-engineers. He has published books in the humanities, the social sciences, and the hard sciences in areas as diverse as artificial intelligence computing, quantum physics, biology, neuroscience, public policy, and literary criticism. Nadeau is currently a professor at George Mason University and lives with his family in the suburbs of Washington, D.C., in northern Virginia.